Romaji Diary *and* Sad Toys

GW00584839

Romaji Diary
and
Sad Toys

by
Takuboku Ishikawa

translated by
Sanford Goldstein and Seishi Shinoda

Charles E. Tuttle Company: Publishers
Rutland, Vermont & Tokyo, Japan

Representatives:

Continental Europe: BOXERBOOKS, INC., Zurich

British Isles: PRENTICE-HALL INTERNATIONAL, INC., London

Australasia: BOOK WISE (AUSTRALIA) PTY., LTD.
1 Jeanes Street, Beverley, 5009, South Australia

Published by the Charles E. Tuttle Company, Inc.
of Rutland, Vermont & Tokyo, Japan
with editorial offices at
Suido 1-chome, 2-6, Bunkyo-ku, Tokyo

Library of Congress Catalog Card No. 84-052395
International Standard Book No. 0-8048-1494-5

First printing, 1985

The Japanese text of *Sad Toys* is a
photographic offprint from *Takuboku Kashū*
(Tokyo: Iwanami Shoten, 1975)
and is used by permission.

Printed in Japan

Contents

Publisher's Note

The publication of this edition of two of Takuboku Ishikawa's finest and most popular works together in translation has proven to be interesting from various standpoints.

Romaji Diary and the collection of tanka, *Sad Toys*, while different forms of literature, are not as dissimilar as they appear on the surface. Takuboku himself wrote that poetry "must be an exact report, an honest diary, of the changes in a man's emotional life," and these tanka are indeed as much a diary as a standard prose one. Both works reflect clearly, honestly, and poignantly the emotions and philosophy of a complex individual living in a time of profound change in Japan.

The tanka in this volume were first published in a book entitled *Sad Toys* (Purdue University Press, 1977). *Romaji Diary* is here presented in full in English for the first time, to the translators' and Publisher's knowledge. The Introduction and the various sets of notes are in large part from the Purdue book, but have been revised and added to where appropriate to fit this new edition.

Acknowledgments

With gratitude to . . .

Professor Akira Ikari, scholar of Japanese literature at Niigata University, Niigata, Japan, for his numerous helpful suggestions on our manuscript;

Saburō Saitō, for his excellent editing of the Iwanami Bunko edition of *A Collection of Takuboku's Tanka*, first published in 1946 by Iwanami Shoten, Tokyo;

Yukinori Iwaki, scholar-biographer, for his informative studies, *The Life of Ishikawa Takuboku*, published by Tōhō Shobō, Tokyo, 1955, and *Ishikawa Takuboku*, published by Yoshikawa-Kobunkan, Tokyo, 1965;

Dr. Takeo Kuwabara, for permission to quote from his excellent essay "The Diaries of Takuboku," found in *Works of Takuboku*, Chikuma Shobō, Tokyo, 1968 (originally published in the extra volume of *Collected Works of Takuboku,* Iwanami Shoten, Tokyo, 1954);

Iwanami Shoten, Tokyo, for permission to photograph the Japanese text of *Sad Toys* found in *Takuboku Kashū*, 1975, and for the use of the original text in our translation of *Romaji Diary*, found in volume 16 of *Collected Works of Takuboku*, 1961 (the suppressed words in this edition were filled in from the Iwanami Bunko edition of 1977); special thanks also to Ryōsuke Yasue, Chief Editor of Iwanami Shoten.

Introduction

BIOGRAPHY

Poverty, illness, and tanka—the traditional thirty-one-syllable Japanese poem—permeate many of the twenty-six years of Takuboku Ishikawa's life, and like the contradictory manifestations that moderns are bombarded with, such an unusual triumvirate represents Takuboku's fall and greatness.

Takuboku's father, Ittei Ishikawa, was the fifth son of a peasant in Iwate Prefecture. In mid-nineteenth-century Japan a needy family living in a poor rural community hoped one of its sons would become a priest, the position being a kind of religious protection against the bleak aftermath of life, to say nothing of the immediate security and status such a career offered. Ittei was taught by Taigetsu Katsurahara, who was versed in Chinese classics and skilled in the tea ceremony and who was himself a poet whose tanka, while conventional, were nevertheless well formed. Even Ittei wrote tanka, typical and unoriginal to be sure, but like his teacher's, excellent in structure:

> I have given up this world
> As full of taint, yet there is nowhere to move.

> What shall I do with this aging me? Neither floating
> nor sinking,
> I drift, tossed by the waves of years.

> How peaceful the village of Tamayama!
> The sunshine so soft, Mt. Kohime in haze.[1]

11

Takuboku's mother, Katsu Kudō, was Katsurahara's younger sister,[2] and she herself had been a very bright youngster. The private school she attended had trained her in calligraphy, reading, and some arithmetic.

In 1874, Ittei was appointed temple priest in a village next to Shibutami in Iwate Prefecture. Only twenty-five at the time, he was exceptionally young for the position. Certainly Katsurahara's influence was a major factor in earning Ittei the appointment. It was in this Zen temple that Takuboku was born on February 20, 1886,[3] the third child in a family with two daughters, Sada (ten) and Tora (eight). As Takuboku's parents had separate family registers because Zen priests in those days were not supposed to marry, the child Hajime (Takuboku is a penname) was listed in his mother's family register as a son born out of wedlock to Katsu Kudō. It must have been quite surprising to Takuboku's classmates in his second year at lower primary school to find Hajime Kudō had suddenly become Hajime Ishikawa. His father and mother had probably decided it was inconvenient and painful for a schoolboy to have parents with different family names. Bastard children were subject to ridicule and hate.

In 1887, Ittei was transferred to the temple in Shibutami, a village which is on the old highway to Aomori, the northernmost city in Honshu. The former priest had died, but the son who would usually be next in line for the post was too young, so Ittei had been selected. Katsurahara had influenced the incumbent of the head temple to appoint Ittei, while Ittei was himself persuading a group of influential parishioners. The parties concerned disregarded the plight of the bereaved family members, who had to leave the temple without any means of livelihood. Usually members of a village have an interim-incumbent until the temple son is old enough to succeed his dead father, but in this instance no such guarantee was provided. Ittei's hard bargaining caused some villagers to dislike him and to have misgivings about him, so the prize carried with it a residue of antagonism.

After moving to Shibutami, Ittei discovered his chief goal was the reconstruction of the temple, which had been destroyed by fire a decade earlier. By the time he was forty, the task was accomplished, an impressive three-year achievement, but one Ittei was never to equal during the remainder of his own sad life.

Takuboku was a small delicate child, but he was quite happy during these early years, doted on as he was by his parents. His sister Tora said that after the boy's birth their mother disregarded her daughters. Another child, Mitsuko, was born December 12, 1888, and she too remarked that her parents were overly partial to Takuboku, who became increasingly wilful.

As a primary school student in Shibutami in 1891, Takuboku established the best record in his class. In those days the lower primary school course lasted four years, so in 1895 Takuboku entered an upper primary school in Morioka,[4] which is about ten kilometers south of Shibutami. Takuboku's uncle on his mother's side boarded him in Morioka for two years during these upper primary school days, and later, in 1899, Takuboku lived with his married sister in the same city.

After finishing his third year of upper primary school, Takuboku successfully entered Morioka Middle School, the five-year course roughly equivalent to Japan's present secondary school system. Takuboku had ranked tenth out of 128 when he entered, but his record steadily declined. In spite of this performance, Takuboku remained a precocious student. One of his achievements was a literary manuscript handwritten in ink and circulated. With a school friend (Koshirō Oikawa, later a famous admiral), Takuboku visited Kyōsuke Kindaichi (1882-1971) and formed what was to be a lifelong friendship with him. Kindaichi, who as a professor at Tokyo University became a well-known expert on the Ainu language, was not only Takuboku's first teacher of tanka but continually helped Takuboku during his miserable years of poverty. Kindaichi had contributed poems to tanka magazines, and he lent Takuboku all the issues of the famous literary magazine *Myōjō*, which Tekkan Yosano (1873-1935) had established in November 1899 and which published many of the memorable tanka written by his wife, Akiko Yosano (1878-1942). *Myōjō*'s October 1902 number carried one tanka by Hakuhin Ishikawa. *Hakuhin*, translated as "white flowers of the water weed," was Takuboku's penname at the time. The November 1902 issue contained two of his tanka; and that of December 1902, three:

With these poems written in blood as proof of my life,
I wander in tears through the fields of autumn.

———

As a dream vanishes soon, so love dies in a moment:
Let those who will say so—I do not mind.

———

Suddenly awake, I closed my eyes, relieved,
Thinking of the darkness at the end of my dream.

In 1901, a student strike erupted at Takuboku's middle school in Morioka. It was Takuboku's third-year class which first protested, demanding reform, and the fourth-year students soon followed. The action, begun at the end of February, lasted about a week. The startling decline in Takuboku's class standing at the end of his third year was probably due to this event and to his literary pursuits.

In that year he had organized a student literary association and had begun circulating a school magazine he called *Mikazuki (Crescent)*. In the autumn of this same year, Takuboku and some of his friends began distributing a new magazine, *Nigitama (Soft Soul)*, the word associated with the ancient Shinto belief that two souls exist in each person, one *(nigitama)* representing the sensitive aspects of mind, the other *(aramitama)* symbolizing the warlike. Added to the young student's romantic tendencies was his interest in Setsuko Horiai, with whom he had become acquainted in his sister's neighborhood in 1899. That interest soon flowered into love.

The first issue of *Nigitama* included Takuboku's essay "Aki no Urei" ("The Sorrows of Autumn") and a series of thirty tanka he called "Akikusa" ("Autumn Flowers"), a few of which follow:

> Do not tell others, little pillow, of my dreams tonight.
> Sometimes I resented, sometimes sorrowed, and
> sometimes I was happy too.

> Softly opening the door to the brightly lit palace room,
> I peeped in, drawn by the *koto* she played.

> I will not curse the world of men, nor will I even regret.
> No longer. The cloud of ideals in tatters now.

Despite this last tanka, Takuboku maintained his sympathy for the downtrodden, which had been first awakened by the student strike. That sympathy found further expression in the sensational incident of December 10, 1901. Shōzō Tanaka, an ex-member of the Lower House, disturbed the entourage of Emperor Meiji on its way to the opening ceremony of the Diet by attempting to hand the emperor a petition urging him to stop the wastes of the Ashio Copper Mine from entering and polluting the downstream farmlands in Tochigi Prefecture. In February 1902, Takuboku and other members of his literary club sent a donation to the suffering peasants victimized by the most famous pollution incident in Meiji (1868-1912) and Taishō (1912-1926) Japan. Throughout his life Takuboku questioned injustice in the legal, political, and economic systems. He was especially troubled by various codes in Japanese family relationships.

Yet it was an incident of cheating on an examination that created the first really crucial event in Takuboku's life. In April 1902, he was reprimanded for "misconduct on the terminal examination." At the end of his fourth year of middle school, he ranked eighty-second in a class of 119. Despite the earlier warning, he cheated again in July. A scholarship student wrote the answers to a mathematics test on two sheets of paper, and as he left the classroom, he handed one to Takuboku. Because this student was deprived of his scholarship, Takuboku undoubtedly felt responsible for the penalty. As for Takuboku himself, he was not merely reprimanded: his examination papers were voided, and his punishment was publicly announced. In October, he suddenly left school "for family reasons" and went up to Tokyo.

Takuboku's withdrawal from Morioka Middle School prevented him from graduating. Since the graduate of a middle school was equivalent in status to today's college graduate, the middle school diploma was a necessary stepping-stone to a better career. The real elite, of course, were the university graduates, but a middle school diploma was almost a prerequisite for work demanding intellect. Takuboku did try to find a vacancy in the fifth-year classes around Kanda, the student quarter in Tokyo, but he was unable to gain admission. Consequently, his formal education ended with his departure from Morioka. As a Meiji dropout, he had difficulty acquiring a good job.

On November 9, 1902, the aspiring poet attended a meeting of Tekkan's Shinshi-sha (New Poetry Association), and the following day Takuboku visited the famous tankaists Tekkan and his wife, Akiko. Later Tekkan was to write in a supplement to the Kaizōsha edition of Takuboku's works (published in monthly volumes with accompanying leaflets in 1938-1939) that the lad was frank, bright, noble, and sagacious, "a very spirited young man." From the time of this visit, Takuboku went every day to the public library where he became absorbed in literature, including works in English, even attempting to translate into Japanese an English translation of Ibsen's *John Gabriel Borkman*. The end of the year, however, found Takuboku ill and poverty-stricken. Three poems written for his middle school alumni magazine suggest Takuboku's mood in leaving home, feeling disoriented, and confronting an intense and passionate loneliness:

> Fallen leaves of late autumn, destined to decay!
> Following them in sympathy, I hurried to start my journey.

> Not knowing where the wind has gone that blew it
> from its twig,
> This stray leaf, bewildered and lost, has fallen on my sleeve.

> Is there a friend in these fields who will cry out treading the
> waste weeds?
> This evening cloud of autumn burning like a flame!

In February 1903, Takuboku's father had to accompany his son home to Shibutami from Tokyo because of illness. Perhaps this physical setback was the earliest indication of Takuboku's tuberculosis. While recuperating, he read Wagner and, under his penname Hakuhin, proceeded to write "On Wagner's Thought," an article in ten installments for the *Iwate Nippō*. In the July issue of *Myōjō*, four of Takuboku's tanka were published, one of which suggests the origin for the poet's adoption of the name he was to use later:

> So thin have I grown,
> As ugly as some slim woodpecker scurrying about
> in the bush.

Takuboku is the Chinese pronunciation of *kitsutsuki* (woodpecker). Most Japanese woodpeckers are beautifully colored, but Takuboku probably envisioned a drab bird, which is usually disliked because it slyly eludes human detection.

Another tanka in the same issue suggests Takuboku's changed condition:

> Will not my parents cry if I tell them my life
> Will perish in the dark with this flame?

In the November 1903 issue of *Myōjō*, twelve more of Takuboku's tanka appeared under the name Hakuhin, two of which follow:

> Only a glance! That single sight I had of her
> Started this wild blaze in my heart!

> ———

> A phosphorous fire on the altar,
> A witch of the land of the dead combs her sinful hair
>   throughout the night!

That month Takuboku was nominated for regular membership in the Shinshi-sha, and in December he published five poems, each fourteen lines long. For the first time he signed his name Takuboku, though four tanka in the same issue bore his earlier penname.

Takuboku published numerous tanka, articles, and critical reviews in 1904. By the end of October, he had returned to Tokyo and remained there with the intention of bringing out his first book of poems. He was regarded as one of the most promising of the younger poets. But a real turning point in his life came on December 26 with his father's dismissal as the incumbent of the temple in Shibutami.

The synod of the Sōtō sect of Zen Buddhism had deprived Ittei of the post for failing to send in the regular donation of fees from temple income. Debts and traveling expenses for his son's illness might have had something to do with this oversight, but the main cause was Ittei's laxity in financial concerns. Stubborn by nature and somewhat naive in the ways of the world, he had disregarded the synod's repeated demands for payment. The dismissal meant that Takuboku had to assume responsibility for supporting the family.

On March 2, 1905, Ittei and the remaining members of his family left their temple home. Takuboku, in Tokyo at the time, was informed of the event by mail. Ittei himself had no plans for the future. Angered by the attitude of some of the villagers and by the indifference of the synod, which had given no consideration to his meritorious service over the past twenty years, he had rashly left the temple. Finding his present difficulties too much to endure, he went to Aomori Prefecture to live with Katsurahara, his teacher-priest and brother-in-law. On March 23, 1906, a letter came from the synod in which Ittei was pardoned for his offense, and hearing the news, he left for Shibutami on

April 10. Later a meeting of parishioners was held, and a decision was made to request Ittei's reinstatement. But a conflict between two factions erupted, one supporting the reinstatement, the other violently opposing it. With the intensification of his financial crisis, with further persecution from some of the villagers, and with added economic hardship caused by the birth of Takuboku's daughter on December 29, 1906 (Takuboku having married in 1905), Ittei once more left home, this time on March 5, 1907, his hope for the reappointment abandoned. Takuboku also moved away soon after. His father returned to Tokyo in December 1909 to live with his son, who was again poverty-stricken at that time. After a quarrel in which Ittei struck his wife, he again retreated in September 1911, though the ultimate reason was the family's unbearable poverty. Ittei did not even attend his wife's cremation in March 1912, but in April that same year, having been living in Hokkaido with his son-in-law's family, he came to Tokyo after learning of Takuboku's serious illness. When the poet died on April 13, his father was present.

Takuboku's departure from middle school, his father's loss of position as temple priest, and the breakup of the family caused Takuboku considerable anguish. A fourth major concern in his life was his marriage to Setsuko Horiai, the sweetheart of his Morioka schooldays.

Urged by the Horiais to speed up the proceedings, the Ishikawa family decided to hold the ceremony on May 30, 1905. At that time, Takuboku was in Tokyo. But on the appointed day, the traveling bridegroom was nowhere in sight. The go-between and the two families were panic-stricken. Finally it was agreed the festivities would take place in spite of the omission of the ceremony. The party opened lamely enough without Takuboku, some of the guests having already departed. Setsuko was calm throughout, apparently confident of Takuboku's good faith. A few days later Takuboku turned up without the slightest trace of embarrassment or guilt. The reasons for his delay remain unclear. Biographer Yukinori Iwaki believes the poet fell prey to anxieties, overwhelmed as he was by the heavy responsibility of supporting others when he was uncertain about providing for himself. In spite of an overweening pride in his literary gifts, Takuboku lacked real drive. He had left Tokyo on May 20; he had hoped to remain in Sendai for ten days and to return home by the thirtieth. The Sendai interlude may be called a failure of nerve, a futile attempt to escape the reality of a future commitment, but his actions show equally the egotism of a man of letters and the strong confidence he had in Setsuko's love.

A further complication arose to mar these marital beginnings. Setsuko's father had been strongly opposed to the connection because he was an old-fashioned moralist who believed in arranged marriage, not in the freedom of choice of the young participants. He had reluctantly given his permission because his sister had threatened him by informing him the lovers might "do anything," implying the possibility of the double love-suicide so common in Japanese society. Takuboku's mother was also reluctant to sanction the match. The later quarrels between the new bride and her mother-in-law were more deep-rooted than the usual antagonism that exists in these complicated Japanese roles.

Since the nineteen-year-old Takuboku was a new family man, he rented a two-room house in Morioka in which the bride, the groom's parents, and Takuboku's younger sister Mitsuko were to live. Five people in two small rooms proved cumbersome, and it foreshadowed even greater difficulties despite the fact that on June 25, 1905, Takuboku moved to a larger house in the city. The rent of five yen a month was a considerable sum, and the poverty of the family continued. Takuboku's mental distress was intensified by the fact that he had become the major support of his family. The newlyweds occupied one room in the five-room house where they enjoyed a brief period of happiness. The husband took pleasure in listening to the violin solos his wife played to him.

The family income consisted of the small sums Takuboku received for writing a series of newspaper articles for the *Iwate Nippō*, presided over by his old teacher. Most of the living expenses, however, came from selling meager family possessions. Takuboku's attempt to start a new literary magazine was perhaps motivated more by economic circumstance than by literary inclination. Single-handedly he made an amazing effort to establish *Shōtenchi (Microcosm)*, whose first number was a brilliant success. Critics in Tokyo were surprised by the fact that many noted writers contributed to this little magazine published in a small city in the north. But the venture was short-lived. Financial considerations prevented the appearance of the second issue.

Takuboku was forced to find some other means of livelihood, and he finally decided to return to his native village on April 11, 1906, to accept, thanks to his father-in-law's help, a position as a substitute teacher at the Shibutami Primary School. The eight yen a month salary was low. That the young Takuboku was overly confident of his pedagogic talents is revealed in a diary he kept at the time. His attitude bordered on the arrogant. Apparently some of the villagers were against his appointment, afraid his personality would lead them into difficulties. He had of course not wanted to become a teacher, nor was he interested in village politics. Some misunderstanding, at any rate, was at work. It may be that Takuboku felt himself persecuted more than he actually was. Although it seems unlikely the villagers wanted to drive him out, Takuboku indicated they did in a tanka in *A Handful of Sand* (see p. 29):

> This sorrow of being driven from my home
> As if pelted with stones
> Will never disappear.

He had a general dislike for the provincial mind one expects in a Japanese village. Though he had a special nostalgia for the rural area of his earliest and happiest years, he hated its inhabitants, mainly because of their treatment of his father.

Setsuko gave birth to a daughter in December 1906, and the financial situation grew even more desperate, especially after the poet's year-long struggle to help his father regain the temple had failed. Determined to begin a new life in Hokkaido, Takuboku tendered his resignation from the school on April 1 that year, but on the nineteenth, in another maneuver typical of him, he persuaded the upper-course primary pupils to follow him to the southern edge of the village and go on strike to expel the principal. Then and there Takuboku taught them the chorus of a revolutionary song he composed on the spot. The commotion that ensued led to the principal's transfer, but instead of granting Takuboku's request to resign, the authorities ordered a dismissal, a further blot on the young man's record.

The breakup of the family occurred next. Takuboku's wife and child Kyōko went to live with his in-laws in Morioka, and his mother moved in with a village acquaintance. In June 1907, Takuboku found a job as a substitute teacher in a primary school in the city of Hakodate in Hokkaido. Despite his low salary of twelve yen a month, Setsuko and Kyōko came to Hakodate on July 7, and the couple set up housekeeping at 18 Aoyagichō. His mother came on August 4.

Misfortune, however, continued to dog him when both the primary school appointment and the side job he had taken as a free-lance reporter were eliminated after a fire destroyed the greater part of Hakodate on August 25. He resigned from the school on September 11 and went to Sapporo to work as a newspaper proofreader. Soon he was invited to join the staff of a paper to be founded in Otaru, a port city near Sapporo. At a salary of twenty yen a month he was jointly in charge of city news with Ujō Noguchi, later a popular poet and songwriter. Takuboku rented two upstairs rooms and lived there with his wife, mother, and child.

Before long, however, he joined in a plot with Noguchi to oust their editor, but the scheme was discovered, and Noguchi was forced to resign. Takuboku, oddly enough, received an increase in pay to become city editor on his own. At the post he displayed his talents to the full, editing the paper as he wished. He was the central figure in this newly established publication, yet characteristically he found himself opposing the chief editor. Takuboku finally managed to have his friend Shintarō Sawada declared editor-in-chief. Unfortunately a conflict within the staff again flared up in December, and Takuboku was physically assaulted by the business manager. Angry, the poet announced his own resignation in the very next edition.

As soon as he resigned from the *Otaru Nippō*, Takuboku and his family were plunged into difficulties. They could not afford to live without an income for even a short period. Usually slow to act, Takuboku was worried this time and anxiously tried to find employment, but his repeated attempts proved useless. At this juncture his friend Sawada persuaded the president of the *Otaru Nippō*, who was also head of a newspaper in Kushiro, to employ Takuboku on the other publication, but Sawada's efforts were undermined by certain conditions Takuboku demanded before accepting the position.

Nevertheless, on January 10, 1908, Sawada visited Takuboku to present him with a ten-yen note offered by the president. The poet was out, but both his wife and mother, their eyes stained with tears, received the money gratefully. Sawada strongly advised Takuboku to accept the appointment for the sake of his family, and he did. Sawada again visited the family about a week after Takuboku had set off for his job in Kushiro. The friend found the women trembling from the cold in a house devoid of paper screens. (Rented houses in Hokkaido were not equipped with these or with *tatami* mats.) Takuboku's family had been forced to sell their own screens, so they were without the added protection against the Hokkaido winter.

Leaving his family in extreme poverty, Takuboku headed for Kushiro, located in the northeast end of Hokkaido. He assumed his new twenty-yen-a-month job as editor-in-chief of the

Kushiro Shinbun. He had been told he would be city editor, but on arrival he found himself in full command. Deeply impressed by the esteem with which the owner regarded him, Takuboku was determined to improve the paper. His talents as a journalist bore fruit, and the *Kushiro Shinbun* soon overwhelmed its rival.

One of the features in the paper was a column about geisha and their amours, which Takuboku himself had originated. To gather material, he visited restaurants and met geisha. In a letter to a friend, Takuboku said it was at Kushiro that he first began drinking sake. Before long he came to spend several days at a time at a "restaurant,"[5] from which he went to work when he became sober and to which he usually returned the same day. Some Japanese restaurants, especially those in rural areas, had overnight accommodations.

Of course it was not merely enthusiasm for his work that led Takuboku into such activities. He knew that naturalism was about to witness its golden age in Tokyo and that many writers were immersed in this new literary movement. To continue as editor of a local paper at the farthest edge of Japan meant isolation from these strong literary currents. It was partly to beguile the irritation caused by such reflections that Takuboku began his life of indulgence, but his lonely existence separated from his wife and child was another partial factor. In a letter to a friend, Takuboku said he had "found solace in the sympathy of a geisha who took away his sake-bottle . . . and prevented [him from] getting dead drunk."

The geisha referred to was Koyakko, Takuboku's Kushiro sweetheart, whose brief connection with him he was to remember all his remaining years. Because he was the editor of a local paper and a well-known Tokyo poet, many women made advances to him, the most aggressive a hospital nurse and another the daughter of the incumbent of a Buddhist temple, but he paid little attention to them. His real attachment was to Koyakko. There had been a woman he had truly admired, Chieko Tachibana, a teacher at a primary school in Hakodate, but his devotion to her remained entirely platonic. She appears in twenty-three poems in his two tanka collections. The following are the most impressive:

> Her black pupils
> Absorbing only the light of this world
> Remain in my eyes

As boys born in mountains
Yearn for mountains,
I think of you when in sorrow.

———

Were I to confess
I wished to see you before I died,
Would you give me the slightest nod?

When Takuboku left Hakodate for Sapporo, he brought Chieko a copy of his first book of long poems, *Akogare (Yearning)*, which had been published on May 3, 1905. Years later, on hearing about Takuboku's illness in Tokyo, Chieko sent him some fresh butter, the gift the subject of one of the tanka in *Sad Toys*.

The relationship with Koyakko, however, was an entirely different matter. Born in Hakodate on October 15, 1890, and given the name Jin, she was the daughter of a dry goods retailer and his wife, Yori. When the girl was nine years old, she was adopted by her mother's elder brother, Matsutarō Tsubo. Upon his death, the young child was informally adopted by the owner of a small restaurant in Obihiro, the Hakodateya, and it was in this establishment that she learned dancing, samisen playing, and other requisites for becoming a geisha. Quite attached to her mother, however, Jin came to Kushiro where her parent had remarried, her husband the owner of an inn. Jin rented a house and became a star geisha on her own, serving for the most part the guests of the Shamotora restaurant.[6] Pretty, accomplished, and sweet-tempered, she had taken as her geisha name Koyakko, *yakko* a common suffix for the profession, *ko* meaning "little" or "child."

She found Takuboku "a small man of undignified appearance with a disproportionately large head," but he was quiet, he smiled when he drank, and women liked him. He easily succumbed to the effects of sake, for when someone pressed him to drink, he did not know how to decline with tact. On such occasions Koyakko often saved him by downing the sake herself. As she was a rather spirited girl, she acted as if she were actually in love with Takuboku when she was teased about her kindness to him. Accordingly, a rumor that they were attached to one another provoked the couple into an even greater intimacy. She came to visit him at his lodgings, and they walked together along the sandy beach at Kushiro. They fell in love in earnest. But due to Takuboku's decision not to remain in Kushiro, their affair was short-lived. The indelible impression Koyakko left on his memory is testified to by the dozen or so tanka about her in *A Handful of Sand*, a few of which follow:

> Waiting till I was dead drunk,
> She whispered to me
> Those many sad things!

———

> When I was drunk and drooped my head
> And when I was thirsty and awoke,
> It was *her* name I called.

———

> On the way back along corridors
> Creaking under these feet in the cold—
> Her sudden kiss!

———

> While pillowing this head on her lap,
> All I had in mind
> Was myself.

Koyakko's tender feelings toward him continued. His diary of October 26, 1908, reveals his surprise on receiving a postcard picturing a geisha, Koyakko herself, and he wondered how she had discovered his Tokyo address. On December 1, she actually turned up at his boardinghouse. They went for a walk and stopped at an Asakusa drinking house, and becoming inebriated and feeling "glorious," he once more escorted her back to her inn, where they kissed on parting. She called again five days later, and again they took a long walk. She leaned against him and sang in a low voice, and later that night they went out to drink with his middle-school friend Kindaichi, who was living in the same boardinghouse at the time. When Takuboku visited Koyakko at her inn the next day, she was waiting for him, and after she sought his counsel about her circumstances, he advised her to become the concubine of her present patron. Eventually, she married this man, and from the union came the birth of a daughter. On February 26, 1909, Takuboku noted in his diary that Koyakko had wired him twenty yen. This period, shortly before he was to take a job with the Tokyo *Asahi* as a newspaper proofreader, was one of financial turmoil for him.

Koyakko was divorced in June 1923 and returned with her daughter to the Ōmiya inn kept by her mother. Changing her family name to Ōmi, Koyakko took over the management of the business. She moved to Toyama in 1962 and a little later to Tokyo, where at the age of seventy-six she died in 1965 in a home for elderly women.

Though only a geisha, Koyakko had apparently gone beyond the usual accomplishments of such women as evidenced by the following tanka she wrote:

You visit this inn connected with Takuboku,
But the woman in the poems, worn to a shadow.

———

Over sixty, and again I live that day of nineteen,
Reading these poems written by my love.

———

As I talk about Takuboku, long outliving him,
Sweet memories of him and of my youthful days return.

Probably Takuboku felt more guilt than happiness in this affair with Koyakko and his contacts with other women, for he was continually worried about his wife, mother, and child; on the other hand, his position as a writer preyed equally on his mind. He keenly felt his isolation from the literary circles in Tokyo where naturalism was nearing its heyday. His desire to become a writer, therefore, overshadowed both family and debauchery, and leaving Koyakko, who had desperately tried to dissuade him, he departed for Hakodate on April 15, 1908. He stopped there to raise travel funds and to find a house for his family while he was away. His friend Daishirō Miyazaki, whom Takuboku had met at a society for tanka poets in Hakodate in the summer of 1907, helped him solve both problems, and the aspiring writer left for Tokyo on April 24.

On reaching Tokyo, Takuboku first stopped at Tekkan's poetry association, the Shinshi-sha, and through the famous tankaist's influence was promised an appointment to the staff of a newspaper. However, the possibility did not materialize, and Takuboku was given the job of correcting poems sent to the Shinshi-sha by amateurs. With no definite prospect for a sufficient income, Takuboku decided to live by writing stories, and he worked at them strenuously. But his optimistic expectations were shattered when, in spite of the efforts of Kindaichi and the recommendation of the famous novelist Ōgai Mori (1862-1922), the manuscripts were continually rejected.

On May 4, 1908, Takuboku moved into the Sekishinkan, the boardinghouse where Kindaichi was living. The poet shared his friend's lodging for the night, and the next day Takuboku rented an upstairs room. Both his desk and chair were given him by Kindaichi. Takuboku had thought it would not be too difficult to pay the expenses at the end of each month by selling his stories. Actually, he had not even accumulated enough money for the first month's rent on June 11. As Kindaichi was talking to him that day, a servant came to ask for the payment. Kindaichi pawned some of his own clothing for twelve yen and lent Takuboku the required sum.

The poet continued to devote himself solely to writing, composing five stories in one month, a total output of more than three hundred manuscript pages, but with none of the stories accepted, Takuboku despaired of ever becoming a writer. His days were spent in further agony when he learned of the suicide of Bizan Kawakami (1869-1908), the philosopher and critic, and the death of the famous short-story writer Doppo Kunikida (1871-1908).

But the night of June 23, 1908, was the beginning of one of those unique creative interludes found only in the talented few. Inspired, Takuboku had composed at least 246 tanka in fifty hours from the early morning of June 24 to 2 a.m. on June 26. Written at this time were such famous tanka as

> On the white sand of a small isle in the eastern sea,
> I play with crabs,
> Tears on my face

> Carrying my mother playfully on my back,
> I take one step, two, no more—
> How her lightness dims these eyes....

> Calling my own name softly, I shed tears:
> It was spring, and I was fourteen,
> And never again would this day come back to me.

One hundred of these tanka written in three glorious days were published in the July 1908 issue of *Myōjō*.[7]

INTRODUCTION

Takuboku's well-known association with the Tokyo *Asahi* newspaper began in March 1909 when he acquired the job as proofreader at a salary of twenty-five yen per month with an extra yen for each night of duty for the early morning edition.

In April, his mother, whom he had left just about a year ago at Hakodate with his wife and child, pleaded in a letter to bring them all to Tokyo. But he could not comply because he was in arrears with his rent for the boardinghouse he had moved into the previous September. His life of self-torture intensified over his guilt in being unable to meet his parent's request. He did not want his family in Tokyo: he was of course irresponsible, yet at the same time he could not be certain he would be able to provide the necessities. Furthermore, if his family came, he would not have, he realized, the freedom required for writing. This disgust with himself manifested itself in dissipation in low-class brothels in Tokyo's Asakusa district. It was during this period that Takuboku kept his *Romaji Diary*. Various entries vividly express his feelings toward his family (see, for example, those of April 7, p. 62, and April 15, p. 84), his desire to escape (April 10, p. 70, and May 16, p. 119), and the occasional threat of suicide (April 16, p. 87).

Takuboku's friend Miyazaki had taken care of the family in Hakodate, and in June 1909 Miyazaki brought Takuboku's mother, wife, and child to Tokyo. Takuboku rented two rooms above a barbershop. During the Hakodate days, the antagonism between the daughter-in-law and the husband's mother, a traditional conflict in hierarchic and feudalistic Japan, had intensified, and the conflict did not end with the reunion in Tokyo.

The relationship between Takuboku and his wife, Setsuko, provides another of those strands of complexity in the poet's life. They became acquainted when he was in middle school in Morioka, and at nineteen they had married. The new bride regularly attended the tanka meetings held at their home, and she even wrote some poems in the *Myōjō* style of the day:

> Awake at dawn
> After a night of sleep
> On the grass in my beautiful robe—
> The cricket's chirp
> And my lover in dreams

This sunflower,
Flower of gold,
Suddenly in full bloom,
Enticed
By my songs of flame!

———

This evening
Of pale light
When the cricket sings:
Autumn has come,
Embracing these breasts.

———

This me, a black lily,
A cursed flower
That blooms in the shade
Of old mountains,
My hair long in summer.

Apparently Setsuko believed a curse was hanging over her lovely head. She had lived with her husband from June 1905 to May 1907, a period of almost two years before Takuboku left for Hakodate on May 4. After this interlude of their first two years of marriage came a series of separations—some brief, some lengthy—which destroyed their intimacy and added to their marital difficulties.

The *Romaji Diary* reveals that Takuboku was not happy to have his family members rejoin him in Tokyo. They did indeed arrive on June 16, 1909, the last line of this remarkable document noting that "we arrived at our new home by jinrikisha." That key moment in Takuboku's life was to prove a kind of breaking point. Several tanka in *Sad Toys* (*Kanashiki Gangu*, 1912), the collection of poems written in the last year and a half of his life, record the conflict between Setsuko and Takuboku's mother:

Placed in the midst
Of a discord impossible to dispel—
Sadly I spent another day in anger

———

If I keep a cat,
That too will sow some seed of strife—
O my miserable home!

The tension between a new bride and her mother-in-law is proverbial in Japanese life, where filial piety demands the husband support, at least openly, his mother in any situation. The wife is expected to remain silent, obedient to all demands made on her. Setsuko undoubtedly bore up like a first-rate Japanese wife, but her own declining health must have proved too exacting, for irritability accompanies illness and restraint has its limitations on a sickbed.

Though Setsuko had arrived in Tokyo in June 1909, she left at the beginning of October, but left by running away with her daughter, Kyōko. Only a note was offered in explanation. She was of course fleeing from the tension of living with her irreconcilable mother-in-law. In addition, since September Setsuko had been ill with pleurisy, and she wanted to have it treated and to get some needed rest. She also wished to help her sister in preparing for her marriage to Miyazaki, who had been so kind to the family during its Hokkaido days. Due to the efforts of Kindaichi and others, however, Setsuko was persuaded to return at the end of the month, but Takuboku had been dealt another severe blow. He had learned that the fragile moments of life can only be grasped by firmly encasing them in tanka—human beings were another matter.

The son born to Setsuko in October the following year died on the twenty-seventh of the same month. It was on the day of his son's birth that the Tōundō Publishing Company had paid Takuboku twenty yen for his second volume of poems, *Ichiaku no Suna (A Handful of Sand)*, published on December 1, 1910. (Each of the 551 tanka was written in three lines, a departure from the traditional form of printing them in one or two lines). Takuboku had to spend for his son's burial the only sum the publishers were to give him for this volume.

The year 1910 can be considered an important year in tanka history due to the publication of *A Handful of Sand*, but it also marks the beginning of the development of Takuboku's interest in socialism.

We have seen from Takuboku's schooldays the rebel in him, protesting, going on strike, maneuvering for power, sympathizing with the exploited. But it was the report of the Kōtoku Incident on June 5, 1910, that profoundly catapulted Takuboku's thought toward social movements. All his earlier activity had been more like some adolescent testing ground. Now the injustice of the world—social, political, economic—struck home forcibly during the so-called treason trial of Shūsui Kōtoku, a journalist and anarchist. Several members of his group had formed plans to assassinate Emperor Meiji. Though Kōtoku was opposed to the scheme, he was somehow involved in it. The Meiji government had of course been suppressing radicals with its own system of censorship and incarceration. Before any of the assassination bombs had been transported to the scene of the crime, the conspirators were arrested. The arrests began toward the end of May 1910, Kōtoku himself taken on June 1. Reports of the sensational event appeared in the newspapers on June 5. The trial, held in December of that year, was secret; not a witness was summoned. The court also took the precaution of seeing that the records did not remain in the hands of counsel. Only five of the defendants were involved in the bomb-making, and it is believed today that Kōtoku had no part in the assassination plot. Nevertheless, he was sentenced to death at the closed trial, mainly because the government had been suppressing what it saw as "dangerous thought." The incident remains the most revealing example of despotism during the Meiji period.

Takuboku's friend Shū Hiraide was a counsel for the defense of these twenty-six socialists headed by Kōtoku. The defense Kōtoku himself wrote while in prison, Takuboku recopied. The task required two days to complete. He began reading socialist literature, including Kropotkin's *A Plea to Youth*. On January 18, 1911, the decision in the case of high treason was unprecedentedly severe: twenty-four of the twenty-six were sentenced to death. But on the following day, due to the "benign order of the Emperor," twelve of the twenty-four had their sentences reduced to life imprisonment. The shock to Takuboku was, nevertheless, great. On January 23, he reviewed the case trial records, and the next day he wrote "The Plot by Japanese Anarchists: The Course of Events and Attendant Phenomena." Eleven of the condemned, including Kōtoku, were executed on January 24; the only female, Kōtoku's mistress, was executed a day later. At Hiraide's house on January 26, Takuboku read through the seven thousand pages of trial record.

During Takuboku's hospitalization from February 4 to March 15, he read Kropotkin's autobiography, *Memoirs of a Revolutionist*. At home the poet perused the back numbers of the *Heimin Shinbun*, which had been put out by the social anarchists Kōtoku and Toshihiko Sakai,[8] and he also spent time going through other socialist journals and literature. Even as his health declined, he wrote about the Kōtoku Incident, and on November 17, 1911, he finished copying Kropotkin's *Terror in Russia*. Earlier in the year Takuboku had written a series of poems revealing his socialist leanings. He called these poems *Yobuko*

to *Kuchibue (The Whistle and Whistling)*. According to Katsuichiro Kamei in his postscript to *The Works of Takuboku* (in
Works of Modern Japanese Literature, vol. 39, Tokyo: Kodansha,
1964, p. 421), these seven poems created under conditions of
illness reveal "not a trace of morbidity ... and little sentimentality or romanticism." Kamei sees in *Whistle* the perfection of
Takuboku's art, poems "tense like a testament, there being
hardly any waste of emotion." This praise seems extreme when
one considers the high quality of Takuboku's tanka, but in
Whistle perhaps the best is "A Spoonful of Cocoa," written on
June 15:

I know
The sad heart of the terrorist—
A single-minded heart
Which finds it impossible to cut asunder speech and act,
A heart that wants to speak with deeds
Instead of words, which one has been deprived of,
A heart that hurls at the foe the body encasing it—
This is the sorrow serious and fervent men forever have.

Sipping cold cocoa from a spoon
After some eternal endless debate,
I know from this slightly bitter taste
The sad sad heart
Of the terrorist.

Takuboku could intuit "the sad heart of the terrorist," though
he was outside any real kind of political activity. It was the
insight of a poet of acute sensitivity who could see into the
fractured structure of a world filled with unrealized moments.
In the first poem in *Whistle*, "After Endless Debate," he com-
pares Japanese youth to their Russian counterparts fifty years
ago, the eyes of his companions bright in hope arguing about the
methods of revolt, yet Takuboku writes—

... no one strikes the table with his clenched fist
And cries, "V Narod!"

V Narod! (Into the midst of the people) may have been true of
men not so lost in endless debate on the theory of property and
the state or on the exploited and miserable, but for Takuboku at
least, the energy needed by the active revolutionary was a
quality he lacked. In "A Heated Argument," the third poem in

the series, Takuboku notes how he himself debated for over five hours with N, a young economist and comrade, about the new society's disposal of power. N finally called his opponent a demagogue:

> But for the table between us
> His hand might have dealt this head a blow.
> His large swarthy face I saw
> Spill over with masculine rage.

Once the argument stopped one hour past that midnight in May, Takuboku felt relieved:

> How fresh the hint of rain in the wind of night
> On these convalescent yet agreeably heated
> cheeks of mine.

Takuboku could argue and suffer defeat in debate, but he could not at this late date act. Critic Kamei calls "My Home," the penultimate poem in the series, an excellent socialist statement: "It is a home like this that lies hidden in the depths of a mind suffering from destitution, and it may be said that all revolutionary passions contain such a yearning for home. It is not 'individualism' but a desire common to all poor people...." Today few will agree with Kamei. In fact, those who emphasize Takuboku as a revolutionary would like to disregard this poem, for it seems to reveal the limitation of Takuboku in this area. It is the expression of a secret desire of a frustrated man wearied from the battle with life. Nevertheless, the poem also shows his honesty and guilelessness. "My Home," we feel, rings with that perpetual desire in Takuboku to escape, to live a life of ease as a student or as a comfortable family man with enough books and cigarettes and leisure:

> Oh, its garden shall be wide, overspread with weeds,
> Oh, the pleasure of the sound of summer rain
> Falling on the wild grass covered with leaves.
> In one corner I'll plant a huge tree
> And at its foot I'll place a bench all painted white,
> And on rainless days I'll go out there
> And while smoking Egyptian cigarettes rich in fragrance
> with thick rings of smoke,
> I'll cut the pages of new books
> Maruzen sends every four or five days
> And pass the time dreamily until dinner's announced ...

The relationship between Takuboku and his wife continued to decline in June 1911. Once more Setsuko wished to visit her parents, for they were moving to Hakodate where her father had found a new job. After innumerable disputes which lasted from June 3 to June 6, the husband's objections won out. He refused to let Setsuko leave. He remembered his anguish during her flight from home almost two years earlier. Had she gone he had vowed to sever his connections to her family.

While this despotic attitude on the part of the male was commonplace in Meiji Japan, Takuboku's conduct may be cited as equally springing from the irritability of tuberculosis patients, who at any moment are likely to flare up into anger. In July, Takuboku developed a high fever, and his wife was also unwell from an illness diagnosed as a mild case of tuberculosis. In January 1912, his mother's lung hemorrhaged. The three adults in the family were suffering from the same illness. Since Setsuko's condition was comparatively slight, she had to undertake all the household chores.

Takuboku's history of ill health can be traced to his delicacy as a child. Certainly the continual pressures he had been under since his departure from middle school had not helped his condition. The *Romaji Diary* contains frequent references to his mental and physical anguish. The long poem entered in the *Diary* on April 10, 1909, notes Takuboku's desire for some illness to attack him in order to free him from responsibility:

> For a year, no, for even a month,
> Even for a week, three days even,
> O you gods, you gods, if you exist,
> Grant only, I beg, this one prayer:
> Damage some part of this body,
> Ever so slightly, painfully even.
> Of that I won't mind. . . . Oh, to be made ill!
> Oh, I beg!

He was to have this perverse wish granted. On February 1, 1911, he underwent a medical examination at the hospital attached to Tokyo University. He had felt unwell for some time, and his case was diagnosed as chronic peritonitis, a condition in which germs from the lungs settle in the abdomen. He had no idea his peritonitis was related to TB, for some types of peritonitis are not of this order. Key moments of his stay in the hospital from February 4 until March 15 are recorded in several of the tanka in *Sad Toys*. During this period his abdomen swelled, and he had to undergo an operation to drain the excess fluid out of the abdominal cavity. Whatever the illness, Takuboku must have long been conscious of the specter of tuberculosis.

The poet's last days were described in the postscript to *Sad Toys*, written by Takuboku's friend Aika Toki: "Several days before Takuboku's death," wrote Toki, "he asked me to find a publisher for his book of poems, as he was penniless. Immediately I went to Tōundō's and persuaded them, though with some difficulty." With the twenty-yen payment in his pocket, Toki hurried to Takuboku's home. Despite the emaciation in the poet's face and body due to the final stages of tuberculosis, Takuboku's eyes revealed his excitement on hearing the news. He felt he had to polish some of the poems, and he also wanted to arrange the series, but only after he recovered from his illness. However, Toki informed his friend that the publisher insisted on having the manuscript at once. Surprised, Takuboku waited a moment in silence before asking his wife to fetch what he called his "dismal-looking" notebook. It was medium-sized with gray flock-paper covers. This notebook Takuboku entrusted to his friend with the words, "From now on I must look to you for help."[9]

Takuboku succumbed to tuberculosis on April 13, 1912, one month after his mother died of the same disease. His wife also died of TB, on May 5, 1913.

ROMAJI DIARY

In Japanese literature the last flowering of the tradition of diary-writing, which dates back to the ninth century, fell to Shiki (Tsunenori Masaoka, 1867-1902)[10] and Takuboku. It is the latter's *Rōmaji Nikki* (diary in Roman letters, as opposed to the Japanese writing system of two syllabaries plus Chinese characters), kept from April 7 to June 16, 1909 (first published in 1948-49), which offers the reader a vivid portrait of a disturbed artist as Japan was itself undergoing radical change during the Meiji era.

Armando Martins Janeira in his *Japanese and Western Literature* says of the Japanese court diaries of the tenth to the fourteenth centuries that their originality is in their subtle and subdued poetic tone as well as their sharp delineation of psychological observations.[11] And in *Japanese Poetic Diaries* Earl

Miner makes a distinction between public diaries written as early as the eighth and ninth centuries that recorded events in classical Chinese and those Japanese diaries of a literary sort that were either private or diurnal. He notes that the Japanese diary as literary art most often concerns love instead of marriage, death rather than participation in mortal combat, the family in lieu of public life. Yet Miner believes that even when the literary Japanese diary is private, its content must be broader, in fact universal, if it is to be read with interest. These human concerns of nature, time, death, love, and family, he feels, must provide some thematic order of universal significance if they are to succeed as art.[12]

In Takuboku's *Romaji Diary* there is observation of certain current social conditions. We learn of Takuboku's interest in the new cinema and the popularity of some cinema commentators. Takuboku gives space to the naturalist movement, which dominated so much of the Japanese literary scene in the latter part of the nineteenth and early twentieth centuries. He speaks of the passing of major writers either by natural death or suicide, of Akiko and Tekkan Yosano, of Gorki and Turgenev. Family, marriage, home roots, love and death and friendship—all these larger social, moral, and philosophical areas—find their way into the diary as they do in other literary diaries. But with Takuboku the inner voice dominates, the personal element overwhelms, the existential dilemma of choice—the voice of disturbed modernity—commands attention.

Perhaps the best commentary on the *Diary* is found in an essay by Takeo Kuwabara. One group of writers, says Kuwabara, interests us so much that we are compelled to know about their actual lives, while a second group fails to interest us in this way. Kuwabara places Takuboku in the former group, his reason being that Takuboku was one of those modern Japanese writers whose works, if not the greatest, are the most intense.[13]

Romaji Diary may actually be considered a kind of novel in diary form; the conception is not too far removed from Takuboku's belief in tanka as a diary of the emotional changes in a poet's life. It is obvious that the *Diary* has all the elements of tanka moments; however, instead of a dispersal of scattered diurnal moments, which we might find in non-literary diaries, we discover the same unity found in classical diaries, but with something modern and disturbing that goes beyond traditional Bildungsroman, because our youthful hero—if we consider the *Diary* as a novel—is a kind of anti-hero. After all, Takuboku does not always turn out to be the admirable young man one hopes will overcome his difficulties in his pursuit of the good, the true, and the practical. It would seem as though something perverse in the hero, a Dostoyevskian personality pursuing illogicalities with a vengeance, were fighting against a program that would lift him from his dilemma, almost hurling himself toward even greater difficulties each step of the way.

When we consider the myriad of moments in each day, we are forced to conclude that the same task of selection faces the tankaist, the diarist, the short story writer, and the novelist. Obviously Takuboku could not plan his diary in the same way that James or Flaubert could speculate on a germ or devise a scenario. Yet the elements of the major problem he faced at this time remained constant: the ambivalence of various possibilities, the chemistry of fatal ambiguities, the eruption of moments and their fatal fallout—all these remain in the diary from its first pages to its last.

The *Diary* is not, of course, a literary work in the usual sense of that term. The author does not pay attention to form, and except for the unity given by the pervasiveness of his troubled mind, episodes are deficient in organic integration. Nevertheless, its great literary value and success lie in the fact that Takuboku wrote it entirely for himself without any expectation or fear that it would ultimately be read by others.

As a short story writer, Takuboku was a failure. One of the reasons was that his characters were not sufficiently alive. He observed them as if he were a superior existence rather than a fellow human sharing their weaknesses. Furthermore, his earlier diaries (written in the usual Japanese script) read like studies in short story writing. (In one story at least, we find a reproduction of a scene in his diary.) He always attempted to justify himself in his diaries, and the reader is sometimes led to wonder what the opposing party would say. In *Romaji Diary*, however, Takuboku was completely honest. He did not need to "judge" others; he concentrated on chronicling his mind and its reactions to people and events. And in this attempt his training as a short story writer aided him. He could accurately describe his own experience; without affectation he could see himself truthfully. Divested of encumbrances, his genius was fully displayed in bringing this unique document to life.

Why was the *Diary* written in *rōmaji*? Donald Keene has commented that such an unusual method of transcription would be comparable to someone's composing a diary in Esperanto today.[14] Takuboku himself provides a partial answer in his entry of April 7:

Why then have I decided to write this diary in Roman letters? What's the reason? I love my wife, and for the very reason I love her, I don't want her to read it. But I don't really mean that! That I love her is the truth, and that I don't want her to read it is equally true, but these two statements aren't necessarily connected.

Am I a weakling then? Not by any means. That is to say, this contradiction arises from the existence of that erroneous institution called Conjugal Relations. Matrimony! What a ridiculous institution! So what am I to do?

The obvious desire for secrecy on Takuboku's part even this early in the *Diary* may seem strange, for Takuboku could not know that the entries would proceed with passages that depict so frankly—incredibly so for 1909—his visits to red-light districts and activities therein, and that offer such highly critical comments on many of his contemporaries. Yet he must have known that because of his own personal honesty he would tell all and that he would be able to if he so wished because of the new method of transcription. Furthermore, in no other diary does Takuboku go into such minute detail on his sexual pursuits. The use of Roman letters permitted him a wide range of freedom.

But to treat the matter of secrecy in terms of his wife alone or his sexual tastes is to limit the *Diary's* range and intention. Because *rōmaji* itself had not yet been popularized, it was not Setsuko alone who would be unable to read it. Takuboku may not have wanted his "friends" to read it either. The following portions (from April 12) on friendship would undoubtedly have disturbed many of Takuboku's close associates:

> I think it's already time to separate from my old friends— yes! from my old pals—and to build a house of my own. . . .
> So don't be loved by others. Don't receive favors from others. Don't make promises to others. Never do anything that requires begging another's permission. Never tell others about yourself. Always wear a mask. Be ready at all times to fight, ready to land a blow to the head. Never forget that when you become friends with another person, a day will inevitably dawn when you must break with him.

While it is true that Takuboku felt the need for secrecy in keeping his diary from his wife and probably from friends as well, Kuwabara believes that there was a further reason for this choice of transcription. Takuboku had tried the same approach in his short story "Mr. Sakaushi's Letter" (see entry of April 19, p. 94); and in a letter dated February 6, 1911, to Tsuneo Ōshima in which Takuboku refers to the necessity of social revolution,[15] Takuboku informs his friend that he intends to begin popularizing *rōmaji*. Takuboku was one of the far-sighted Japanese of his era who seriously considered reformation of the Japanese language. Kuwabara notes that unless we take this fact into account, it is difficult to understand Takuboku's conduct on the day that he had his first hemorrhage: on that day he copied out *A Compendium on the Right Use of Kana for Representing Kanji Sounds.*

Kuwabara believes that Takuboku, by adopting *rōmaji*, could be liberated from three categories of repression: (1) mental and ethical repression, for the diary would not be read by his family; (2) the repression of traditional Japanese literature; and (3) social repression in general, which would also include the first two categories. Takuboku could create a world whose activities would be surprisingly free. The adoption of Roman letters not only enabled him to write boldly; it made inevitable the removal of archaic words of Japanese origin and unfamiliar words derived from classical Chinese, and it led to the creation of a new, freer style of written Japanese. In fact, his style did become freer, and he was able to adopt fresh and popular expressions even when he wrote in the traditional manner. The use of *rōmaji* enabled Takuboku to produce a more natural flow of language.

After presenting this strongly persuasive hypothesis, Kuwabara goes on to consider the major theme of the diary as the classic struggle between "freedom" and "self-consciousness." While it was true that Takuboku wandered alone to Kushiro in Hokkaido and then to Tokyo to find the means by which to establish his family in decent surroundings, a Takuboku letter of July 7, 1908, notes his desire for freedom and his inclination to desert his family and become a hero who "fully tastes all the sorrows and joys, all the pleasures and pains in life most boldly, most straightforwardly, most deeply, and most widely." That he wrote only twice to his family since the beginning of 1909, that he sent his wife and mother almost no money, that he spent desperately needed funds on prostitutes—funds that ought to have been directed to his family struggling in Hokkaido—all are part of the poet's personal warfare, yet these very conditions underscore the complexity of his crisis and strengthen for us the other end of this dual chemistry, namely, the artist's recognition of the necessity of providing for his family.

Kuwabara finds more to sympathize with in Takuboku's dilemma than he does to complain about. He feels that *Romaji Diary* not only describes the poet's experiment in living, but also his experiment in literature. Takuboku, as a man of letters, attempted to analyze himself by means of writing, but found that he needed a new style, both truthful and tense. It was by writing in *rōmaji* that he succeeded in creating a style which fulfilled his purpose. Kuwabara also points out that although Takuboku's frank description of his life was impossible without the existence of naturalist literature, it is only Takuboku who, with his sharply innate self-consciousness, tested naturalism to the utmost and surpassed it by negating that medium.[16]

What Kuwabara means by this last statement is that Takuboku's naturalism always "contained a gleam of neo-idealistic romanticism," an illustration of which is his brief interlude of happiness won by sleeping with a prostitute. We can add a number of details to support this "neo-idealistic" tendency, especially in the last quarter of the diary (see the entry of May 2, p.112) when Takuboku befriends two young men and attempts to keep them from the Tokyo pit of despond. Penniless even with a job, he paid for part of their boardinghouse fees, helped them move, tried to devise plans for their survival, and even thought of spending time in their room writing stories he hoped to sell in order to maintain them and himself.

When he began his *rōmaji* diary, Takuboku must have resolved to write something never written before. In the entry for February 21, 1909, of an earlier diary, he refers to a change which had occurred in his thought toward the end of the previous year. And in the *rōmaji* entry for April 10, he says that he spent the last one hundred days fully armed even though there was no war. During that period he parted from his friends, one after another. He was at war with the real world around him and with his real self. For that purpose he had first to destroy his own facade, an extremely painful task for him. He performed on himself a kind of vivisection. Whether this pained his wife or friends did not matter as long as he did it in *rōmaji*. He looked squarely at himself for the first time in his life. He liberated himself from his usual narcissism and sentimentality. He ceased to be a bystander and viewed himself and the world around him through non-tinted glasses. The experience was a trying one, but that experience, that experiment, aided him in taking a step forward as a writer who would later be able to produce *Sad Toys*.

The poet left his diaries to Kyōsuke Kindaichi. "I will leave them to you," Takuboku informed his friend. "If you think they are no good, burn them. Otherwise, you need not." Kuwabara further informs us that Takuboku's wife, just before her death, gave them to her brother-in-law, saying, "My husband told me to burn them, but my attachment to them has prevented me from doing so after all." Kuwabara speculates that it was not pure accident that the diary in Roman letters and the other diaries have become accessible. Something in Takuboku himself forced her to preserve them despite her husband's instructions, something that forced their publication after they escaped destruction. Kuwabara defines that something as "a power which engenders in the reader's mind a deep affection for the writer."

TAKUBOKU AND TANKA

In "Various Kinds of Tanka," an article which Takuboku had serialized in the Tokyo *Asahi* newspaper from December 10 to December 20, 1910, he pointed out that tanka poets ought to be free to use more than the traditional thirty-one-syllable rhythm of 5-7-5-7-7. Even the content of tanka need not be limited, Takuboku insisted, and he urged poets to disregard "the arbitrary restrictions which dictate that some subjects are not fit for tanka and will not make one." Modern readers may be surprised when Takuboku, in this context of defining tanka, suddenly lapsed into the nihilistic frame of mind so deeply rooted in him: "What can I do with those many things which really inconvenience me and pain me? Nothing. No, I cannot continue my existence unless I live a miserable double life, submitting with resignation and servility to these inconveniences. Though I try to justify myself, I cannot help but admit I have become a victim of the present family, class, and capitalist systems and the system of trading in knowledge." It was in this mood of pessimism and defeat that Takuboku turned his gaze from the clock at which he had been staring "to a doll thrown down like a corpse on the *tatami* mats. Tanka are my sad toys," he concluded.

The definition of tanka that Takuboku himself provided in "Poems to Eat," an article serialized in the Tokyo *Mainichi* newspaper from November 30 to December 7, 1909, was that "Poetry must not be what is usually called poetry. It must be an exact report, an honest diary, of the changes in a man's emotional life." Takuboku loaded his poems with events from his own personal history. The detailed biographical aspects of that life, like the I-novel which forms so much a part of Japanese literature, cannot be ignored. In an I-novel, the author-hero exploits with a fair degree of accuracy the details of his own life. Takuboku's life is tanka, his tanka his life.

Were Takuboku's tanka merely "toys" he played with in times of misery and sadness? Or did he feel his tanka were "toys" because they had no social value? An examination of Takuboku's life provides a kind of synecdoche on the eternal struggle of the artist in society, and while *Sad Toys* contains penetrating moments into that sad life, these poems go beyond it to provide tanka with a much greater range than it had in its twelve-hundred-year history. Along with the famous Akiko Yosano, Takuboku became a supreme tanka-reformer. The words *sad* and *toy*, contradictory and clever and yet edged with pathos—that of a child who cries over his toys—contain on closer scrutiny a much deeper significance when viewed in the light of Takuboku's diaries, letters, and articles.

What is there in Takuboku that breaks the heart yet bears along with this fragile feeling a strength that cannot crumble into sentimentality? The slippery wire Takuboku walked along remained taut. That fragile yet taut line was of course tanka. We must ascertain Takuboku's view of tanka, his sad toys; many of the 194 tanka in this posthumous volume serve as examples of the evolution of an idea of tanka that was to radically modernize it and lift it from the mechanical reliance on technique that had brought tanka to its last dying gasp in the Meiji period.

In our *Tangled Hair: Selected Tanka from "Midaregami" by Akiko Yosano*, we noted how Akiko and her husband, Tekkan, had removed tanka from the stranglehold of history and mere technicality. The earlier court poets had made the *Kokinshū*, Japan's second oldest anthology (completed 905), their sacred book:

> ... as time passed, many words and phrases were totally incomprehensible to the mass of readers. Those families versed in the art of tanka capitalized on the inscrutable expressions in these poems and monopolized the field. The prestige of the poetry families was heightened; moreover, the financial rewards were great. For hundreds of years the heirs of these families were initiated into the well-guarded techniques of the art. As a matter of course, poets and their poems were conservative in the extreme.
>
> In 1871 what later became the Imperial Poetry Bureau

was established under the Ministry of the Imperial Household, the commissioners of the bureau descendants of these very court poets and their disciples. The commissioners were rigid formalists absorbed in preserving tradition yet quite deficient in creative energy. Until the end of the second decade of the Meiji era..., poets were completely dominated by the Poetry Bureau School, or, as it was later called, the Old School. The poets of the Old School were removed from the dynamic life of Meiji as it experienced the impact of Westernization. Their poems, deficient in real feeling, were concerned only with the beauty of nature. Suddenly aware of the rapidly progressing materialism of the new age, the Old School poets began to feel something of its impact and tried to adapt their art to the new era. But inadequate in talent and sensibility, they were unable to keep pace with the times, even though they introduced into tanka the telegraph and the railroad. Their newness never went beyond mere subject matter.[17]

Early in his career Takuboku met Akiko Yosano and her husband, Tekkan. The young Takuboku soon saw the limitations in Tekkan's work; he liked Akiko's much more and admired her talent. But he felt he was going beyond their direction as he continued to create tanka as diary, the record of a man's life, a tanka without restriction of subject, its form open to certain kinds of change. That is to say, we feel Takuboku was carrying tanka to its very outermost limit before it broke down into prose. Takuboku's tanka still remain poetic, obviously, but it is a poetry almost lapsing into prose, into the commonplace; and perhaps the more prosaic and commonplace the subject, the more Takuboku would have called it "his" kind of tanka.

In letters, diary entries, and articles, Takuboku probed his attitude toward tanka. What was this poetic form and who were the people who composed it? In his early days he had difficulty in deciding what the content and the mood of the poem ought to be. "Once," he tells us in his article "Poems to Eat" as he continues along this line,

I used to write "poems." It was for a few years from the age of seventeen or eighteen. At that time there was nothing for me but poetry. My mind, which was yearning after some indescribable thing from morning to night, could find an outlet to some extent only by making poems. And I had absolutely nothing except that mind. —As everyone knows, poetry in those days contained only conventional feelings besides fantasy, crude music, and a feeble religious element or something equivalent to it. Reflecting on my attitude toward poetry at that time, I want to say this: a very complicated process was needed to turn actual feelings into poetry. Suppose, for instance, one derived a certain sentiment from looking at a sapling about three meters tall growing on a small plot lit up by the sun: he had to make the vacant plot a wilderness, the sapling a towering tree, the sun the rising or setting sun, and he had to make himself a poet, a traveler, or a young man in sorrow. Otherwise, the sentiment was not suited to the poetry of those days, and he himself was not satisfied.

With this early attitude that poems ought to emerge from the "inspiration" of the "poet," Takuboku discovered he could not write poems when he felt "inspired," but only "when I was in a mood in which I despised myself or when I was driven by some practical circumstance, such as nearing a deadline. I wrote many poems at the end of every month, for then I found myself in circumstances which made me despise myself." He came, he continues in "Poems to Eat," to reject such words as *poet* and *genius*, and when he recalled those youthful days in which he had written "poems," the regret at no longer being able to turned to sorrow and then to self-scorn. Forced to make a living, Takuboku became a stranger to poetry:

From my home to Hakodate, from there to Sapporo, then farther on to Kushiro—in that way I wandered from place to place in search of a livelihood. Before I knew it, I had become a stranger to poetry. When I met someone who said he had read my old poems and who talked about the bygone days, I had the same kind of unpleasant feeling one has when a friend who had once indulged in dissipation with him talks about an old flame. The actual experience of life caused a change in me. When a kind old politician who took me to the office of a newspaper in Kushiro introduced me to someone by saying, "He is a poet of the new school," I felt in his goodwill the greatest contempt I had experienced till then.

What revived Takuboku's interest in poetry and other forms of literature was the naturalist movement in addition to his own boredom in thinking of literature as fantasy (that is, removed from reality). His own tormented grasp of the reality of his own life caused him to further accept the spirit of the new naturalism at work in Meiji Japan. He did not object to the attempt to bring into poetry words from everyday life, yet he drew a line—and this is extremely important in the evolution of his own tanka: "Naturally poetry is subject to a certain formal restriction. When poetry is completely liberated, it must become prose."

For this reason Takuboku's later tanka, especially those in *Sad Toys*, are more often than not a mixture of colloquial and formal diction, though even in this last volume many are formal in tone. When he came to Tokyo after living in Hakodate, "that colonial town in the north, where the crude realities of life were left unveiled," he often said he too would write colloquial poems in the new style, but his words were simply for those hard-liners who regarded the form of tanka as fixed, cemented in the techniques of history and tradition. In Tokyo, where the difficult life he lived is so movingly described in his *Romaji Diary*, he apparently wrote four or five hundred tanka during that year, the pleasure from them "somewhat like that which a husband beaten in a marital quarrel derives from scolding or teasing his child without reason." His boardinghouse life, which sometimes hurled him toward the pit of suicide, made him appreciate more fully the spirit behind the new naturalism and the new poetry, the name he gave to the latter being "poems to eat": "The name means poems made with both feet upon the ground. It means poems written without putting any distance from actual life. They are not delicacies or dainty dishes, but food indispensable for us in our daily meal. To define poetry in this way may be to pull it down from its established position, but to me it means to make poetry, which has added nothing to or detracted nothing from actual life, into something that cannot be dispensed with."

Poetry had become for Takuboku as indispensable as food. In this context, of course, his tanka had to be much more than mere toys. He hacked off the outer protective shell that had made the genre into something curious and rare for the elite few, and he turned it into something to be seized by the very teeth, all moments of life available to it. And this meant that the rarefied name "poet" had to be eliminated: "... I deny the existence of a special kind of man called poet. It is quite right that others should call a man who writes poems a poet, but the man should not think himself a poet. My way of putting this may be improper, but if he thinks himself a poet, his poems will degenerate; that is, they will become something needless to us.

First of all, a poet must be a man. Second, he must be a man. Third, he must be a man. Moreover, he must possess all that the common man possesses." Nor must the content of poetry be "poetic" in the refined connotation of its earlier meanings:

> ... to say that poetry is the purest of arts is tantamount to saying that distilled water is the purest water. It may serve as an explanation of quality, but it cannot be a criterion in deciding its value or necessity. Future poets should not say such a thing. At the same time they should firmly decline preferential treatment given to poetry and the poet. Like everything else, all literature is in a sense a means or a method to us and to our life. To regard poetry as something high and noble is a kind of idolatry.
>
> Poetry must not be what is usually called poetry. It must be an exact report, an honest diary, of the changes in a man's emotional life. Accordingly, it must be fragmentary; it must not have organization. (Poetry with organization, i.e., philosophy in literature, is the novel deductively and the drama inductively. The relationship between them and poetry is what exists between a daily balance of accounts and a monthly or yearly settlement.) The poet must never have preoccupation like the priest looking for material for a sermon or a whore looking for a certain kind of man.

In "Various Kinds of Tanka," Takuboku introduces a letter written by an unhappy schoolteacher living in some out-of-the-way village in which the writer describes his boring life in a community he feels is without taste, declaring he will do his utmost in studying tanka and will contribute at least one tanka a day to the *Asahi*. Takuboku considers his correspondent a fool "to think writing tanka is something great." At the same time, however, Takuboku feels a kind of envy toward this man who is free from the pain of self-scrutiny. Takuboku continues: "From the fact that he said he would do his utmost in the study of tanka in spite of his unsatisfactory circumstances ... I found that he was a man who had never seriously thought how pitiable he was or why, though he called himself 'pitiable' ...."

The schoolmaster, Takuboku discovered, continued to send daily contributions to the tanka column Takuboku was in charge of. The poet found himself perversely waiting for the mail to see how long the man would "be able to continue his meaningless effort." The writer did continue to send an "enormous" number of tanka which Takuboku judged as "no more than mere representations in thirty-one syllables of natural features suited to poetry. There was hardly one good enough to print." What Takuboku concluded was that the man's poems might truly become poems by a living person if the writer squarely faced the fact of his own "pitiable" quality and "unflinchingly thought through how pitiable he was and why."

At the end of the article Takuboku reflects on the "reality" of tanka:

Smoking a cigarette and resting one elbow on my desk, I was idly looking at the hands of the clock, my eyes tired from writing. And I thought the following: When anything begins to inconvenience us, we had better attempt to boldly reconstruct it so as to remove the inconvenience. It is only right that we should do this. We do not live for others but for ourselves. Take, for instance, the tanka. We have already been feeling it is somewhat inconvenient to write a tanka in a single line. So we should write it in two lines or three according to its rhythm. Some may criticize us by saying this will destroy the rhythm of tanka itself. No matter. If the conventional rhythm has ceased to suit our mood, why hesitate to change it? If the limitation of thirty-one syllables is felt inconvenient, we should freely use lines with extra syllables. As for the content, we should sing about anything, disregarding the arbitrary restrictions which dictate that some subjects are not fit for tanka and will not make one. If only we do these things, tanka will not die as long as man holds dear the momentary impressions which flash across his mind, disappearing a moment later during his busy life. The thirty-one syllables may become forty-one or even fifty-one, yet tanka will live and we will be able to satisfy our love for the fleeting moments of life.

Thinking thus, I remained motionless while the second-hand of the clock completed a circuit. Then I felt my mind getting more and more somber. What I now feel inconvenient is not merely writing tanka in a single line. Nevertheless, what I can freely change now or will be able to change in the future are only the positions of the clock, the inkstone case, and the ink-pot on my desk, and, besides these, tanka. They are all matters of little importance. What can I do with those many things which really inconvenience me and pain me? Nothing. No, I cannot continue my existence unless I live a miserable double life, submitting with resignation and servility to these inconveniences. Though I try to justify myself, I cannot help but admit I have become a victim of the present family, class, and capitalist systems and the system of trading in knowledge.

From the clock I turned my gaze to a doll thrown down like a corpse on the *tatami* mats. Tanka are my sad toys.

It seems that Takuboku had to find some means of justifying his life as a writer of tanka, for the words of the novelist Futabatei Shimei (penname of Tatsunosuke Hasegawa, 1864-1909) that a man cannot devote his life to literature had considerable impact on the young poet, though Futabatei himself could not break away from his craft. Takuboku tried stories and socialism, but in neither could he succeed. And yet even as he was successful as a young tanka poet, it almost seems as if he was fighting this talent in himself. "The Glass Window," an article published by Takuboku in June 1910, a year after the cessation of his *Romaji Diary*, sharply explores this contradictory tendency. Takuboku begins the article by claiming there is nothing interesting left in the world. He has discovered that even the cigarettes he incessantly smokes have become less appealing. His walks outside are directionless, and on his return home he carries only "dissatisfaction in [his] mind .... It was as if [he] didn't know what to do with [his] life." As he reviews the past, he once more notes his contempt for poets or literary men:

Three years passed. Five years passed. Before I knew it, I had ceased to have sympathy for men younger than I who wanted to become poets or literary men, titles the sound of which had once thrilled me. Before I knew their personalities by seeing them or considered their literary endowments, I found myself feeling pity and contempt and at times distaste for them. As to those people living in the countryside who do nothing but pass their time writing poems and yet have such strong pride as cannot be imagined by outsiders and who write me vague, enigmatic letters—I sometimes felt that the world would become a much cleaner place if I dug a big hole and buried them all.

He felt the gap between the Philistines and the literati or the gap between the actual world and the life in literature itself. He notes in this article the rise of naturalism as a movement to bring literature closer to actual life, yet Takuboku concludes that naturalism could not fully bridge the gap between the two. Perhaps Takuboku meant that inevitably naturalism could not remain a literary movement, for the gap that must remain between the created form and life as it is actually lived is one "which even an operation by the most ingenious surgeon could not suture." Takuboku claims that it is only by this gap that literature can preserve its territorial integrity forever (should that line be crossed literature could not call itself such). Nevertheless, Takuboku could not help pointing to the deep sorrow men who create literature must feel because of this gap. And still he had to admit he was most content when he was busily at work at his desk completing one piece of work after another:

> When I am too busy, I sometimes feel dizzy. At such moments I scold myself by saying to myself, "How can you lose your head because of this?" and I concentrate my attention, which is apt to be distracted, on my work. Though the work may be uninteresting, I have no other desire and no dissatisfaction. My brain, eyes, and hands work in combination so efficiently I myself am surprised. It is so pleasant. I think to myself, "I want to be busier, much busier."
>
> After a while the work is completed, and with a sigh of relief I have a smoke. I become aware of a healthy hunger. I feel as if I were still seeing myself working hard. Again I think, "I wish I had been busier!"
>
> I have various hopes: I want money, want to read books, want to obtain fame, go on a trip, live in a society which suits me. I have many more additional desires, but all of them put together cannot replace the joy of being immersed in work, forgetting all desire, all gain.

Innumerable times as he returned home by streetcar, he thought: "I wish I could work all my life from morning to night without even time to speak or think, and then die a sudden death." Yet these thoughts, too, like tanka, were only moments of the floating world:

> But sometimes a quite different feeling suddenly occurs to me. I feel as if I have once more begun to experience the throbbing pain of a wound I had forgotten. I cannot control the feeling, nor can I divert my attention from it.
>
> I feel as if the world which had been bright were growing dark rapidly. Things which gave me pleasure cease to do

so; things with which I was contented cause dissatisfaction in me; things I need not be angry with make me angry. There is nothing I see or hear that does not increase unpleasantness. I want to go to the mountains, I want to go to the sea, I want to go to a place where no one knows me, I want to be lost among people who speak a language I don't understand at all. It is at such moments that I laugh to my heart's content at the unbounded ugliness, at the unbounded pitiableness, of this being called myself.

Despite these contradictions Takuboku could not after all abandon tanka. His article "A Dialogue between an Egoist and His Friend"[18] further explores this ambivalence toward tanka. As the egoist Takuboku had said, tanka would die out, but this event would not occur for many years because the form would continue to exist in the same way a man is said to have lived long when he becomes an octogenarian. Only when the Japanese language was unified would it become possible for tanka to die, and the Japanese language would unify itself only when the confusion existing in its mixture of colloquial and formal in its written forms was eliminated. As for other aspects of tanka structure, Takuboku repeated his belief that tanka itself might contain more than the traditional thirty-one syllables and need not be patterned in the traditional one or two lines. In fact, he claimed that because each tanka is different in tone, each might have different line divisions. In one of the most revealing sections of this dialogue, Takuboku (speaker A) notes the convenience of tanka, its length, its capturing of moments, its preciousness in allowing preservation of the fleeting and momentary and ephemeral:

A. Yes. Each second is one which never comes back in our life. I hold it dear. I don't want to let it pass without doing anything for it. To express that moment, tanka, which is short and takes not much time to compose, is most convenient. Yes, it is convenient indeed. It is one of the few good fortunes we Japanese enjoy that we have a poetic form called tanka. (Pause) I compose tanka because I love life. I make tanka because I love myself better than anything else. (Pause) Yet tanka will die. I won't theorize, but it will collapse from the inside. Still, it will not die for a long time. I wish it would die as soon as possible, but it will not, not for a long time to come.

As if to heighten the contradiction, Takuboku once more expresses his desire not to compose tanka:

A. Honestly speaking, I don't want to let myself make such a thing as tanka.

B. What do you mean? You are a tanka poet after all. Why not? Do your best.

A. I love myself far deeper than to let myself compose tanka.

B. I don't understand you.

A. Don't you? (Pause) But it becomes rather foolish when expressed in words.

B. Do you mean that you cannot devote yourself to such a trifling thing as tanka?

A. I have never intended to devote my whole life to tanka. (Pause) What can I devote my life to? (Pause) I love myself, but I don't trust myself very much.

These attitudes toward tanka may best be summarized in a letter Takuboku wrote to Fukashi Segawa, a medical student at the time and a former schoolmate at Morioka Middle School (letter dated January 9, 1911):

First of all, I want to write about the fact that we have both changed in the same way. You said you had drifted farther and farther from poetry, and the same is true with me. The tanka I am now writing are different from those I wrote in the old days. You have ceased to write poetry, and I have become unable to—I have become unable to write such poems as I did in the old days and as the young still do today, just as I can no longer repeat the love affairs I had in the old days. Not that I don't feel any nostalgia for those bygone days when I was happy dallying with my own sentiments .... But I cannot repeat such foolish efforts again.

The tanka I am writing nowadays have hardly any raison d'être—I know that quite well. It makes little difference, so to speak, whether I make them or not. I don't know whether you keep a diary or not, but now I am writing tanka as if I were writing a diary. Perhaps there are well-written diaries and badly written ones, but the value of a diary does not vary according to the writer's skill. A diary is of value only to the writer, and the value is quite irrelevant to the outsider. "I felt so and so" or "I thought so and so"—this is all that my tanka purport now. They have no other meaning, none above that.

Therefore, it makes no difference whether I compose them or not. When I say this, I am not just theorizing. In fact, I don't mind at all if I don't feel like making any tanka for days or even months. I remain quite indifferent. But because I am obliged to lead a dissatisfied daily life, it often becomes imperative to seek the proof of my existence by becoming conscious of my *self* at each moment. At such times I make tanka; I console myself a little by turning the self at each moment into words and reading them. Accordingly, the day in which I make tanka is an unhappy day for me. It is a day I spent purposelessly, a day in which I could not obtain any satisfaction except by finding my real "self" at each moment. You see, even though I write tanka now, I want to become a man who has no need to write any.

You wrote you understood me. And I believe it. From what I have written above, I believe you must have grasped my attitude toward tanka. But there is one circumstance which causes me sorrow. My tanka have a meaning quite different from the tanka of other people. Nevertheless, because I write tanka people regard me as a tanka-poet, and I myself sometimes feel like one. Whenever others treat me as a tanka-poet, a certain rebellious spirit is engendered in me. I cry inwardly, "I'm not such a special curiosity, but a man, an independent man worthy of the name." And yet, a moment later, I sometimes feel proud by comparing my tanka with those of others. I have hardly any respect or sympathy for the life of a man who lives to make tanka. I regard it as crippled and hollow. So I am well aware that it is meaningless to compare my tanka with his. I also think that it is to debase myself to make such comparisons. Yet I often do; sometimes I am impressed by his work, and sometimes I feel proud of mine. This is what makes me sad, and it reveals my weakness at the same time. This weakness induces me to promise I will write a given number of tanka by a fixed date.

In Takuboku's first collection of tanka, *A Handful of Sand*, 551 poems had been included; yet in *Sad Toys*, posthumously published from the notebook in which the poet kept his tanka (the first two in the volume added by his friend Toki from a slip of paper found there later), there were only 194. (We ought to keep in mind the fact that Takuboku did not give his second and last tanka collection the title *Sad Toys*. Toki had wanted to call the posthumous volume *After "A Handful of Sand": From the End of November 1910*, but the publisher wisely refused because readers might have easily confused it with the earlier collection. Toki finally selected the title from the memorable last line in the *Asahi* article.)

Illness, poverty, the demands of his job as a proofreader, his attempt at writing stories, and the pursuit of socialism provide some explanation for the smaller number of tanka; yet these very conditions, painful as they were, lent themselves to the creation of "sad toys." Is it not possible to speculate that Takuboku made greater demands than ever on tanka, demands that pared life down to the essentials of a "self" he was perpetually trying to find? We have seen how Takuboku spent a triumphant three days in his earlier career in which he had set down at least 246 tanka. In the slightly less than seventeen months remaining in his life after the publication of *Handful*, he probably demanded more from each tanka so that he was much more critical of the effort. He saw the moments slipping by, each one in itself containing infinite possibilities for the creation of tanka:

a family at a time of discontent:

Husband's mind on travel!
The wife scolding, the child in tears!
O this table in the morning!

———

an appreciation of the most trivial:

How precious the winter morning!
Soft against my face,
Steam from the hot water in this bowl ...

———

a moment of emptiness bordering on nihilism:

As if these hands, these feet, were scattered—
O this sluggish waking!
This sad waking!

———

the sudden isolation of midnight:

Awakened at midnight
And wondering if Fate rode me—
O the heaviness of this quilt!

the image of one's hands:

> These poor thin hands
> Without power
> To grasp and grasp hard!

———

a crisis of intense concentration to keep oneself
from raging:

> On this day in which my wife behaves
> Like a woman unleashed,
> I gaze at these dahlias ...

Takuboku felt the necessity of preserving the most ephemeral element in man's life, the individual moment, whether that moment was high or low, bright or dark, inspiring or frustrating, and he set for himself a task no other tanka poet before him had undertaken—that of extending tanka's range, of revising its form and content, of blending the unique mixture of colloquial and formal which adds so much to the complexity of the Japanese language. He carried his tanka to a point where the poem was almost destroyed because it came so close to breaking down into prose. At times he wished tanka might collapse, and he felt that it would at some future day, but he refused to allow himself to be the one to make that disastrous move. He called his tanka "sad toys," but even toys so easily broken can become precious and indispensable, for his tanka were also "poems to eat." Takuboku gave to the Everyman in each of us moments we can immediately recognize and value as commonplace, real, honest, compassionate, unflinching, and human.

Sanford Goldstein
Seishi Shinoda

Notes

1. All translated passages in the Introduction and its Notes are by the translators.

2. The father of Takuboku's mother was born into a family of lower-class samurai called Kumagai, but he was adopted by the Kudō family. He had four sons and three daughters, of whom Katsu was the youngest daughter. Naosue, the second son, did not like serving his feudal lord. When Naosue's mother died, he entered a Buddhist temple to become the disciple of a priest. Later he returned to Iwate to be the incumbent of a temple. In 1872, the Meiji government ordered all priests to adopt family names. At that time Naosue adopted the name Katsurahara. He should have adopted his father's earlier name Kumagai, but he preferred Katsurahara, the name of a distant family ancestor who was a prince.

3. Takuboku wrote on the flyleaf of one of the notebooks in which he kept his poems, "Born February 20, Meiji 19 (September 20 in the old calendar, Meiji 18)." This entry shows that Takuboku believed that for some reason, in spite of the official register, he was actually born on September 20, in the old calendar, in the eighteenth year of Meiji. The date is October 27 in the new calendar. Such discrepancies between the actual date and the registered date of birth were not at all rare in those days. Some parents neglected to register the birth of a child for a time, but when they did, they entered a fictitious date which fell within the prescribed period. Accordingly, some scholars believe that Takuboku was born on October 27, Meiji 18, i.e., 1885. But Takuboku's biographer Yukinori Iwaki denies this date. According to him, it is established beyond doubt that the family moved to Shibutami village in the spring of the year following Takuboku's birth, and the chronicle preserved in Ittei's second temple, Hōtokuji in Shibutami, and the village register as well, record that the movement took place in the spring of Meiji 20 (1887). Hence it must be considered conclusive that Takuboku was born in 1886. Aika Toki in the postscript listed Takuboku as twenty-eight. He believed Takuboku's year of birth was 1885. By using the old Japanese way of counting that every Japanese becomes a year older each January 1, Toki arrived at the figure twenty-eight.

4. During the Meiji period, upper primary school had courses of study that were two, three, or four years long, but after finishing the second year, students were qualified to take entrance examinations to the five-year course of middle school. However, students who grad-

uated from schools in the rural areas and who wished to further their education found the limited training they had received insufficient to really compete in these examinations. In Japan's first school system in 1872, lower primary school was four years and upper primary school was the same; but the program was not this systematic in actual practice, and a three-year "simplified" course was permitted in upper primary school. In 1890, a new primary school act was enforced in which the lower course was three to four years, the higher two, three, or four. This latitude was due to the fact that there were not enough school buildings and teachers.

5. In large cities, *ryōriya* (restaurants) and *machiai* (where a patron could pass the night with a geisha) were kept distinct. Before World War II, Japan's licensed prostitutes were called *shōgi* but were more commonly referred to as *jorō*. They lived in special districts (*yūkaku*) where licensed brothels were located. These prostitutes were not allowed to go outside the *yūkaku*, so they were sometimes called "caged birds." The women Takuboku was to buy in the Asakusa red-light district in Tokyo were cheaper, unlicensed prostitutes who were ostensibly waitresses at bars. The authorities knew what these women were but did not interfere with their trade unless it became conspicuous. Near the famous pleasure quarter of Yoshiwara, which was next to Asakusa in Tokyo, was a district of cheap brothels. Geisha, on the other hand, were not prostitutes but entertainers at parties. They were paid for their skill in dance, music, and conversation. Sometimes, though, they slept with their guests for love or for money. Restaurants could not be used on such occasions, so the guest and geisha went from these establishments to the *machiai*. In rural Japan, however, regulations were not so strictly adhered to.

6. Usually a few (sometimes several) geisha lived in a *geisha-ya* (geisha house) owned by the *okami* (mistress or proprietress). These geisha were given board and clothing by the *okami*, but she was reimbursed from geisha fees paid by customers. Because a geisha's clothing was costly and because a good many outfits for frequent change of costume were needed, many geisha found themselves in debt to the proprietress and were obliged to find a "patron," usually a special customer. But some geisha who were very popular could follow their profession on their own by having their own house. Koyakko seems to have earned a good deal of money because she was able to be independent.

7. According to biographer Iwaki, Takuboku composed 55 tanka from the night of June 23 to dawn of June 24 (1908), 50 in the forenoon of June 24, and 141 on June 25. Thus the total number of tanka composed would be 246. This figure is based on what Takuboku wrote in a notebook in which he set down his tanka. But in a diary entry for June 24, Takuboku wrote: "Last night I began writing tanka after going to bed. My enthusiasm increased hour by hour, and I wrote all night through. At dawn I took a walk in the graveyard of Honmyōji Temple. I felt incomparably refreshed. My enthusiasm continued, and I composed more than 120 tanka from last night to 11 o'clock. I sent about 100 of them to Mr. Yosano...." On June 25, Takuboku wrote in his diary: "Inside my head all is tanka. Everything I see and everything I hear turn into tanka. Today I composed 141 tanka by 2 a.m. Forty of them are about my parents. I composed them in tears." Thus Takuboku's figure of the number of tanka written in this three-day period is more than Iwaki's figure of 246. In spite of Iwaki's assertion that 114 of these tanka appeared in *Myōjō*, only 100 of the 116 poems in *Myōjō* were composed during this unusual three-day period.

8. The *Heimin Shinbun* was published by the Heimin-sha, headed by Kōtoku and Sakai. At first it was a weekly paper of eight pages (from November 15, 1903, to January 29, 1905, its last issue no. 64). On January 15, 1907, it was revived as a daily, but because of some internal strife between two factions, the reissue was short-lived. The last issue, April 14, 1907, was no. 75. *Heimin* means "common people" as opposed to the privileged. No longer used, the word has been replaced by *jimmin* or *minshū*.

9. The postscript to *Sad Toys* is dated June 9, 1912; *Sad Toys* was published June 20, 1912.

10. We offer the following passages from Shiki's diaries:

> Besides pain in a certain part of my body, which has plagued me for some years, I have come to suffer a fresh pain in the side. The pain has increased so much since last year that it has been impossible to continue writing. The frustration of being unable to give vent to my thoughts has tormented me. "What's the use of living on like this? Isn't there some way to relieve my boredom in sickbed?" Wondering thus, I happened on an idea. What if I jotted down whatever came into my mind during an interval between fits of pain? The entries would be twenty lines at most, and short ones would be ten, five, or sometimes only one or two lines. It would be better to write even such things than not write at all. I decided to give it the title *A Drop of Ink*. I am not, however, presumptuous enough to think I will be able to meet the reader's expectations with such childish writings. But it will give me a slight comfort to find my writings in the newspaper when I open it in my sickbed every morning.

> my old brushes
> too worn out
> to paint the second bloom
>   [from *A Drop of Ink*, January 24, 1901]

———

> While I could not move about, I didn't mind lying in sickbed, nor did I think my illness was very hard to bear. But since I have recently become unable to move an inch, mental agony has been added to physical pain. Almost every day I suffer so much that I become frenzied. In order to avoid the torment, I use every

device, but in vain. And the frustration adds to my agony. My head becomes muddled. My endurance, reaching its limits, explodes. Then nothing can be done about it. I scream, I cry. That makes me scream and cry the louder. The torment is beyond description. I think the agony would go if I went mad, but that doesn't happen. What I desire most is to die. But I don't die, and there is no one who will put me to death. My pain decreases slightly at night, but as soon as it abates and I get drowsy, I think of the pain I'll have on awakening the following morning, for it reaches the extreme when I awake. Isn't there anyone who will relieve me of my agony? Isn't there anyone who will relieve me of my agony? [from *My Six-Foot Sickbed*, June 20, 1902]

11. Armando Martins Janeira, *Japanese and Western Literature* (Rutland and Tokyo: Charles E. Tuttle, 1970), p. 75.

12. Earl Miner, *Japanese Poetic Diaries* (Berkeley and Los Angeles: University of California Press, 1969), pp. 4-5.

13. Takeo Kuwabara, *Works of Takuboku* (Tokyo: Chikuma Shobō, 1968), pp. 192-207 (original ed.: *Collected Works of Takuboku*, extra volume; Tokyo: Iwanami Shoten, 1954).

14. Donald Keene, *Modern Japanese Literature* (New York: Grove Press, 1958), p. 211.

15. Ōshima, a member of Tekkan's Shinshi-sha, was also a member of the Bokushuku-sha (Clover Club) in Hakodate. He eventually became the leader of the group; he also gave the club's journal its title, *Beni Magoyashi* (Red Clover). With the breakup of his marriage, he returned to his home in the country, leaving the work of editing the journal to Takuboku, who had by then arrived in Hakodate. Ōshima was well educated, and Takuboku's letters to him are written in a respectful style.

16. Kuwabara, pp. 206-7.

17. Akiko Yosano, *Tangled Hair: Selected Tanka from "Midaregami"* (Lafayette: Purdue University Studies, 1971), pp. 1-2.

18. The article was first published in the November 1910 issue of *Sōsaku* magazine.

Romaji Diary

Tokyo

Branch House, Gaiheikan
359 Shinsaka
1 Morikawachō, Hongō

Wednesday, April 7

From out of the west came a savage wind in a clear sky. All the windows on the third floor rattled incessantly, and through the crevices particles of sand from the ground far below swept into my room with a rustling sound. And still the scattered white clouds in that sky didn't move. In the afternoon the wind finally subsided.

With springlike sunshine warmly illuminating the ground-glass windows, it was the kind of day that might have made everyone sweat if it hadn't been for the wind. The old keeper of the lending library, rubbing his nose with the palm of his hand, came in on his regular rounds. "It's real windy," he said. "But before the day's over, every last cherry tree in Tokyo will be blooming. That's how nice it is out, you see, even with the wind."

"Spring has come at last," I said.

The old man was of course totally unaware of the deep feeling behind my words. "Yes, yes!" he replied. "But spring, you see, is like poison to us. It's bad for business. Loafing's better than reading. Besides, it's natural for readers of books to keep them out a long time."

I had a five-yen note in my purse,[1] all that remained of the advance I had received at the office yesterday. I couldn't get that sum out of my mind all morning. It's probably the same kind of nagging anxiety that a man who usually has money feels when all of a sudden he's broke. In either case it's stupid. And though there's no difference in the degree of stupidity, there's a world of difference in the happiness of each.

Having nothing else to do, I made a chart of *rōmaji* spellings.

61

From that chart images of my mother and wife living beyond the Sea of Tsugaru came floating toward me. "Spring has come. It's April. Spring! Spring! The flowers are blooming. Already it's a year since I came to Tokyo. And still I'm not ready to send for my family and support them!" This is the problem that continues to flit in and out of my mind nowadays.

Why then have I decided to write this diary in Roman letters? What's the reason? I love my wife, and for the very reason I love her, I don't want her to read it. But I don't really mean that! That I love her is the truth, and that I don't want her to read it is equally true, but these two statements aren't necessarily connected.

Am I a weakling then? Not by any means. That is to say, this contradiction arises from the existence of that erroneous institution called Conjugal Relations. Matrimony! What a ridiculous institution! So what am I to do?

How sad!

A postcard from Chieko Tachibana in Sapporo telling me she was cured and checked out of the hospital last month on the twenty-sixth.

Today is the final and decisive match for the tennis team from Kyoto University. They've been staying in the rooms next to mine. All the players left in high spirits.

After lunch I took the streetcar to the office as usual. I read proof in a corner of our wide editorial room with the old-timers, and at about five-thirty, after finishing the proofreading for the first edition, I started back. That's the daily routine I go through to earn a living.

Today the old geezers were discussing double love-suicides. What a bitter irony! After they talked about how they suffer when their legs get cold, old Kimura, his face all lewd and vulgar, said, "Ishikawa, you're thinking, 'What rubbish these old men are gabbing about,' aren't you?" I laughed my "Ha, ha ha." That was a fine irony too.

On the way home I walked along the main thoroughfare of Hongō to do some shopping. In one day half the cherry trees on the university campus[2] had bloomed. It's really spring everywhere.

For some reason or other the sound of footsteps back and forth along the crowded street exhilarated me. So many beautiful women in beautiful kimonos were out walking that I wondered where they had suddenly sprung from. It's spring! That was my thought. And then I was reminded of my wife and my dear Kyōko. I had said I would definitely send for them by April. And I haven't. No, I haven't been able to.

God, literature is my enemy, and my philosophy is nothing but the logic with which I mock myself! It seems I want many things. Actually, however, isn't there only one thing I really want? Money!

The tennis players in the rooms next to mine were defeated after all by the Tokyo University team.

Around eight o'clock I went with Kindaichi to see a movie at a recently built theater out on the main street. All the men who did the commentary were poor.[3] One of them, who reminded me of my middle school friend Shimodomai, amused the audience with a few off-color jokes. As I watched the man perform, I kept remembering Sakichi Miyanaga, whose desk was next to mine when I was in my first year at middle school and who since then seems to have been making his way through those depths of society we know nothing about. Once I heard a rumor he had become a movie-theater commentator.

When we returned after ten, the room next door was in an uproar. One of the players had returned drunk from a party given for the team and had gone on a rampage, smashing electric bulbs in the rooms and breaking the lattice-work frames of the sliding paper doors.

Outside my room I met Sakaushi, a member of the team and an old friend. He had been a classmate at upper primary school and was now a student in the Department of Science and Technology at Kyoto University. I hadn't seen him in eight years. The three of us—Kindaichi was the other—went into my room and, often laughing uproariously, engaged in childish banter until one or so in the morning. Eventually the noise next door subsided. A night of spring—the night of a day of warm weather in which all the cherry blossoms had fully bloomed in a single day—that night wore on.

Alone and awake in the metropolis where the entire race of men was fast asleep, I realized, as I kept track of the breathing of others during that quiet spring night, how meaningless and trivial my life was in this narrow three-and-a-half-mat room.

What will I look like when, sleeping all alone in this narrow room, I am overcome by some indescribable exhaustion? The final discovery of man is that he is far from great.

Such a long time in this narrow room, nursing a weary anxiety and a foolish desire to seek out, by force if necessary, something to interest me—more than two hundred days have come and gone. When will I be able to . . . No!

Lying in bed, I read Turgenev's short stories.

Thursday, April 8

I got up and washed, and even two hours later, they had not brought in my breakfast tray. So busy serving the students in the next room, the maids had probably forgotten me. The very fact that they have forgotten is an insult. Still, under my present circumstances it's right for them to forget me and insult me. With this thought in mind I laugh everything away.

I reflected: In situations of this kind I had remained silent up to now, merely smiling. I had never once become angry. And yet was that because I am by nature tolerant? Probably not. It was because of my mask. Or else it came from some even more cruel intention. This was my thought, and then I clapped my hands to call the maid.

The sky was calm and clear. As usual during the cherry blossom season, the streets seemed lively. Sometimes a gust of wind swept up particles of dust and fluttered the gay kimonos worn by flower-viewing passers-by.

On the streetcar on my way back from the office, I met Hinosawa, who holds a degree in engineering. A genuine fop. The minute I sat down beside him in my old padded kimono with its frayed sleeves was exactly the right moment to say something sarcastic to him in his brand-new Western suit.

"Well, did you go flower-viewing?" I asked.

"No, I've got no time to look at flowers."

"You don't? That's nice."

What I said was quite commonplace. Something anyone would say. But I had intended it as a fine irony—to say something commonplace to this commonplace man. Of course there was little likelihood Hinosawa would understand, and he remained quite unflustered. That was what amused me.

Sitting opposite us were two old ladies. "I don't like the old women of Tokyo," I said.

"Why's that?"

"They're distasteful. Somehow I feel lousy looking at them. There's something un-old-ladylike about them, not like the old women who live in the country."

Just then one of the women began glaring at me from behind her dark glasses. Even the people around me were paying attention. I experienced a vague delight.

"Do you really think so?" said Hinosawa, his voice as low as possible.

"Speaking of women, there's nothing like the young women of Tokyo. All old women are horrible!"

"Ha, ha, ha, ha!"

"I like movies. Do you?"

"I've never taken the trouble to see any."

"They're interesting. You ought to go have a look sometime. Suddenly it's light and suddenly it's dark, you know? It's rather funny."

When he asked if it wasn't bad for your eyes, I could clearly see the dark color of confusion on his face. I couldn't help feeling slightly triumphant. This time it was my turn to "Ha, ha, ha!"

Thinking I would mend my torn kimono, I went out around eight to buy some needles and thread. Hongō had that energetic pace befitting a spring night. In addition to the usual night stalls, I discovered many stands selling plants.

Everyone was walking along shoulder to shoulder in apparent enjoyment. Without buying the needles and thread and even as I heard an inner voice crying "Stop! Stop!" I finally took out my purse and bought this notebook I am writing in, a pair of *tabi*, some undershorts, a roll of letter paper, and two pots of pansies at five sen each. Why must I hear that inner voice crying "Stop!" even when I purchase necessities? That voice says, "You'll be left without a penny!" and, "They're having a hard time in Hakodate!"

I brought one of the pansy flowerpots into Kindaichi's room. "When I went in to see you yesterday," my friend said, "I kept wanting to tell you something, but I just wasn't able to." That was how his interesting chat began.

"What's it about? I haven't got the foggiest notion what you mean."

My friend finally started after hesitating a number of times. What he told me follows:

It was on the first night of this month that the ten or so students from Kyoto University had come to our boardinghouse and occupied Rooms 7 and 8, that is, the rooms between mine and Kindaichi's. All the maids had been quite excited, intent on serving only them. Especially Okiyo. Since Okiyo, the prettiest of the five of them, was in charge of the third floor, she spent all her time, morning to night—sometimes till midnight even— with the spirited young students. Every one of them made a fuss over her, continually calling out, "Okiyo-san, Okiyo-san!"

Some of them even used indecent language to her, and Kinda-ichi figured that a few of the students had tried tickling her. I had grown used to the ill treatment suggested by the sporadic, curt behavior of the maids and had thus more or less assumed an attitude of indifference toward whatever they did, so I hadn't felt that these goings-on were particularly unpleasant. But each time Kindaichi heard sounds in the rooms next to his, he was tortured, he said, by unutterable feelings of jealousy.

Jealousy. What a subtle word. Unable to suppress these feelings, my friend had come to think himself a despicable person steeped in jealousy, the holidays from the first to the fourth of the month spent, he said, in absolute anguish. When he had gone to work at Sanshōdō on the fifth, he heaved a sigh of relief and felt, to use a favorite saying of that pathetic poetaster in the editorial section there, "Much more at ease here than at home." From that time on Kindaichi had regained some of his usual equanimity.

Okiyo had come to work at our boardinghouse at the end of February. She's fattish in a sensual way, has a healthy complexion, and reveals something impudent and unyielding in her slightly squarish, thick-eyebrowed face. They say she's twenty years old. At any rate, it seems that when she first arrived, she made a real effort to approach Kindaichi. But Otsune—another interesting one—was intent on dissuading her, so it seems Okiyo abruptly changed her mind about my friend. I was able to infer this much from Kindaichi's words. Afterwards, apparently, he was continually watching her with the feeling a man has when the small bird that has flown into his house suddenly escapes. It seemed to me that Kindaichi, inexperienced as he is in dealing with women, had not realized that Okiyo's innately lascivious yet somewhat domineering attitude had gained control of his rational faculties. On the last day of last month, Kindaichi—having never once offered the maids a tip—gave something only to Okiyo. Apparently, she told the other servants about it after she went downstairs. The next day Otsune's attitude, Kindaichi said, had undergone a complete transformation. A really ridiculous and pitiful tale. Nevertheless, the very fact that it is ridiculous and pitiful makes it interesting. It was at this point that the university students had arrived.

The two of us agreed that Okiyo is a strong woman. Of the five maids, she works the hardest. On the other hand, they say that at the stroke of ten, she makes it a rule to go to bed no matter how much the other servants still have to do. No man can equal her in her work habits. And so before any of the maids had realized it, she was dominating them. She seems like an unyielding woman who seldom cries. Her character is that of the powerful.

As for Kindaichi, though, there's no denying he's a very jealous person, and what's more, a very weak one. And there's no denying there are two sides to a man's character. Though gentle, good-natured, kind, and considerate, he is, on the other hand, a quite jealous, weak, and effeminate man with petty vanities. Well, that's beside the point. The students all left today except for two. Tonight, they were sleeping separately in Rooms 7 and 8.

I had stayed up late. It was about one-twenty. I was busily engaged in writing when suddenly I heard footsteps stealing outside my room, someone breathing short and hard. Well! Breathlessly I cocked an ear.

The breathing outside my door sounded, on this very quiet night, as violent as a storm. For a while there was no indication that the person would move on. Whoever it was seemed to be spying out the conditions in the various rooms.

From the first, however, I didn't think it was a thief. Not by any means!

Suddenly the shadow of a woman, her hair done up in a huge *shimada* hairdo, was clearly shadowed against the sliding paper door at the entrance to my room.[4] It was Okiyo. Strong as she was, I could tell by the violence of her breathing after she had stolen up the stairs how violently her heart was beating. The corridor lamp had caused her silhouette to fall against my door. The door of the room next to mine moved quietly on its hinges. The woman entered. A faint voice mumbled, "Mm-mm." It seemed to me she had awakened the dozing man. Before long, she slightly opened the door she had closed and was apparently spying on my room. And then with the door left as it was, she once more entered the room.

Again I heard that "Mm-mm." And then faint voices. She went to the entrance of the room and slid the door shut. I thought I heard her take two or three steps; then nothing more caught my ear.

A clock striking one-thirty in a distant room. A rooster's faint cry.

I felt as if I were suffocating. The two in the next room must have thought I had fallen asleep. If I had offered the slightest sign that I was awake, how embarrassed they would have been. I was in a real fix. So trying as hard as possible not to make a sound, I first took off my *haori* and socks and rose slowly to my feet, but I found it quite difficult to get into bed. It was about ten minutes before I finally managed somehow to crawl in. Even then I still felt somewhat suffocated. I was really having a difficult time!

In the next room quick, warm, irregular breathing was faintly audible, like the breathing of a lion from far off. They were in the midst of rapturous pleasures.

Hearing those sounds—those strange sounds—I didn't feel the least bit moved. From the very first I had felt as if I had discovered some good material for a story.

"That man's really something!" I thought. He had probably remained behind just to make a conquest of Okiyo. Even so, that woman—how bold *she* was! Tomorrow, first thing in the morning, should I tell Kindaichi about it? But that would be cruel. No, it would be more amusing to tell him. The clock struck two.

Before long I fell asleep.

Friday, April 9

Almost all the cherry blossoms are in bloom. It was a perfect springlike day, warm and quiet, the distant sky hazy in this season of flowers.

As I was glancing at Chieko-san's postcard, which hadn't moved me in the least when it had arrived the day before yesterday, I felt an uncontrollable yearning for her. And I thought, "If only I could meet her just once before she becomes someone's wife!"

Chieko-san. What a fine name! And her walk, so graceful and light and yet young and girlish! Her clear voice! The two of us had talked together only twice. Once at the house of Ōtake, the principal, when I went to bring him my resignation. And once in her room at Yachigashira with its reddish-brown curtains hanging in the window. That's right, it was when I brought her a copy of *Akogare*. Both meetings were in Hakodate.

God! It's been twenty months since we parted!

I told Kindaichi about last night's incident. The storm it generated in my friend's mind will not pass away in a mere day or two, of course. It was evident that he didn't find the situation as amusing as I had. I soon learned that the man's name was Wakazono. He left around nine tonight. I was in my room with Kindaichi, and we heard the man's parting words to Okiyo. From their conversation I gathered that his rivalry with someone called Watanabe had made him remain behind to make a conquest of her. Immediately after Wakazono left, Okiyo, humming a tune, went about her work.

At the office, today's first edition was finished rapidly, so I came back early, at about five. I forcibly suppressed an unbearable desire to go out.

In the streetcar on the way home, I saw a child who very much resembled my Kyōko, whom I haven't seen since my departure last spring. The child was blowing a whistle with a rubber balloon attached to the end, and each time she blew it, she looked at me and hid her face, smiling as though she was embarrassed. I found her so cute and lovable that I could have hugged her. The nose, cheeks, and eyes of the child's mother so closely resembled my own mother's—in fact the woman's entire face did—that I felt my old mother must have looked just like that when she was young. The face, though, wasn't elegant.

It's a spring night sweet as milk! A precious letter came from Jinko Tsubo—Koyakko of Kushiro.

Frogs are croaking in the distance. The first frogs! The sounds of frogs remind me of the garden of Ozaki-sensei's house in Shinagawa, which I visited five years ago, and then of Hideko Hotta, who now lives on the coast at Kunohe.

Lying in bed, I read the short stories in this month's *Chūōkōron*.

Saturday, April 10

I read in bed until past three o'clock last night, so it was after ten when I got up this morning. A wind from the south was raging in a clear sky.

The fact that recent short stories have degenerated into a kind of new descriptive essay, or rather that we can't help regarding them as such when we read them—in short, that we are dissatisfied with them—shows how the prestige of naturalism as a view of life has been steadily declining.

Times change. We can't deny that at first naturalism was a philosophy we pursued with the utmost zeal. But all too soon we perceived contradictions in its theory. And when we advanced beyond these contradictions, we found that the sword in our hands was no longer the sword of naturalism. At least I could no longer be content with the attitude of an onlooker. The attitude of a writer toward life must not be that of a spectator; a writer must be a critic. If not, he must be a man who designs his own life. Moreover. . . .

The positive naturalism I have arrived at is exactly a new idealism as well. For a long time we have treated the word "ideal" with contempt. We have discovered to our cost that the ideals we once cherished were indeed only a pathetic daydream. It was no more than a *life illusion*.[5] However, we are living, and we have to live. The ideal we have again erected with our own hands after destroying everything to the full is no longer a pathetic daydream. And even if this ideal is after all only a *life illusion*, we cannot live without it. Were I to abandon this need, which comes from the innermost depths of my heart, there would be nothing left for me but to die.

The last passage I wrote this morning does not really express what I mean. At least it's not of primary importance to me. I do not believe that man's projects, whatever they may be, can be great. It was when I didn't yet know what greatness was that I thought literature was greater and nobler than anything else. Can anything done by man be great? For one thing, man is neither great nor noble.

I want only freedom from care. This I realized tonight for the first time. Yes, that's so. Quite definitely so. What I want can't be anything else!

Oh, this freedom from care! The feeling of such peace of mind, what could it possibly taste like? For a long time, ever since I began to comprehend what was going on around me, I have forgotten what peace of mind is.

Nowadays, it's only on streetcars to and from my office that my mind is most at ease. When I'm at home, I feel, for no reason at all, that I must be doing something. That "something" is what bothers me. Is it reading? Is it writing? It seems to be neither. No, reading and writing seem to be only a part of that "something."

Is there anything I can do besides read and write? I don't know. At any rate, I do feel as if I must always be doing something. Even when I'm indulging in idle carefree thought, I always feel as if I am being dogged by that "something." Yet I can't concentrate on anything.

When I'm at the office, I keep hoping time will pass as quickly as possible. It's not that I particularly dislike my work or that I feel my surroundings are unpleasant. It's that I am pursued by the feeling I must get home as soon as possible and do something. I don't know what I'm supposed to do; and still, from somewhere behind me I feel myself pursued by that "something I must do."

I am keenly sensitive to changes in nature in terms of season. When I look at a flower, I feel, "Good heavens, that flower's come out!" That simple experience stabs me as sharply as an arrow.

I feel, furthermore, as if that flower will open in an instant and its petals will fall as I'm looking at it. Whatever I see or hear, I feel as if I'm standing on the brink of a surging stream. I'm not at all calm. I'm not composed. For some reason or other, my mind can't stand still, as if it were being pushed from behind or being pulled forward, and I feel as if I must start running.

Then what is it I need? Fame? No. Projects? No. Love? No. Knowledge? No.

Then is it money? Yes, money is one of the things I need. But it's not an end—it's a means. What I am seeking for with all my soul is freedom from care. That must be so!

In other words, I'm probably exhausted.

A sort of revolution that erupted in my mind at the end of last year proceeded at an enormous rate. In spite of the fact that there was no enemy worthy of the name in front of my eyes, I spent those hundred days continually armed. Everyone, no matter who it was, seemed to be a foe. There were times when, without exception, I wanted to kill all the people I knew, from the most intimate on down. The more intimately I knew the person, the more I hated him. That "everything would be fresh and new" was the "new" hope which dominated every day of my life. My "new world" was a "world of the strong," that is, "a world dictated by power."

At that time naturalism as a philosophy had abandoned the inner citadel of "passivity" and charged into the wide plains of "activism." "The strong one" had to cast off the old armor of restriction and convention and barehanded, without help from others, had to fight gallantly. With a mind like steel, without tears, without laughter, and without consideration for anything, he had to push on recklessly in the direction he had aspired. He had to discard like dust all the so-called human virtues, and he had to do in cold blood what a human being cannot do. And for what? He himself did not know. No, he himself was his own object and aim and also the object and aim of all mankind.

Those one hundred armed days passed while I did nothing but shake with excitement. Whom did I conquer? How much stronger had I become? Oh God!

In short, I became exhausted. Even without fighting, I had grown weary.

There are two ways of going through the world, only two. One, *all or nothing*, is to fight against everything. This way means to win or die. The other way is not to fight against anything. That way means never to win but never to be defeated either. A man who is never defeated has freedom from care. The man who always wins has spirit. And neither one will ever fear anything. But thinking in this way doesn't make me feel the least bit cheerful, nor does it lift my spirit. It makes me sad.

My character is ill fated.

I'm a weakling. I'm a weakling even though I have a sword sharper than anybody else's.

I can't restrain myself from fighting, but I can't win. In that event there's no other way except to die. But I hate death. I don't want to die! Then how am I going to live?

I wish I could live like a peasant, knowing nothing. I have been too smart.

I envy those who have gone insane. I am too healthy in mind and body.

God! I wish I could forget everything, each and every thing. But how?

The desire to go where no human being exists has tempted me quite often of late. For a week, for ten days, for even a day, even half a day, it would be superb to lie down just by myself in a place where there are no people, where at least no human voices are audible, no, where at least I hear nothing which has any connection to me, where there is little fear that anyone will want to see me.

In order to put these thoughts out of mind, I often go to a place crowded with people—the movies. On the other hand, I also go when I have a yearning for human beings—for young women. But I can't find real satisfaction there. Only while I'm watching movies, especially those that are the most stupid and juvenile, can I forget everything by forcing my mind to revert to that of a child. But once the movie is over and the lights flash on to suddenly reveal innumerable figures swarming around, the desire to search for some livelier place, for some more exciting place, wells up all the more powerfully. There are times when I smell directly under my nose the fragrance of a woman's hair, times too when I am clasping a warm hand. But at just such moments I'm making a mental calculation of the contents of my purse. No, at that time I am considering how I can borrow money from someone! When I clasp a warm hand and smell the powerful fragrance of a woman's hair, I am not satisfied with that: I want to embrace a soft and warm and perfectly white body. Oh, the feeling of loneliness when I go back home without fulfilling that desire! It's not merely a loneliness stemming from unfulfilled sexual desire; it's a deep, terrible, despairing realization which forces me to see that I am unable to obtain anything I want.

When I had money, I went, without the slightest hesitation, to those narrow dirty streets filled with lewd voices.

From the fall of last year to the present moment, I have gone about thirteen or fourteen times and bought about ten prostitutes. Mitsu, Masa, Kiyo, Mine, Tsuyu, Hana, Aki. . . . There are some whose names I've forgotten. What I desired was a warm body, soft, perfectly white; what I desired was a pleasure that ravished both my mind and body. But all these women, some middle aged, some mere chits about sixteen years old, had slept with hundreds, with thousands, of men.

Their faces without gloss, their skin cold and rough, these women are inured to men, are insensitive to all stimuli. For small sums of money the only thing they do is rent their privates to men for a while. There is no other meaning than that. Without even untying their kimono bands, they lie down as they are and merely say, "Go ahead." And without even the slightest shame they open their thighs. They don't care in the least if anyone is in the next room or not. (This, however, is an irony of theirs that interests me!) Those genitals, which have been pounded by thousands of men, are flabby, the contractile action of the muscles gone. In them mere discharge takes place. There isn't an iota of pleasure ravishing either body or mind.

My itch for a strong stimulus was not allayed even when I was receiving that stimulus. Three or four times I stayed overnight with a prostitute.

The skin of eighteen-year-old Masa's body was as dry and rough as that of a poverty-stricken, middle-aged woman. The narrow six-by-six-foot room did not even have a light. The room was so stuffy and close that it had only the odor of flesh. Before long the woman had fallen asleep.

I was so unbearably irritated I couldn't sleep. I put my fingers in the woman's vagina and roughly churned around inside. Finally, I put my five fingers in and pushed as vigorously as possible. Even then the woman did not wake up. Perhaps she was so inured to men that her vagina had become totally insensitive. A woman who had slept with thousands of men! I was more and more irritated. And then all the more forcefully I pushed in my fingers. Ultimately my hand entered as far as my wrist. At that moment the woman awoke saying, "Mm, mm."

Suddenly she was clinging to me. "Ah . . . ah . . . ah, that was good. More . . . more. Ah . . . ah . . . ah!" A girl of eighteen no longer able to feel pleasure from the usual stimuli. I wiped my hand against her face. I wanted to insert both my hands or even my foot into her vagina and rip it apart. And—and I wanted to see, even in a vision, her body covered with blood, lying dead in the darkness. Men have the right to murder women by the cruelest methods. What a terrible, disgusting thought that is!

It's already clear that I can't go where there are no human beings, so not one thing gives me satisfaction where I am. And though I can't endure the pain of this life, I'm unable to do anything about that life. Everything is restraint, my responsibilities heavy. What am I to do? Hamlet said, "To be or not to be." But the question of death in today's world has become much more complicated than in his time. Oh, Ilya! The Ilya in Three of Them.[6] His attempt was the greatest man is able to perform! He tried to escape from life. No, he did escape. With all his strength he dashed out of life, out of our human life—human existence—on to the endless dark road. And he died, his head smashed against a stone wall! God!

Ilya was a bachelor. I've always thought it enviable that he was. That's the sad difference between him and me.

I'm exhausted now. And I'm searching for freedom from care. That freedom from care, what's it like? Where is it? I can't, even in a hundred years, return to the innocent mind free from pain that I had long ago. Where is peace of mind?

"I want to be ill."

Lurking in my mind for a long time has been this desire. Disease! This word, detested by man, sounds as precious to me as the name of the mountain in my native province.[7] Oh, for a life of freedom, released from all responsibility!

"I wish my family would die!" Even though I've desired that, no one dies. "I wish my friends would regard me as their enemy." For that I wish too, but no one regards me seriously as their foe. All my friends pity me. God!

Why am I loved by others? Why can't I hate men with all my soul? To be loved is an unbearable insult!

But I'm tired. I'm a weakling!

> For a year, no, for even a month,
> Even for a week, three days even,
> O you gods, you gods, if you exist,
> Grant only, I beg, this one prayer:
> Damage some part of this body,
> Ever so slightly, painfully even.
> Of that I won't mind. . . . Oh, to be made ill!
> Oh, I beg!

On a soft white bed
To sink down and down,
My body gently, lightly,
Sinking to the bottom of the valley of content—
No, if not on a soft bed, then on worn *tatami* in
                   some home for the destitute,
That too will do.
Oh, to lie down at my ease,
Without thought
(And without regret should I die like that).
Oh, for a sleep so sound without awareness,
Even if one should come and steal this arm, this leg!

And how would I feel if I removed this heavy garment of
                   responsibility?
Just that image brings on sleep.
Oh, to remove this kimono I wear,
This heavy robe, weighted with duty—
Oh, the rapture of that!
This body of mine hydrogen-light
And gentle and soft,
Perhaps in flight, high, high, in the great heavens.
"A skylark," everyone below may say!
Ah!

———

Death! Death!
My only wish!

What! A real putting to death?
Wait, merciful gods!
For one moment wait!

For bread, a slight sum,
Five sen will do—five—five—
If you are merciful enough to take the time to kill me,
Please give me five sen.

   It's a night with a warm breeze hinting of rain. In the distance the croaking of frogs.
   A postcard from Mitsuko telling me that she's gone to Asahi-kawa. No matter what she calls what she's doing, my younger sister has become a parasite living off that foreigner! In the metropolis when the cherry blossoms are at their best, her elder

brother wears an old padded kimono frayed at the cuffs. And in the heart of Hokkaido, my young sister buried in six feet of snow is singing hymns!

At three in the morning a soft rain.

Sunday, April 11

I woke up at about eight. It was Sunday, and all the cherry blossoms in Tokyo were out, not a bud unopened, yet not a blossom beginning to fall. The sky was serenely clear, the day warm. It was a day in which two million Tokyoites would forget everything in order to spend their time enjoying flower-viewing excursions.

For some reason or other I felt fresh, light-hearted, the spirit and joy of youth seemingly spilling from my body. I wondered where last night's mood had gone.

Kindaichi, restless as a bridegroom, was diligently getting into his Western suit. The two of us left together around nine.

We got off the streetcar at Tawarachō and walked through Asakusa Park. Though it was still only morning, the crowds were large. Just for the fun of it, I tossed in one sen for a fortune-telling slip. It said, "All will go well." That started me on my lark. We boarded a steamboat at Azumabashi and went up the Sumida as far as Senju-ōhashi. The long embankment at Mukōjima, which I was seeing for the first time, was buried under clouds of cherry blossoms. Beyond Kanegafuchi the view took on something of a pastoral effect. Mt. Tsukuba was not visible in the spring haze. As far as the eye could reach, plains of cherry blossoms!

Just this side of Senju was a long steel bridge which had been painted red. On both banks were green willows. We disembarked at Senju and strolled around the area a while. With my kimono tucked up high and my hat at the back of my head, I gave my friend plenty to laugh at.

We returned by boat to Kanegafuchi and walked toward Tokyo with countless numbers of people. The banks of the river had been transformed into a tunnel of flowers. At that time too I walked along with the bottom of my kimono tucked up and my hat tilted way back.[8] It had no meaning whatever. I merely felt like doing that kind of nonsense. I was enjoying Kindaichi's embarrassment. Tens of thousands of people dressed in their best outfits were walking in succession under that tunnel of flowers. Some were already drunk, clowning around in various ways. We discovered a beautiful girl and trailed her a long time, sometimes actually going ahead of her. The rows of flowering cherry trees continued interminably, and the processions of people, these too were interminable.

Again we boarded a riverboat, at Kototoi this time, and came to Asakusa. Then, after lunching at a sukiyaki restaurant, we went our separate ways. I had to attend a tanka meeting at Mr. Yosano's house.

As I expected, the meeting was a bore. Hiraide said last night's Pan Society gathering had been a great success.[9] Yoshii, who came late, kept on saying, "Last night a policeman reprimanded me for being drunk and urinating off Eitai Bridge into the river." Apparently all the Pan members had gone out on a drunken spree.

As usual, we made tanka on the subjects proposed by the members. In all there were thirteen of us. It was about nine when we finished our selections. Since I don't feel like making any serious tanka nowadays, I wrote my usual comic offerings. A few examples:[10]

> Bristling over the way
> My moustache droops,
> So like the man's I now hate!

> On my nerves of late
> The eyes of that guy I always meet
> Strolling in his red coat!

> Creaking leather inside these shoes,
> I feel queer, uneasy,
> As if treading on frogs.[11]

> Takes a three-year course of study
> Before giving a great big yawn
> In my superior's face!

To leave home, cross plains,
Traverse mountains, seas,
Oh, I want to go somewhere!

———

Took her hand without a pause:
Surprised, she resisted
And never came back.

———

Isn't there a gadget like a pen in your eyes
That aids
This perpetual flow of tears?

———

That guy used to stammer, hands trembling,
When he saw a woman—
He's miles from that now!

———

Lying on green grass by this bank
And hearing from the distant sky
Sounds of a band!

Akiko-san had invited us to continue composing all night. I devised some unconvincing pretext and hurried home. I found Aomi in Kindaichi's room and talked idly there for about an hour. And then I returned to my room.

Remorse suddenly welled up in me: "Another precious day spent uselessly!" If I had wanted to see the cherry blossoms, why hadn't I gone alone and seen them to my heart's content? Tanka meetings! How dull and stupid!

I'm a person who rejoices in solitude. I'm a person who's a born individualist. Any time spent with others seems to me empty unless the time has been spent fighting. To waste one hour with two or three or even more men! It's natural for that hour to seem empty or at least half-empty.

Formerly I was happy when someone called on me. I tried to please him as much as possible so that he'd come again. What a ridiculous thing that was! Now when someone comes to see me, I'm not particularly happy about it. I think I'm only happy when some guy comes who can lend me something when I'm out of cash. But if at all possible, I don't want to borrow money. If it were possible to live without being pitied by anyone or helped by anyone, helped or pitied not only monetarily but in everything, how happy I would be! If that were the case, I could live without saying a word to anyone.

I had felt, "A wasted day!" Somehow, though, I was afraid to continue with that line of thought. The top of my desk was a mess. Since I had no books to read, the only task at present was to write some letters to my mother and others, but I was equally afraid to do that. I always feel as though I want to console those pitiful people by writing something to please them, anything at all. I haven't forgotten my mother and wife—far from it, I think about them every day. Nevertheless, I wrote them only one letter and a card this year. Setsuko mentioned this in her letter the other day. She's still working at the school that she had intended to resign from in March. She said that even though it was only the beginning of the month, she had only twenty sen to give Kyōko for her allowance. That was why I borrowed from the company a little more than the advance I needed. I had intended to send her fifteen yen out of it. And while I kept hesitating to write, a day passed, then two. . . . Oh God!

I went to bed at once.

This morning a man by the name of Arai from Gumma Prefecture had come to see me. He said he was going to bring out a magazine entitled *Fallen Chestnuts*.

Monday, April 12

As bright and clear today as it was yesterday. The cherry blossoms, which had not yet begun to fall, were enjoying their third day of life under a windless sky. The cherry tree below my window has put forth light green shoots above its blossoms. The leaves on the elder tree have become quite large.

After I go down the slope and come out on Tamachi Street, there's a shop on the right that sells *geta*. As I passed in front today a joyous sound suddenly came to me as though it were emerging from some precious memory. Spreading before my mind's eye was a wide field of green grass. A skylark inside a cage suspended from the eaves of the clog shop began chirping. I walked on for a minute or two remembering my dead cousin and Oideno, the place where I used to go hunting with him.

I think it's already time to separate from my old friends—yes! from my old pals—and to build a house of my own. There are two kinds of friendship. One, a friendship in which each party seeks something in the mind of the other. And the second, a friendship in which someone is approached because of mutual tastes, opinions, or interests. In the first type, differences in taste, opinion, or interest or differences in status and occupation will never be an obstacle to camaraderie unless they lead the two individuals into a situation in which they are forced to directly and seriously compete with each other. A friendship between two such people lasts a comparatively long time.

A friendship of the second type, however, is considerably different. Of course, in some situations a friendship formed in this manner changes into the first along the way and continues a long time. But generally this latter relationship is, in a sense, a kind of business connection. It's a commercial relationship. It's not a direct relationship between A and B, but a relationship between A's property or rights—for example, his tastes, his opinions, and his interests—and those that B possesses. The mutual relationship between shops and banks continues as long as no change occurs in their actual business conditions. Once some change does occur in either party, the transactions must be broken off. That is the natural order of things.

It is a misfortune to lose friends, provided the relationship has been of the first variety. If the loss is in a relationship of the second kind, it is by no means a misfortune, though it may not necessarily be called a blessing. If a man lets this latter rupture occur passively, it's an insult to him; if he takes the initiative in rupturing it, it's a victory.

Those I referred to as "old friends" are actually the newest friends in my past, no, *were* the newest. I don't of course regard Mr. Yosano as an elder brother or a father. He's merely a person who has been helpful to me. The relationship between the man who helps and the man who is helped will continue only as long as the helper remains more influential than the man helped or the two men go their separate ways. In a situation in which both pursue the same path and some rivalry exists between them, the friendship dies. I now have no respect for Mr. Yosano. Though we are both following literature as a profession, I feel we are walking along different paths. I do not have any desire for a closer relationship with him, nor do I feel any particular need to separate from him. I want to thank him for his past kindnesses if the opportunity arises.

Akiko-san is quite another matter. I sometimes think of her as an elder sister. The two of them are quite distinct from others.

Most of the other friends I have gained from my association with the Shinshi-sha are in a quite different category from the Yosanos. I have already quarreled with Hirano. And Yoshii is a carbon copy of those self-indulgent dreamers who try to overwhelm you through sheer bluff—and a most pathetic carbon at that. If what they call literature were the same as what I call it, I would not hesitate to throw away my pen at a moment's notice. As for the rest of those friends, they are not worth mentioning.

But all this is idle. There's no use thinking about it.

All I have to do is do what I want, go where I want, in short, follow my own needs.

Yes. Only what *I* want!

That is all! All of all!

So don't be loved by others. Don't receive favors from others. Don't make promises to others. Never do anything that requires begging another's permission. Never tell others about yourself. Always wear a mask. Be ready at all times to fight, ready to land a blow to the head. Never forget that when you become friends with another person, a day will inevitably dawn when you must break with him.

Tuesday, April 13

When I awoke for a moment early in the morning, I heard the maids opening shutters here and there. I didn't hear anything else. And then falling asleep again, I indulged, until eleven, in the sweet slumber of a spring morning. A quiet balmy day of haze in this season of flowers. Before long all the cherry blossoms in Tokyo will begin to fall. Otsune came in and wiped the windows clean.

A sad letter from my old mother:

April 9

Ishikawa-sama,[12]

The letter you wrote to Miyazaki-sama the other day made me glad. Every day I'm waiting for your order to come to you, and it's already April. Until now I've been taking care of the baby and doing the cooking, though I can't do it good, and with Kyōko growing up more every day, I don't have the strength to bring her up any longer. Can't you send for us to go to you? Please tell me. This month on the sixth and seventh there was a big wind and lots of rain. The rain leaked into the house and there wasn't a dry spot, so I had to spend all day standing carrying Kyōko on my back. It was miserable. April two Kyōko caught a cold and still isn't over it. Her mother goes out at eight and doesn't come back until five or six. I been very troubled to hear the child cry for her mother. Beside that I have no spending money. Even one yen will do. Please send it quick. About what time will it suit you to send for us? Tell me that by all means. If you have no answer, I'll shut up this house and all of us will come to you, so be prepared for that.

We can no longer stay in Hakodate, I tell you.

Katsu

The letter from my mother in unsteady and tottering *hiragana* full of mistakes![13] No other person would have been able to read it! When she was a child, I understand she was the best pupil in a private one-room schoolhouse on Senbokuchō in Morioka. After she married my father, she probably didn't write a single letter in forty years. The first letter I received from her was in the summer the year before last. I had left her by herself in Shibutami and had gone to Hakodate. My old mother, unable to bear living in that hateful village, remembered the *hiragana* she had forgotten long ago and had sent me her sad letter! After that, when I was at Kushiro at the beginning of last year, I received one dated from Otaru. Today's letter is the fifth she has sent since I came to Tokyo. Compared to her first letters, the mistakes are fewer and the characters better. This fact makes me sad. Ah, my mother's letter!

Today was by no means a happy day for me. When I woke up, despite feeling sluggish from oversleep, I had felt carefree and comfortable; my blood was circulating rapidly and without stagnation through my entire frame. But that feeling lasted only a while. From the moment I read my mother's letter, I ceased to feel refreshed. Various thoughts occurred to me.

My head felt heavy, as though I was suffering from something like the oppressiveness of spring, and I was impatient with the tediousness of my own thoughts: "I don't expect to be able, after all, to discharge this heavy responsibility. . . . I'd rather give it up now!" That was what I had been thinking.

I have it! I'd write a newspaper novel in thirty installments or so. Maybe that would soon bring in some cash. But I couldn't pull my thoughts together. I had only one streetcar ticket left. I decided to stay away from the office today.

The keeper of the lending library came in, but I didn't have the necessary six sen. Nevertheless, I borrowed a book called *The Sky Battle* and read it.

The Foundation of a New Metropolis

In time a world battle will come.
Warships of the air will swarm phoenix-like in the sky,
And below, destruction of cities and towns.
A long continuous war! And half of mankind, bones!
And afterwards, oh, afterwards,
Where shall we build our New Metropolis?
On history's ruins? On thought? On love?
No. No.
On earth. Yes, on earth. In a realm
Of no distinctions, no rules, not even of man and wife,
Under this boundless blue blue sky!

Wednesday, April 14

Fine weather. I decided to send in a sick-report to Mr. Satō and take today and tomorrow off. Last night Kindaichi returned the two yen I had lent him the other day, so I wasn't hard up for cigarettes today. I began writing my story. I called it "Magnolia," but later changed it to "The Wooden Horse."

The appetite for writing and the sexual appetite seem closely related. When the keeper of the lending library came and showed me some oddities, somehow I found myself wanting to read them. So I borrowed a few. One was *The Flowery Night of the Hazy Moon*; the other, *Trade Secrets of Love*. For about three hours I copied *The Flowery Night of the Hazy Moon* in Roman letters in my notebook.

In the evening Nakajima and Shun Uchiyama, that pint-sized poet I had heard so much about, came to visit Kindaichi, so I went in too.

What a nose Uchiyama has! Its tip is planed flat. It's like some ungainly taro stuck in the middle of a face. He keeps talking,

talking incessantly. He's like a performing street beggar with a moustache. And he's also dwarfish. Of the countless number of pathetic men I've seen, not one has been as pathetic as him. Truly pathetic and clownish and guileless. In fact, he was so much in excess of these qualities, so excessively pathetic, that I felt a perverse desire to give him a really good thrashing. Whatever he expressed in total seriousness sounded ridiculous. When he drew in mucus through that ungainly nose of his after saying something facetious, it sounded like he was whimpering. A poet! He was more like a festival street performer wearing a headband and dancing before a crowd of children under a shady tree and singing songs in a whimpering voice.

It had begun to rain. Already it was almost ten.

Nakajima's a socialist, but his socialism is rather aristocratic—he went home by jinrikisha. Uchiyama, a socialist in the true sense of the word, looked every inch a poet as he walked back in the rain under an oil-paper umbrella he had borrowed.

In my heart was a vague dissatisfaction—and in Kindaichi's too. Plucking cherry blossoms from the vase in the alcove, we scattered petals all over the room, even on the bedding laid out on the mats, and then we continued playing around, screaming like kids.

I covered Kindaichi with the bedding and gave him one blow after another. Then I fled to my room. And immediately I thought, "What we did just now was a kind of destructive act against the existing order!"

I went to bed after writing three pages of "The Wooden Horse." I was yearning for Setsuko, but not because of the lonely sound of the rain. Because of having read *Flowery Night!*

Kotō Nakajima had told me he'd sell my manuscripts for me.

Thursday, April 15

Does my need for Setsuko come merely from sexual appetite? No! Never!

My love for her has sobered. That's a fact, a deplorable but inevitable fact.

But love is not all one's life. It's part of it. Love is a pastime. It's like singing. There are times when every person, no matter who, wants to sing. And while he's singing, he's happy. But man cannot merely keep singing his entire life. And if he continues to sing the same song, he'll get fed up with it, no matter how pleasant the tune. Moreover, there are times when he can't sing no matter how much he wants to.

My love has cooled. I have stopped singing that once-delightful song. But the song itself does remain a delight. It must be so forever.

It's true that I have grown weary of singing only that song. But that does not mean I have developed a dislike for it. Setsuko is really a good woman. Where in the world is there another like her, good, gentle, steady? I could never think of having a better wife than Setsuko. Yes, I have longed for other women besides her. And there have been times when I wanted to sleep with other women. As a matter of fact, I sometimes thought about sleeping with other women while I was sleeping with Setsuko. And I have—I have slept with other women. But what does that have to do with Setsuko? It doesn't mean I was dissatisfied with her. It merely means that man's desires are not simple. I love her now just as much as I did in the past. The person I have loved most has been, after all, Setsuko, though she has not been the only one I have loved. Even now—especially of late—I have frequently longed for her.

Is there any other wife in the world that has been placed in as miserable a circumstance as Setsuko?

The present system of matrimony—all the social systems—full of error! Why must I be shackled because of my parents, my wife, my child? Why must my parents, my wife, my child, be sacrificed for me? But all that is quite different from the fact that I love my parents and Setsuko and Kyōko.

Quite a nasty morning. It was past ten when I got up, relinquishing a sleep of spring as dear as love. Rain, a strong rain, was splattering against my window. The air felt damp, clammy. I went to the lavatory and came back surprised. All the trees, which until yesterday had been as bare as trees in winter, had put forth their young leaves. Clusters of trees at Nishikatamachi had cast off the robe of flowers they had worn until yesterday and had donned a dim gossamer-like garment of young leaves.

A single night of spring rain had transformed the world to green.

Again this morning, pressed for the rent!

How long must I continue this kind of life? Immediately this thought made my spirits sink. I didn't feel like doing anything. Still, before long the rain cleared, and I felt like going somewhere, and I did. I took the inverness that Kindaichi had once told me to pawn in an emergency and brought it to Matsuzakaya's. They gave me a loan of two yen fifty sen on it, but I had to pay fifty sen out of that for interest on a previous loan. I wondered then where I ought to go. I wanted to head out of Tokyo, but where? As I had done when I had gone flower-viewing with Kindaichi, should I take the riverboat from Azumabashi to Senju-ōhashi and walk alone in that rural landscape? Or if I find a vacant house somewhere, should I steal inside and try to sleep until evening!

At any rate, my feelings at the moment were that it would be unpleasant to be in a place filled with people. In order to make up my mind, I toured the stalls in an outdoor market. Then I boarded a streetcar for Ueno.

Ueno, which would have only a few people after the rain. I went there with only that thought in mind. All the cherry blossoms had fallen, leaving only their calyxes. What an ugly color! But the green of the maples! It seemed as though they were exuding some indescribably stimulating vigor of early summer from the depths of an ugliness like that found on a face after tears. Behind a shrine a policeman was questioning a woman leper who appeared to be about forty years old. How I wished to go somewhere! I walked on with this thought in mind. A shrill sound struck my ears. The whistle of a train at Ueno Station.

I wanted to ride a train! That was my thought. I wanted to ride somewhere, anywhere, with no destination in mind and to a place I have never been before.

Fortunately, I had about three yen in my purse.

God! To ride a train! As I walked about with this persistent thought, drops of rain began falling. It cleared up before anything started in earnest, but by that time I was touring an emporium at Hirokōji. And then, thinking how foolish I was, I went inside a Western-style restaurant and ordered something.

Just as I got back home after buying a pack of manuscript paper, a notebook, and a bottle of ink, Kindaichi also returned. We went to the bath together.

"The Wooden Horse"!

Friday, April 16

What a stupid thing to do! Last night, until about three in the morning, I copied in my notebook *The Flowery Night of the Hazy Moon*, that pornographic novel of the Tokugawa period I had borrowed from the lending library. Poor me! I couldn't restrain my desire for that violent pleasure!

I got up this morning around ten-thirty, a strange fatigue clinging to my mind. Then I read Miyazaki's letter. Oh God!

Either everyone in my family must die or I must! It's one or the other. I actually thought so. I wrote him my reply. The basis of my life was laid out: money to get away from this lodging house, money to set my family up in some house, and money for their travel expenses. If I had only that sum of money, all would be fine. That was what I wrote. And then I wanted to die. I enclosed in the letter to Miyazaki one yen for him to forward to my mother. Although I'd been thinking for a while that I would send it, I didn't until today—out of distaste for writing to my mother—no, out of fear.

I took the day off to copy the remainder of *Flowery Night*, continuing my work of last night.

It grew dark out. Kindaichi came in and presented a number of statements to arouse my interest in writing. For no reason at all, I started fooling around thoughtlessly, recklessly.

"Nothing is more reassuring to man than thinking his future is indefinite!" And I came out with my "Ha, ha, ha, ha!"

Laughing, Kindaichi collapsed in a heap on the floor. Tapping my fingers on my rib cage, I asked, "Do you know what—what tune I'm playing now?"

I kept doing all the ridiculous things I could think of until Kindaichi returned to his room. Then I immediately picked up my pen. Thirty minutes passed. Again I couldn't subdue the serious conviction that I'd never be able to write my story, that my future was hopeless. I went into Kindaichi's room and again committed a great many absurdities. I drew a big face on my chest, I changed my own face into several different expressions, I whistled an imitation of the bush warbler and the cuckoo—and then, finally, I picked up a knife and pantomimed a murder in a play. Kindaichi fled the room. Certainly I must have been thinking of that terrible thing at just that moment!

I turned off the light in the room. I stood inside the shutter-box,[14] the knife raised overhead.

Later, when we saw each other in my room, both of us were disgusted with what had just passed. I felt I had no fear of suicide.

And so what did I do the rest of the night? *Flowery Night!*

About two a.m. A fire in the farthest part of Koishikawa. A single pillar of light red smoke heading straight up into a black sky.

A fire! God!

Saturday, April 17

Around ten I was awakened by Namiki. I had pawned the watch I had borrowed from him, and so I hadn't yet returned it. When his voice summoned me from a deep sleep, I felt inexpressibly moody. A person who has committed a crime might have the same feeling if the place he is hiding in, a place where he had felt perfectly safe, is suddenly raided by the police.

Needless to say, to have any kind of interesting conversation with him was impossible. Of course he didn't press me for the watch, but I felt the immense gap between our two personalities. We talked about Gorki and other topics, and then he left around twelve.

Thinking I would definitely work on my story today, I stayed away from the office—no, it was because I wanted to have a holiday that I decided to scribble. At any rate, I did try to write something entitled "Red Ink," which I had thought through the night before. It was to be an account of my suicide. I set down about three pages in my notebook, and then I couldn't write a single word more.

Why couldn't I? Because it was absolutely impossible for me to objectify myself. Yes, absolutely impossible. Anyway, I couldn't write, I couldn't get my idea in shape. I did try to write an essay entitled "Mokichi-ism," which I had thought I'd do when I was writing "On Coming Up to Tokyo," but . . .

I met Kindaichi in the bath. He said his trip to Sakhalin would probably materialize, since he had just received a phone call from Dr. Jinbo. Kindaichi looked surprised, and I couldn't help feeling that way myself. He told me it would probably be during the spring if he went. Apparently he was going as a part-time employee of the Sakhalin Agency to do research on the languages of the Gilyak and Orochi.

After finishing my bath, I felt sad as I sat at my desk. Kindaichi's hesitation about going to Sakhalin was due to the fact that he had been able to earn his living in Tokyo. It was because he was still single and still had many hopes. "If only I could be Kindaichi," I thought. If only!

Before long he came in with the second volume of Doppo's *Collected Works*. He said he felt like crying. He said he'd been thinking only about me all day. I saw his eyes looking compassionately at me.

I asked him to read me a few of Doppo's stories, including "Fatigue." Afterwards he told me many things about Sakhalin. About the Ainu, about eagles flapping their wings in the morning sky, about ships, about the great forests where no human had ever set foot. . . .

"How much will the travel expenses be?" I asked.

"About twenty yen."

"Hmm," I thought to myself. "When you get there," I said, "will you find me a job? Anything will do. Policeman would be fine!"

My friend looked at me, a pitiful expression in his eyes.

When I was alone, I again found myself continuing my unpleasant train of thought. The money was already half gone. Already I had received an advance from my company. And I couldn't write!

It occurred to me to polish up my poems for *Subaru*, but as soon as I spread out my paper, I lost interest. I wanted to write a story about a man arrested by the police for sleeping in a vacant house, but I didn't even feel like lifting my pen.

I wanted to cry! I really wanted to cry!

"I will absolutely give up literature!" I said to myself.

"What will you do after giving it up? What will you do?"

"Die!" There was no other answer.

"What am I to do?" I thought.

Was there anything I could do? Was it preferable to go work on some local newspaper?

But even if I did, it seemed it would not be easy to earn enough money to send for my family. If so, wasn't the primary question that of my family?

There was, at any rate, really only one problem: how to free myself from this oppressive responsibility of earning a living. That was it.

To have money or else absolve myself from responsibility. One or the other.

Perhaps I'll have to carry this problem on my back until I die! In any event, I'll think about it after getting into bed. (One a.m.)

Sunday, April 18

I woke early, but didn't feel like getting up. Since the shutters were closed, my room was in semi-darkness. I was fidgeting in bed until eleven, the mere question of whether or not to go to the office too much to deal with. Should I go? I really didn't want to. Or should I not go? No, no, that would be wrong. While the matter remained unsettled, I heard the maid cleaning the room next to mine, so I had to get up. While I was washing, that bitch Otsune passed me in the hall after she had put away my bedding. "I'll clean your room for *you* after lunch. You don't mind, do you?"

"No," I replied, pretending an indifferent tone.

But inwardly I said, "'For *you?*' Bitch!"

A card came from Setsuko. Again Kyōko hadn't felt well, so my wife had taken her to the doctor and found once again it was her stomach and intestines. To make matters worse, the doctor called it chronic. Setsuko felt uneasy because I wasn't there. She writes that she wants a letter from me.

I decided to go to the office after all. One reason was that I had changed my mind after reading Setsuko's letter, but besides that, I didn't want the maids to think, "He's loafing again today!"

"Well, if you don't feel like it, you can go somewhere else on the way and enjoy yourself!" With this thought in mind, I left, but once on the streetcar, I had my ticket punched for Sukiyabashi and ended up going to the office.

In the streetcar I discovered a cute girl about three years old. As soon as I saw her, I thought of Kyōko. Setsuko would leave home in the morning and return at evening. And for the entire day only my mother and Kyōko in that wretched hole of a house! Grandmother and grandchild. When I thought about the entire day they would spend together, my eyes grew dim with tears in spite of myself. Nothing is more pleasurable to a child than food. When Kyōko would get tired of their monotonous and gloomy routine, she would most probably badger her grandmother for something to eat. But there would be nothing to give her. "Grandma, grandma!" she would cry. My mother would try to distract her, but Kyōko would not listen. "There, there," my mother would say. And lo, she'd come up with a piece of pickled radish!

In my mind's eye I saw the indigestible food entering my darling Kyōko's mouth and harming her delicate stomach and intestines.

As I had been absent for five days, my excuse a trumped-up illness, I felt somewhat ashamed on entering the office. Of course there wasn't the least bit of trouble. Somehow, once inside, I felt secure, since I didn't have to think about useless things. At the same time I envied those who had no ties, those who had to take care only of themselves with the money they earned.

In my spare moments away from proofreading, interest in the operations of the newspaper stimulated me. I felt Otaru was the city with the most promising future in the newspaper industry. I imagined how pleasant it would be if I put all my energy to work by starting a newspaper there.

My wild imaginings were endless! Tidal waves in Hakodate[15] . . . trips to Sakhalin with Kindaichi . . . meetings with political offenders in North Sakhalin, which is Russian territory.

On my way home I saw a deaf-mute on the streetcar. She wrote the word *Koishikawa* in her notebook and, showing it to the conductor, received a transfer.

My younger sister. A long letter had come from Mitsuko, who after leaving her parents, sister, and brother, had gone to Asahikawa this month with an English lady called Evans.

> . . . I have recently become somewhat accustomed to this city, so it's a lot easier to bear. Still, when I am basking in the soft spring sunshine coming in through the windowpanes, I don't think of anything except my memories of Shibutami, our hometown.
>
> I remember the time when, at your bidding, I went walking along the mountain paths looking for violets. Perhaps you sometimes remember life in those days. . . . On my desk is a lovely adonis. While I was looking at it today, I couldn't help remembering our hometown. We often walked around the graveyard searching for violets and adonises, remember? . . . And I recalled so many things. I relived again the resentment I had felt when you had scolded me long ago—please forgive me. There will never be another occasion which will cause you to scold me, even if I want you to!
>
> Why at those times did I not receive your scolding meekly? At this stage of my life I regret that more than anything else. How I wish to be scolded by my elder

brother! But that is no longer possible. Truly, my attitude was wrong. . . . Are you now corresponding with anyone in Shibutami? I myself want to write to Kiyoko Akihama, but I haven't sent her a single letter since I came to Hokkaido.

By the way, we are going to visit Otaru and Yoichi again around the middle of May to attend meetings of women's societies and moral training groups. . . .

My eyes blurred. If I were to tell my sister my feelings as they actually were at this moment, how glad she would be! The only letters I now read to my heart's content are hers! Those of my mother and the letters of Setsuko—they're too sad for me, too hard to bear. Sometimes, if it were possible, I even want to avoid reading them. And what's more, I have now lost those friends with whom I exchanged letters that appealed so much to the heart of each of us. It's true that I read the letters from women who sometimes write me—a few young women—but theirs aren't sincere.

My sister! My only younger sister! I am thoroughly responsible for her. And yet I haven't discharged that responsibility in the least. At the beginning of May the year before last, I was dismissed from my school in Shibutami for organizing a student strike, and it was decided that my younger sister would live with our elder sister in Otaru. We went together as far as Hakodate, my intention being to go to Hokkaido to find a job. The Sea of Tsugaru was rough during the crossing. My younger sister, seasick and pale aboard ship, was tended by me. I made her take some pills. Ah! that was perhaps the one time I acted like a brother toward my one and only younger sister.

She's already twenty-two. If things had gone normally, she would obviously have gotten married, and she'd be holding a cute child. But things didn't turn out that way. I don't know how many times up to now she's made plans to support herself. Unfortunately, all those plans have ended in failure. My unlucky sister, who resembles me too much, was not made, after all, to conform to the actual world! Finally she sought God. No, perhaps she was searching for a job through God. She's now working for "God," supported by some cold foreign woman. Next year she's going to enter a mission school in Nagoya after taking their examination, and in a year she'll "dedicate her life to God" and become a missionary.

Is my sister, who is so like me, really suited to becoming a teacher of religion?

Possibly because our personalities are so similar, my sister and I have been on bad terms ever since we were little. It would probably be hard to find anywhere a brother and sister who were on such bad terms with each other. Sometimes she spoke to me like a younger sister, but I myself have never spoken to her like an elder brother, even from the time she was safely inside her straw crib![16]

In spite of all that, my sister doesn't feel any resentment against me. And what's more, she says she wants to be scolded by me as in the old days, and she deplores the fact that it's no longer possible to be. I wanted to cry.

Shibutami! Shibutami! which I can't forget even as I try to forget it. Shibutami! Shibutami!

Shibutami, which raised me and then persecuted me!... I felt like crying and I tried to cry. But the tears wouldn't come. My father and mother, who spent the most important part of their lives there, eighteen years—on those two sad, elderly people Shibutami left memories too bitter and painful. My older sister, who's dead now, lived there for only three years, maybe five. My second elder sister at Iwamizawa has forgotten Shibutami along with her once-gentle heart. She feels that it's shameful to remember the village. And Setsuko was born in Morioka. Is there anyone anywhere who like myself has been unable to forget Shibutami? The only person in this wide world who hasn't is Mitsuko!

Tonight, I can't suppress my love for my younger sister, my poor younger sister. I want to see her! On seeing her, I want to say something an elder brother would say. I want to talk with her about Shibutami to my heart's content. I want both of us to return to those days long passed when we knew nothing of the bitterness, the sorrow, and the pain of the world. Nothing else is necessary! Sister! Sister! Will the day ever come when our family, all together, will talk happily about the old days in Shibutami?

It had begun raining without my realizing it. The raindrops sounded lonely. If only I could gather together my father, whom I haven't written to in a year, and my mother and Mitsuko and my wife and child and all of us have dinner together, no matter how simple the meal would be.

It seems Kindaichi's trip to Sakhalin will be only for the summer vacation. Today he went to Ōmiya with members of the Linguistic Society.

Monday, April 19

How this boardinghouse has perfected its ill treatment of its guests really takes the cake! I woke this morning around nine. When I came back from washing up, there wasn't even a fire in the brazier. I even had to put my bedding away. As I was lighting a cigarette with a match, the landlord's child came along the corridor. I ordered the youngster to bring me some burning coals and hot water. Twenty minutes later a maid brought in my meal. There wasn't a scoop for the rice. I pressed down on the bell. No one came. Again I rang. No one. After a considerably long time Otsune brought in the rice scoop and, almost hurling it at me, went out without a word. The *miso* soup was already cold.

Beneath my window the flowers on the elder tree were in bloom. Long, long ago when I was living in the temple at Shibutami, I remember cutting off the branches of this tree and making pipes from the twigs.

Whenever one of the maids behaves rudely to me, I think, "The slut! What if I paid all the money I owe and then threw them a tip? What flattering looks they'd assume then!" But will that time ever come?

I began writing a story entitled "Toyokichi, School Servant," which I later changed to "Mr. Sakaushi's Letter," but before I had jotted down five lines, it was noon and I left for work.

Nothing new there. It was amusing to see Old Mishina, the elderly novelist, trying various ways to get to know me. Kobayashi, the office boy, asked me, "What were the months that the stories you wrote appeared in *Subaru*?"[17]

After returning home, I began writing "Mr. Sakaushi's Letter" in Roman script, but by around ten my brain got fatigued and I stopped.

Tuesday, April 20

In the corridor Otsune was talking to someone. I had not heard the voice of the other party before. It was a thin voice, a naive voice. It sounded like another new maid had come. All this happened at about seven o'clock. That was the first thing I was conscious of today.

While I was dozing, someone entered my room. "Must be the new servant," I thought to myself dreamily. I breathed softly a few times and opened my eyes slightly.

As I had thought, a round-faced girl perhaps seventeen years of age was carrying in some coal for the brazier. "She looks like Osada-san," I thought, immediately closing my eyes. Osada-san was the daughter of the man in charge of the Shibutami post office. At that time, 1903, she was, if I remember correctly, fourteen, so now she must be—that's right—already twenty. Into whose family had she married?

While pondering this question, I remembered Shichirō Kanaya. And I drifted off to sleep.

Soon I woke again, though not so fully as to open my eyes. Rudely parting the sliding doors to my room, Otsune came in. She was taking the coals out of my brazier. When I opened my eyes, she said, "I'll bring some in later."

"You really do abuse me, don't you, you slut!" Intending to speak only to myself, I had blurted out these words. Otsune, coloring, said something. Mumbling to myself, I rolled over on my side.

During the forenoon my head was clear enough to allow me to write two pages of "Mr. Sakaushi's Letter." Then I went to work.

The city editor's staff was buzzing with activity because a train had overturned just this side of Kawasaki last night.

I left for home at the usual hour. Before long a telephone call came from Hiraide. It was to urge me to get my manuscript in for the tanka number. I gave him a random reply, but when I thought to myself, "Tanka! What rot!" I felt ridiculous remaining in my room, and I went out alone. I stayed at a movie theater on 5-chōme until nine. After that, inside a streetcar aimlessly for an hour.

In the morning I had brought my scarf to a pawnshop and got sixty sen for it. Then I had gone to a barbershop and had my hair cut short. I bought a towel and a bar of soap at some shop, and as I was about to enter the public bath just opposite, the affable wife of the bathhouse keeper told me, "Today's inspection day, so we won't be ready until eleven."

Wednesday, April 21

In bed last night I read a little of Tengai's *Star of a Millionaire*. His attitude in saying that he studied the world of business for a year with the thought of writing a book about it is in itself quite wrong. A second-rate novel. But as a writer he does have a formidable talent for arranging his episodes like an architect. An author with a poor imagination would be no match for him.

While I was reading the book, Kindaichi came in and asked if I had any hot water. He told me Bin Ueda was going to publish a magazine article entitled "The Novel is Not Literature."

"There! I told you," I said. "At last he's been forced to make that distinction. He couldn't abandon his classical view—or his taste—that poetry is the purest form of literature, yet he couldn't help recognizing the power of the new literature. And so he was probably obliged to make such a dualistic distinction!"

From today on Okiyo will again be in charge of our third floor. I got up early.

It's the season when the green foliage of the cherry trees is so beautiful. When I open a window, the colors of the haze-like young leaves stimulate my vision.

Yesterday on the streetcar I saw at least two men wearing straw hats. It's summer.

At nine o'clock I went to the public bath on Daimachi. This was the bathhouse I often used when I was living at the Sekishinkan after coming up to Tokyo. It hasn't changed at all: its large full-length mirror and its pleasant spray-shower are still there. The only thing that has changed is that the girl, perhaps seventeen, whom I saw last year and who looked like she was fond of men, wasn't on the attendant's stand.[18] Flickering on the plate-glass window was the shadow of green leaves cast by the fresh morning sunlight. I felt as I had the year before. The bathhouse attendant was the same fellow as then. I realized that the hot Tokyo summer was just about on us. That one summer at the Sekishinkan! It was a period when in spite of extreme poverty, I was enjoying my "semi-bachelorhood," happy to be freed from the responsibility of supporting my family. No, trying not to remember that responsibility. It wasn't long before I had cast off the woman I was intimate with at that time.[19] Now she's a geisha at Asakusa. Many things have changed in this one-year period. I gained several new friends, and then I broke with them.

While diligently washing my body, which seemed healthier than it had been at this time last year, I was steeped in these recollections. Oh, the violent struggle of this one-year period! *And, the dreadful summer is coming again on me—the peniless novelist! The dreadful summer! alas! with great pains and deep sorrows of phigical [physical] struggle, and, on other hand, with the bothomless rapture of young Nihilist!*

As I came out of the gate of the bathhouse, the expressful faced woman who solled me the soap yesterday said to me "Good morning" with something calm and favourable gesture.

The bath and the memories bring me some hot and young lightness. I am young, and, at last, the life is not so dark and so painful. The sun shines, and the moon is calm. If I do not send the money, or call up they [them] to Tokyo, they—my mother and wife will take other manner to eat. I am young, and young, and young: and I have the pen, the brain, the eyes, the heart and the mind. That is all. All of all. If the inn-master take me out of this room, I will go everywhere—where are many inns and hotels in this capital. To-day, I have only one piece of 5 rin-dōkwa: but what then? Nonsence! There are many, many writers in Tokyo. What is that to me? There is nothing. They are writing with their finger-bones and the brud [blood]: but I must write with the ink and the G pen! That is all. Ah, the burning summer and the green-coloured struggle![20]

From today on, due to the revision of the train timetables, the deadline for the first edition is earlier, so we have to remain until the second edition is ready. Report for work at twelve, leave at six.

In the evening Nakamura stopped in at Kindaichi's room. I went in to talk with them. Heard this man will join the *Asahi* newspaper staff after he graduates.

By phone, pressed for my manuscript by Hiraide.

Thursday, April 22

Because I retired early last night, I got up at six this morning. Then I wrote some tanka. The day, which had been so fine, clouded up in the afternoon.

In the evening I chatted with Kindaichi, made some tanka, went into Kindaichi's room again at ten, and had a hearty laugh reading him the tanka I had composed. We had a good time and made quite a row, and then I returned to my room and went to bed.

Friday, April 23

When I woke around six-thirty and went to wash up, the beautiful woman in Room 19, who Kindaichi said had bowed to him in the lavatory, was just coming out after washing. Hang it! "Too late, Yuranosuke!"[21] I was washing my face, using the metal basin she had used, and thinking, "What a foolish thing you're doing!"

I wrote some tanka. It wasn't pleasant to realize that writing tanka was the only thing I had a good command of.

It began raining around eleven. What with the absence of the two old men, Kimura and Maekawa, I was too busy at the office even to smoke until the first edition proofreading was approved.

From about the time I was on my way home, it had become quite cold out. Moreover, I was so hungry that my kneecaps were shaking while I was on the streetcar. There I happened to meet Naganuma, an acquaintance from my middle school days. Wearing a bowler hat above his pale fat face and dressed in the fashionable style of a company employee or a civil servant, he looked arrogant. It seemed he was already a father. I gave him my card, writing my address on it, though I knew the bastard would never visit me.

Lately I've often been meeting former acquaintances on the streetcar. Just yesterday when I was about to get off at Sukiyabashi, a young man wearing a stiff *obi* and seated near the exit said to me, "Excuse me, but didn't you live at Morioka, Mr. Ishi— . . . Ishi—?"

"That's right, I'm Ishikawa."

"My name's Shibanai."

Kaoru Shibanai, that cute kid! On asking him where he was living, he said he was staying in Akasaka at the home of the former principal of Morioka Middle School, Tada. I had to get off the streetcar without having had sufficient time to tell him my own address.

Kindaichi seemed hard at work on a draft of tomorrow's

lecture. As soon as I got home and finished dinner, I set to work making tanka. All told, with those I had been writing recently, I had by about twelve o'clock set down seventy poems to which I had given the title "Seventy Poems: Don't Ask Me Again,"[22] and then I went to bed satisfied.

The feeling after working all day without interruption, whatever the work may be, is incomparably pleasant. No doubt the really deep meaning of life lies there!

Saturday, April 24

Though it was a fine day, the thermometer only rose to about 63 in a wind from the north.

During the morning I selected forty poems out of the 698 tanka on "Fall" contributed by *Subaru*'s readers. On the way to the office I dropped these off at Hiraide's along with last night's "Seventy Poems: Don't Ask Me Again."

Among today's news items was a report of the crossing of the Pacific by a training squadron.[23] The article said that on the morning of the Springtime Worship Festival of Imperial Ancestors, all hands gathered on deck, faced West, and paid homage to our Imperial Ancestors. Old Mishina, the novelist who can hardly hear, said, "West isn't in the direction of Japan," and he refused to listen to any other argument. And Old Man Maekawa was quarreling with Round-Eyes Katō about Maekawa's absence without leave the day before. Maekawa resembles my father.

I returned a little later than usual. On top of the writing pad on my desk was something that looked like a letter. With heart throbbing as I flipped the switch on the lamp, I found it was from Chieko Tachibana in Sapporo! I had yet to send a reply to her postcard informing me of her release from the hospital.

She wrote, "Though I saw you only briefly in Hakodate, I am happy . . . from your letter that you have not forgotten me." And she wrote, "I have become well enough to go out for walks lately." And also, "I remember the old days." And then, "If you have time, at least a postcard. . . ."

Kindaichi came in. He was beaming, probably because today's lecture had gone well. We talked about many things, but something in his eyes kept telling me, "Keep writing your stories." He said, "Write a sequel to 'The Footsteps.'" While he talked to me about the enthusiasm I had shown a month ago, he seemed to be blaming me for my loss of real interest in everything of late.

"I'd love to come up to your expectations at once, Kindaichi, but all my rivals have vanished! Somehow, it's not worth the battle."

"Rivals! That's absolutely right!"

"My rival at that time was Ōta. He really was."

"He most certainly was!"

"The transaction between Ōta and me came to a halt with unexpected swiftness.

> Duality, duality! If that failed to explain
> He was keen on setting up triality!
> Oh, my clever friend!

When I wrote that tanka, who do you think I had in mind? Mr. Ueda, and after him, Ōta. I wrote three or four other tanka besides this one to spell out my ideological break with Ōta."

"So, you've already cast him aside then?"

"He has ceased to be a rival. And that's why I'm so disappointed. Rivals! Rivals! At a time when there are no authorities, it's terrible not to have strong rivals! In that area Doppo was great, really great."

Even this talk, however, did not cause my pulse to beat even a trifle faster.

Sunday, April 25

I have only one interest at present: to go to my office and for two or three hours do proofreading without a moment's rest. When my hands are not occupied, my head feels empty and time endless. I have even become accustomed to the roar of the rotary presses, which at first gave me such a thrill, so much so that they do not now ring out powerfully in my ears. When I thought about that this morning, I felt sad.

Am I not losing interest in everything? To lose interest in everything is to be abandoned by everything. And what if the time comes when *I have had lost from everything?*[24]

Last night I told my friend, "I've been running and I'm short of breath. At present I'm walking at a slow pace."

Today the great smokestack of the ordnance factory is not disgorging any smoke.

I went to the office and received my monthly salary—seven yen in cash. My IOU for eighteen yen was returned to me as well.

Last month I could only look at the twenty-five yen because all of it was handed back to Mr. Satō, so I had returned home without even a fraction of a sen.

Since it was Sunday, I went home after the first edition was finished. Then around four, I went to visit Mr. Yosano at Surugadai. He was out, having gone to see a play at a training school for actors, but as I was talking to Akiko-san upstairs, Yoshii called. The subject of Yoshiko Hirayama came up.

Akiko-san said that her husband's poems which were to appear in the coming tanka number were likely to bring on a good deal of comment from the public.

When I asked why, she said, "We quarreled the other day. All he does is dote on Nanase while being very cruel to Yatsuo, though I don't know why. And because he treats her so cruelly, she's becoming more and more nervous, crying even more, so I had him promise me he would not scold her for a week, but in spite of that he slapped her on the face, so I said that if he was that cruel to a child, I'd return to my parents, and then he got angry. His present tanka are about that situation. In many of them there's the line 'I was deserted by my wife' or something like that."[25]

"Is that so?" I said laughing.

"By the way, Miss Yamakawa died."

"Miss Yamakawa!"

So the hapless woman poet Tomiko Yamakawa had at last died! Soon after Mr. Yosano came home, I took my leave.

Having left laughing over something we had been talking about, I walked a few steps before my tongue came out with a "Tut, tut!" I said to myself, "All right! I'm different from them. Wait and see, you fools!"

I bought a strip of twenty streetcar tickets.

I had a slight headache. I asked Kindaichi to go out for a walk with me. At Hongō 3-chōme, I asked him, "Where'll we go?"

"Hmm!"

We had our transfer tickets punched for Sakamoto and went to the Yoshiwara. It had been the second or third time for Kindaichi, but it was the first time in my life that I had set foot into this quarter that never sleeps. It was not as vast or as breathtaking as I had expected. We took a stroll around the district. There was no denying its appeal.

Soon after the great clock of the Kadoebi struck ten, we left the flowerlike district and went by jinrikisha to Asakusa. I suggested we take a walk around the garden at the foot of the Tower,[26] but both of us had lost interest, and since we felt terribly hungry, we stopped at a sukiyaki restaurant. We got back a little after midnight.

"When I wake up in the night, the sound of raindrops seems like the whispers of lovers in the next room, and I have vague feelings—I feel as if a beautiful woman were sitting by my bed," Kindaichi said suddenly, something like that.

"Some vague feeling! I don't know how many years it's been since I've forgotten that kind of sensation!"

My friend also said something that implied he definitely wanted to stay overnight in the Yoshiwara.

"Great! You ought to. But what about marriage?"

"I'd get married any time if I could find a suitable woman. After I do, though, I probably won't have to go to such places!"

"No, I disagree. I think you ought to, even after you get married."

"You may be right."

"And, you know, Asakusa—that's merely a place for gratifying one's carnal desires, so to speak, so it doesn't matter who the girl you're with is. But if it's the Yoshiwara, I'd like to sleep with a real beautiful one. The place has historical associations, and it's all artistic. You go to bed inside a room which is the last word in splendor, a coverlet lining of burning red silk that seems as though it's about to go up in flames, a crimson red mattress so soft you feel as if your body is sinking when you lie on it, and just as a beautiful lantern is casting its deep shadow and you're suddenly awakened from an indescribable feeling of ecstasy, a beautiful girl is sitting gracefully by your bed. Magnificent!"

"Irresistible!"

"When you go to the Yoshiwara, you must have a beautiful girl. If it's at Asakusa, on the other hand, she must have, above all, a well-developed physique and privates without a flaw."

For nearly an hour the two of us talked about "that vague feeling" and about a girl whose surname was Kuji, who had been a student at Morioka and was said to be working in the Yoshiwara.

Monday, April 26

When I opened my eyes, I found the fire in the brazier had gone out. I felt as if the inside of my head were wet and clammy.

Just as I was thinking how to brighten my mood, a postcard from Namiki arrived.

As I read it, my head returned to its dampened state, utterly dark and cold. His card asked me to return, within the month, the watch I had borrowed from him—that watch I had pawned.

God! Never before had the question of death been so directly near me as today. Should I go to work or not? . . . No, no, first, before that decision, was the question of whether to die or not. . . . Well, it wouldn't do to remain in my room. I'd go out, somewhere else.

It occurred to me to head for the bathhouse. Because I couldn't bear this unpleasant feeling. Because the good feeling I had when I had gone there the other day would come back to me. So I'd go to the bathhouse. And afterwards I'd think about the other question. So I went to the public bath on Daimachi. Until that moment I had actually intended to die.

It was comfortable in the bath. I thought I'd stay as long as possible. I felt that the moment I left this place, my fearful problem would pounce on me and force me to kill myself or do something else. I felt as if my body were my own only as long as I immersed it in the hot water. I felt I wanted to remain in the bath a long, long time. But it took me an unexpectedly short while to wash.

What should I do! Leave the bathhouse or stay a bit longer? If I left, where in the world could I go?

Through the glass door I could see the girl on the watcher's stand. It was the girl who had been on the stand last year when I used to come here frequently. I hadn't seen her there the other day, though—that snub-nosed but round-faced girl with the healthy complexion, a girl apparently fond of men. In less than a year she had filled out so much that I hardly recognized her. It seemed to me her body was throbbing with the fire of a girl in her prime. The transformation in this young girl's body made my imagination go off in several directions.

Thinking about whether I should get out of the bath or not had diverted my mind from the question of dying, and a psychological change occurred in me. After dashing myself with cold water, I felt considerably lighthearted. When I weighed myself, the scale registered 45.1 kilograms. I had gained a kilogram and a half in less than a week.

I left the bathhouse after lighting a cigarette. The air felt good on my skin. The desire to write welled up, and I went to Matsuya's and bought a pack of writing paper.

Soon after returning to my room, I received a letter from Miyazaki. I——. He said he would send my family to Tokyo in June. I needn't worry, he said, about their traveling expenses or anything.

It seemed as if I had spent the entire day trying only to brighten my mood. I had a slight headache, and I frequently felt as if the world were becoming dark, murky.

While I was eating my dinner after returning from work, Kindaichi came in. He too said it was one of those nights when he didn't feel like studying.

"Let's enjoy ourselves just for tonight!"

And so the two of us left around eight and went to Asakusa without saying just where we were heading. We saw a movie at the Denkikan, but it was so dull that we left early, and then we walked along the quarter near the Tower. For some reason, a number of pretty girls attracted my attention. We were dragged into a certain shop but managed to make a quick escape. Then after we entered another shop, a girl full of gestures kept asking us to treat her to something. We ate some sushi.

The Shin-matsumidori! This was the shop Kitahara and I had drunk at the other day. Kindaichi and I went in around ten-thirty. One of the girls, Tamako by name, said she remembered my face. She was a pretty girl with a certain refinement, even in her words. She told us about her past, bitterly complaining about her lot and the harsh treatment by the mistress of the house. I ran my fingers over the strings of a samisen I found hanging on a wall, and the upshot was I took the instrument down and clowned around with it. Why had I done such a thing? Was I in high spirits?

No! Somehow the feeling overwhelmed me that there wasn't a place in the entire world for me. "I have a headache, so just for this one night I'll enjoy myself." These words weren't true. So what was I searching for? A woman's body? Saké? Probably neither. If not, what? I myself didn't know.

My self-consciousness made my mind sink even deeper. I didn't want to fall into the terrible abyss. Nor did I want to return to my room: it was as if some disgusting thing were waiting for me there. It was as if Hongō were some absurd distance away and to return there was too troublesome. And so what was I to do? I knew there wasn't a thing I could do. The feeling that there was no place for me in the whole wide world had made me play the fool for the sake of being a fool.

"I'm quitting the fifth of next month," Tamako said, her face sad.

"You ought to. If you're thinking of leaving, it's best to leave immediately."

"But I have debts."

"How much?"

"When I got the job, they totaled forty yen, but they piled up gradually and now they're a hundred. And I've never even had a kimono made for me. . . ."

I felt as if I couldn't bear this any longer. It seemed there was nothing else for me to do except cry or joke. At that moment, though, I couldn't tell any jokes. And of course I couldn't shed tears.

The voice of the mistress at the counter abusing Tama-chan. Outdoors, some vulgar voice singing *naniwabushi*, the jeering, jocular voices of loungers outside who had passed the shop, and a tune sung by a woman whose voice seemed to have come from some hollow place.

"This is life, huh?" I said to Kindaichi.

I ordered some saké. I downed three cups in rapid succession. In a moment I was drunk, and just like a sick bird fluttering its wings, I was struggling to keep myself from falling into the dark abyss.

The disagreeable mistress of the shop came over. I handed her two yen. I went into an adjoining room and for about five minutes slept with a girl called Oen. Tama-chan called me and I went back into the other room, where I found Kindaichi lying down. I didn't feel like saying anything. A feeling as if I had finally fallen into the abyss. . . .

We left. The streetcar went only as far as Kurumazaka, and we walked home from Ikenohata. Leaning against my friend, I felt as if I were going along some road of inexpressible sorrow. I was also drunk.

"Some people cry when they're drunk. Tonight I think I understand that feeling."

"I know."

"After we get home, Kindaichi, will you put your arm around me and sleep with me?"

We walked along the dark street by the University Medical School while we talked about Pale Face.[27]

When we knocked at the gate on returning to our boardinghouse, I felt as if I were tapping my own chest and hearing something unpleasant.

Tuesday, April 27

I awoke with a start to find Okiyo standing by my bed. I sprang up even though I was so tired I could have wept.

A cloudy day.

I remembered everything about last night. It was a fact that I had slept with a girl called Oen; it was also a fact that I had derived no pleasure from it. It was a fact too that when I had again come into the main room, Tama-chan's cheeks were slightly flushed. It was equally a fact that while returning with Kindaichi, he had told me he had not slept with her but had kissed a woman for the first time in his life. And it was a fact that I had been trying to escape from some terrible sorrow assaulting me by pretending to be quite drunk while walking home, and it was a fact that the sorrow in the depths of my mind which I had wanted to leave intact without touching was the sorrow of wasting three yen to no purpose.

This morning I made up my mind that never again would I spend any money and time on women. Such, after all, had been my mask.

Even after arriving at the office, I somehow felt restless until around four. It was because I thought I would try to get an advance of twenty-five yen on next month's salary and yet dared not suggest it even though I had gone downstairs to. The company vault closed at four. When the clock above my head rang out its four beats, I heaved a sigh of relief.

A glimpse of a red shadow was reflected on the windowpane as I was trying to quiet my mind after spreading some manuscript paper on my desk. I had just heard the sound of a fire bell. It was about eight o'clock, and directly opposite my window I could see the fire that had broken out in Koishikawa. The fire raged furiously, and a clamor started in the street below. Fire! With my window wide open I was looking on as though I were seeing something pleasant I had not witnessed for a long time.

Around nine-thirty I was called to the phone. It was Kindaichi. He had gone with Nakajima and some others to the Shōkatei restaurant in Nihonbashi, and he asked if I would join them. I set off at once.

After being jostled on a streetcar for about forty minutes, I reached my destination and found four men with a young geisha. Uchiyama, the Nose, was singing a *shinnai*, his voice quite unlike his appearance.

Kindaichi and I left after an hour or so and returned home by streetcar.

Wednesday, April 28

A carp streamer had been hoisted on a house below the cliff. An early summer wind turned the windmill and made the carp pennant swim above the green foliage of the cherry trees.[28]

I got up early and visited Mr. Satō at his home on Kasumichō to ask for an advance on next month's salary. It was impossible at this time, he said, so he requested I wait until the beginning of next month. On my round trip on the streetcar I found my eyes assailed by the bright colors of young leaves. It *was* summer!

Nothing new after I got to the office. I had spent my last yen at that unexpected party the previous night. Now, only one defaced five-rin copper coin in my purse.[29]

I wouldn't be able to pay tomorrow's streetcar fare.

Thursday, April 29

I decided to take the day off. I began writing a story called "The Bottom." Since I didn't go out even after the noon hour, Kindaichi came into my room. "It's because you don't have any money for the streetcar that you haven't left yet for the office, isn't it?" he asked.

"Yes," I replied, "that's one reason. . . . Forgive me, but I've really warmed up to my work today."

"You mean it? If that's the case, then get on with it!" With these words my friend left the room.

Though I was interrupted by Isen Satō for about two hours in the afternoon, my pen kept moving without a pause.

I spent the evening in Kindaichi's room.

Friday, April 30

If I go to the office today, I won't have any money for cigarettes. As for receiving an advance, that's out of the question until tomorrow. If I stay home, I'm afraid they'll dun me downstairs, since it's the last day of the month.

Perplexed about what to do, I finally decided to take the day off.

I wrote the first three installments of "The Bottom."

Recently a very short girl called Sumi-chan has come to work in the house. Though they say she's seventeen, she looks like she's only fourteen or so. She went back home for a while last night, and after a scolding from her mother and elder brother, she rushed outside, heading toward the seashore at Shinagawa with the intention of killing herself. They say she finally returned here alone without attempting anything. I heard it was around half past three when she got back.

She's terribly strong-willed and saucy, yet she's quite lovable. "Okiyo-san's a darling," Sumi-chan said of one of the maids older than herself. "That what's-her-name—Otsune-san. Her face is like this," the girl said on another occasion, imitating Otsune by putting on an ugly comical face.[30]

In the evening they came, as I expected, to press me for payment. I asked the landlord to wait until tomorrow night.

At around nine Kindaichi lent me two yen fifty sen. From that moment my enthusiasm to write passed away. In bed I read Futabatei's translation of Turgenev's "Rudin." I went to sleep nursing some deep emotion.

Saturday, May 1

Yesterday it drizzled all day, but it cleared up beautifully, and for the first time in a long while I could see Mt. Fuji. It was a little cold out due to a northerly wind.

In the morning I spent my time reading "Rudin" and "The Floating Plant." Ah, Rudin! To think about Rudin's character is tantamount to proving that I'm a man unable to do anything in this world.

When I got to the office, Mr. Satō was absent. The face of Katō, our boss in the proofreading section, looked somewhat bloated. I remained silent, deliberately refraining from apologizing for yesterday's absence.

My advance met with success, so I borrowed twenty-five yen. That meant there would be nothing to take home the next payday this month. I paid one yen sixty sen for last month's cigarettes.

I left the office at six-thirty. In the morning Namiki had come to my room to talk about that watch of his, so how should I use my twenty-five yen? If I took the watch out of hock, I wouldn't have enough to pay the boardinghouse; and if I gave them twenty yen, it would be impossible to retrieve the watch. This trivial question filled my mind, and I couldn't come to any conclusion. Actually that triviality proved more difficult than deciding to die or not. At any rate, unless I settled the matter, I couldn't go back home.

I boarded a streetcar at Owarichō. For Asakusa.

"Transfer?"

"No."

So answering, I asked myself, "You going again?"

I got off at Kaminarimon and ate dinner at a sukiyaki restaurant. Afterwards I went to a movie, but it wasn't the least bit interesting. At a magazine shop I bought the *Subaru* tanka number.

Even as I was thinking to myself, "Don't go! Don't go!" my feet were heading toward Senzokumachi. I secretly slipped past the Hitachiya and came out in front of a new shop on the corner called the Kinkatei, and it was just at that moment that a white hand thrust itself from the lattice of the shop and caught me by my kimono sleeve. Before I realized it, I was on my way in.

God! That girl! Hanako. Age seventeen. At a glance I immediately thought, "It's Koyakko! Her face is just like Koyakko's, only she's a few years younger."

A moment or two later I left the place with a bedraggled old woman who sold cakes. She pulled me about here and there until we came out along a tall brick wall behind the Senzoku Primary School. On both sides of the narrow lane were back-street tenement houses with all their doors closed. There was no traffic, as if the street had been consigned to oblivion. The moon was shining.

I thought, "I've finally come to the very depths of this miserable world!"

"Please wait here," the old woman said. "I'll go open the door." For some reason she kept looking around. Evidently she was afraid of the police.

She quietly opened the door of the nearest room in that deadly silent tenement building and came back part way. I saw her beckoning me in the moonlight. She showed me into that forbidding building and went out saying, "I'll keep watch from over there."

Hanako had arrived before me, and no sooner had I gone in than she threw her arms around me.

It was a small dirty place. Even at a glance I could see that the walls were dirty, the straw mats rotting, and that the room had been built without a ceiling. A small lamp on the edge of an oblong wooden brazier dimly lit up the miserable conditions of the room. An old clock ticked away monotonously.

When I entered a narrow two-mat room partitioned off by sooty sliding paper doors, I found the bed already laid out. Even the slightest laugh rattled the doors.

I looked intently at the girl's face in the dim light and saw looming in the semi-darkness a round white face exactly like Koyakko's. I was so taken with it that my eyes narrowed in ecstasy.

"She resembles her, she really does!" Repeatedly I whispered these words to myself.

"Look, my hairdo's all ruined, so don't keep staring at me like that!" the girl said.

The skin of that young girl was so soft it fascinated me. The clock in the next room kept on ticking.

"You tired already?" she asked.

I heard the old woman quietly entering, but nothing more came to me.

"What's she doing now?"

"Crouching in the kitchen. I'm sure she is."

"She's pathetic, isn't she?"

"Don't mind her."

"But she's really pitiful!"

"Well, yes, she's pathetic. She's really all alone."

"You'll be like that too when you get old."

"Oh no, not me!"

After a while she said, "Stop staring at me!"

"You really do look alike."

"Like who?"

"My kid sister."

"Oh, I'm so happy!" Hanako said, burying her face against my chest.

It was a strange night. Until then I had slept with many women. But I had always been irritated, as though I was being urged on by some unknown force. At such moments I had always jeered at myself. Never before this night had I experienced such feelings of fascination, such indescribable feelings, so much so that my eyes had narrowed in delight.

I no longer thought about anything. Enraptured, I could feel my body warming to its very core by the heat from the girl. Furthermore, the act of copulating, which had done nothing recently but leave me with unpleasant sensations, was performed twice this night in sheer pleasure. And even afterwards not a trace of disgust remained in me. We sat up in bed and smoked.

"Look," she whispered. "After you leave, turn to the left and wait for me at the corner of the second alley."

At the dead end of an alley in that world of misery, I stood by the side of a hydrant in moonlight pure as water. She finally came running along the darkened half of the street, her clogs sounding lightly. The two of us walked side by side. Occasionally she drew near me to say, "Really, please do come again. You hear?"

It was midnight when I returned to the boardinghouse. I had, oddly enough, no feelings of regret. I felt only some "indefinable ecstasy."

There was no fire in my room, and my bed had not been laid out. I slept as I was.

Sunday, May 2

Otake came in to wake me. "Excuse me, Mr. Ishikawa, the master's just about ready to leave, and he told me to ask about the rent."

"Well of course. I came back so late last night I went straight to bed." Rubbing my sleepy eyes, I took out my purse and gave her only twenty yen, adding, "I'll pay the remainder around the tenth."

"Will you?" Otake said, her eyes cold and knowing. "Could you please tell him yourself at the office? We're always being scolded about it."

I turned over in bed without answering directly and said, "Oh, what a fine time I had last night."

It was about nine when a small maid came in to tell me that a Mr. Iwamoto was here to see me. Iwamoto! Who could that be?

I got up, stowed away the bed,[31] and after calling him in found he was, as I suspected, Minoru, son of the deputy village master at Shibutami. He had come over with a young man born in Tokushima Prefecture who happened to be at the same inn. Minoru had traveled to Tokyo hoping his aunt living in Yokohama would help him, but after letting him stay for two weeks, she had given him, he said, travel funds and told him to go back home. But he had no wish to and with the intention of securing employment in Tokyo had put up at an inn in Kanda three days ago, quite troubled, though, because he had not known my address until today. The other person, Shimizu by name, had also turned up in Tokyo after quarreling with his family.

Summer insects, lured by flame, leap into it and die. These men had so ignorantly been captivated by what we call the metropolis that they had dashed toward it. Sooner or later they would be burned to death or would run for their lives. Of the two possibilities, one was inevitable. I felt a sharp pang of sorrow.

Without giving them any advice about their recklessness, I kept repeating, "Don't be impatient. Take it easy." That was because I knew a time would definitely come when they would want to commit suicide. Minoru had only two yen thirty sen, Shimizu one yen eighty.

There was absolutely no connection between Shimizu and me. I would probably be putting myself to unnecessary trouble helping the two of them if they stayed together. But I didn't have the heart to force them to separate when I saw the helpless expression on Shimizu's honest face.

"How about your inn? Can you leave any time you want?"

"Yes. We paid up last night. We definitely thought we could manage something by today."

"Well, first you have to find a place to live."

At about ten-thirty I went out with them. After searching all over, we found a boardinghouse called the Toshimakan at 8, Yumichō 2-chōme. The landlady agreed to their each paying eight yen fifty sen per month for one six-mat room for the two of them. I handed her a one-yen deposit.

I took them to lunch at my favorite tempura shop. Having decided to take the day off, I sent Shimizu to their inn to pick up their baggage, and I went with Minoru to Shinbashi Station to get

石川啄木 著

ローマ字日記 悲しき玩具（英語版）

貧困と流離の天才歌人・啄木が赤裸々に綴った「ローマ字日記」と短歌史に新しい生命を刻んだ歌集「悲しき玩具」

石川啄木 悲しき玩具 ローマ字日記 タトル出版

TUT BOOKS

their checked luggage. When we got back, Shimizu was already waiting. We talked about various things until around three and then I came back to my room. My purse was completely empty.

The stories about Shibutami that I had heard today from Minoru revived so many memories that it was almost unendurable. He said the principal of the primary school had formed a secret relationship with N-san, and a quarrel in the teachers' room caused by jealousy had taken place. N-san, who resigned last year, seemed to have become pregnant, and recently a rumor had circulated that she was slightly deranged.

Minoru told me Seimin Numada had been punished for trespassing and had been put on probation for three years. Not one of the rumors concerning the other people Minoru told me about failed to move me. Even Isoko, my "woman of the firefly," had become the wife of the younger brother of the village doctor and was living in Hirosaki.

I also heard to my surprise that my story "The Shadow of a Bird" was known by the villagers.[32]

In the evening I tried to write a letter to Iwamoto's father. For some reason I couldn't. I tried writing to Chieko-san at Sapporo, but that too I couldn't do. When I opened the window in my room, a soft night wind caressed my heated cheeks, and from the depths of the screech of some streetcar rounding a curve, there floated before my eyes my native town.

Monday, May 3

I sent in a sick-report and spent the day in bed. That slut Otake abused me terribly: the entire day passed without her bringing me any coals for my fire. Every now and then Sumi-chan came in for an innocent chat. That bitch Raku-chan went by looking at us suspiciously.

A nasty day! I lay my head, my heavy head, against my pillow like a man in despair, like a man totally worn out. I excused myself to all visitors.

Tuesday, May 4

Again took the day off. Kept writing the entire day. I began "A Day Spent with the Gate Locked," but gave it up, began "Reminiscence" and dropped it, began "An Interesting Man?" only to stop that, and "Memories of my Boyhood," only to leave that too. This showed how agitated I was. Finally I threw down my pen. I went to bed early. I couldn't sleep, of course.

Towards evening Namiki came over. Then Iwamoto and Shimizu dropped in for a moment and left. From first to last with them as usual, I talked about nothing in a carefree way.

Wednesday, May 5

Took the day off again.

Wrote and wrote, but unable to finish anything. It was already evening when I completed an essay, "Looking at My Hand." Sent it to Reisō-sha in Maebashi.

Thursday, May 6

Again took the day off. Rained all day yesterday and today, to the inconvenience of those who went to attend the festival at Yasukuni Shrine.

In the morning I had been awakened by Iwamoto and Shimizu. They looked depressed.

"This won't do at all!" I thought. "I've got to do something for them. That's it! I'll take next week off and work hard at writing. This room isn't suited for that. I'll go into some empty room at Iwamoto's and write from morning till night. In the evening I'll come back here and sleep."

I thought that if I could make some money, the three of us could rent a house and cook for ourselves. I got Kindaichi's approval after telling him about my plan.

With a pad of writing paper and a bottle of ink I at once went to Yumichō. But I couldn't write anything today, so I merely listened to various topics the boys brought up. The more I listened, the dearer the two of them became. They sleep in one bed. And in the light of a small dark lamp, they talk about the future.

Mohachi Shimizu is an honest man with considerable steadiness of purpose. He said that for two years he had been working in his elder brother's shop in Seoul in Korea and that he had run away because he desperately wanted to study.

Various thoughts whirled in my mind as I listened to the talk of these two men, but I used all my will power to suffocate the worries swirling in the depths of my mind. Suddenly I found myself engrossed in listening to Shimizu's words, and I asked, "How much would the travel fare be?" How pathetic I am!

Around eight that evening I returned home and after talking to Kindaichi in his room for a while went to bed.

I made up my mind to write today because it's the only way I can go now. This thought makes me feel terribly melancholy. My salary for the month has already been advanced. There's no other way to get any money, and next month my family will be coming. I'm now in the abyss. The abyss! Either I will die or climb out. One or the other. And I have to rescue those two young men!

Friday, May 7

I had the maids wake me at seven, and by nine I was at Yumichō. They gave me eighty sen for some books at a secondhand bookshop, and I bought a big oil lamp, a chess set, and some cigarettes. Oh, the girl at the Kikyōya![33]

It was glorious just to chat. Not only that, but the weather was bad, so I couldn't get much writing done anyway. Nevertheless, I did write about ten pages of "The Inn" and began something else called "A Handful of Sand."[34] At least the day wasn't wasted. Returned around nine at night. Oh, the girl at the Kikyōya!

A letter from Iwamoto's father asking me to take care of his son. And a precious letter from Jinko Tsubo in Kushiro, a card from Yoshiko Hirayama, and a card too from Isen Satō.

Saturday, May 8, to Thursday, May 13

What have I done during these past six days? Nothing. What I did merely proves, after all, that it's impossible to change my present condition no matter how impatient I am to.

I went to Yumichō three times in all. While I was with the two boys, I tried to write, but my pen didn't make as much headway as I had hoped. On the tenth I stopped going and wrote in my room. I gave up on "A Handful of Sand" and began "Sapporo," but it's not finished even after fifty pages or so.

I've been absenting myself from the office under the pretense of illness. Even when word came from Mr. Katō telling me to come in, I sent him a letter that I had stomach pains. Yesterday, when I went to Yumichō, I found the boys in distress over the demand for their rent, so I sent Iwamoto to Mr. Katō to ask to borrow five yen for me from Mr. Satō, and with it I paid the lodging house. At a used bookstore I sold "The Heathens," which Kitahara had presented to me.

I gave Shimizu various kinds of bitter advice, and I wrote directly to his elder brother for him. I made Shimizu promise to look for a job, regardless of what it was. As for Iwamoto, I had asked Hiraide's family, since he was away from home, to find someone who would employ the boy as a student-dependent.

An interminable bleakness often blackened the way before me. I was at least trying to keep the thought of death at arm's length. One night, wondering what I ought to do, I suddenly felt all was pitch dark before me. To go to the office was meaningless, nor was it any use to stay away. I tried inflicting a cut on my chest with a razor I had borrowed from Kindaichi, and with the wound as a pretext I had thought to stay away from work for a month or so and thoroughly think through my circumstances. I had tried cutting myself just below the nipple of my left breast, but it was so painful I wasn't able to. I did manage to inflict two or three slight scratches. Surprised, Kindaichi wrested the razor from me and, dragging me out by force, pawned his inverness and took me to our favorite tempura shop. We drank. We laughed. Around midnight we came back home, but my head was heavy. I felt all I had to do was switch off the light and I would see that terrible thing before me.

Another pathetic letter in *kana* from my mother. She thanked me for the one yen I had sent her last month. She asked me to send her some money if it was convenient because she wanted Kyōko to have a summer hat.

A moment came when I even thought of escaping from Tokyo right then and there. And a moment came when I felt I wanted to go to the country to raise silkworms.

With the rainy season approaching, there was no letup in the gray drizzle. I didn't complete even one piece of writing during these several days of depressing weather.

Nor did I meet any friends. No longer did I have any use for them. In fact, they must be angry with me after reading my poems in the tanka number.

Often, thoughts about Shibutami.

Even though I was so very much moved by my younger sister's letter, I haven't even sent her a postcard. To Iwamoto's father only a card. I haven't written to my family. Nor anything to Chieko Tachibana. I had thought I'd write her, but I had nothing to say.

In the evening I went into Kindaichi's room, and the subject of women came up. I couldn't concentrate in the least and didn't write anything on returning to my room before going to bed, so I decided to read Ryūkei Yano's *The Unnecessary*. His temporary good and genuine good! What, in the final analysis, is genuine good?

I know now that I have no confidence, that I have no aim, that from morning till night I'm driven by vacillation and anxiety. I have no fixed point in me. What will become of me?

A useless key that does not fit! That's me! Wherever I bring myself, I can't find the keyhole that fits me!

Dying for a smoke!

Friday, May 14

Rain.

I was awakened by Isen Satō. With five in his family he has to find work.

After Satō left, Shimizu came. He said he had a job making the rounds of customers for a Nihonbashi wine dealer.

I sent for Iwamoto and told him to write out a record of his personal history and bring it to me.

The weather was unpleasant, but somehow my mind settled.

I've become so used to taking off from work it no longer pains me. On the other hand, my thinking's become so flabby I can't write a thing. Somehow I've become strangely indifferent.

Two times my mouth bled profusely. A maid said it was probably from a rush of blood to the head.

At night I copied a pamphlet entitled *A Compendium on the Right Use of Kana in Representing Kanji Sounds*.

I thought I'd write something about Shibutami, but try as I might, I couldn't warm up to the subject, so I went straight to bed.

Saturday, May 15

I was awakened at nine by Iwamoto. A "trusting to your judgment" letter had come to me from his father.

Today's papers reported that Tatsunosuke Hasegawa (Futabatei Shimei) had died aboard ship on his return to Japan. All the newspapers tried to outdo each other in praising his virtues as they expressed their grief over the death of this man, great in some indefinable way.

It's been very cold lately, but today it's warmer. The sky has also cleared up.

I spent the entire day doing nothing. From the bottom of my mind, which has become terribly dulled, a presentiment rises like a ghost before me that soon I will have to carry out my terrible action.

In the evening the two boys dropped in. Shimizu had arranged to live as an apprentice at the wine dealer's on Kyōbashi. He said he'd move tomorrow.

Soon after they left, Toshimaro Obara, a writer who's visited me once, stopped in. His eyes are like a rabbit's. I was so bored as he talked on about various trivialities that I hardly answered. Around ten-thirty he finally left.

"Everything changes according to the way you look at it," Obara had said. "People think that day by day they are shortening the fifty or sixty years allotted to them, but I believe life means adding one more new day after each succeeding day, so the passing of time doesn't pain me in the least."

"When all is said and done, the happy person is someone like you. A person like you can feel assured deceiving himself in such a way," I had replied.

At about eleven I went into Kindaichi's room, and we spoke of Futabatei's death. My friend said he couldn't understand why Futabatei disliked literature, why he disliked being called a literary man. My poor friend could not understand the deep yearning and pain in life. Feeling unbearably lonely, I returned to my room. Ultimately it's impossible for a man to make another man understand him fully. In the final analysis, camaraderie between one man and another is merely superficial.

Realizing that the friend who I had thought understood me as thoroughly as I had him was unable, ultimately, to understand the anguish and pain at the bottom of my heart made me feel unbearably dreary. We are each separate, each alone!

This thought left me indescribably sad.

I was able to imagine what had been in Futabatei's mind as he was dying.

Sunday, May 16

Got up late. The rain kept me cooped up indoors and spoiled my precious Sunday.

I went into Kindaichi's room to convince him to change his view of Futabatei, and I succeeded. Iwamoto dropped in again today.

Not only did I not go to the office, I didn't do anything. I had no cigarettes. Absentmindedly, I thought again of going back to the country. I dug out some newspaper from my hometown to glance through and thought of various ways to edit a local sheet.

In the evening I told Kindaichi about my present state of mind. "I'm not fit for city life," I said. I mentioned I was seriously considering going back to the country.

My friend shed tears for me.

The country! The country! That's the place I ought to die in. I'm not suited to the violence of city life. To devote my entire life to literature! Impossible! It's not that I couldn't if I tried, but that the life of a literary man is, in the long run, nothing but emptiness.

Monday, May 17

A terrific gale all morning. Took the day off.

In the afternoon Iwamoto dropped in for a while and left.

Items in today's paper about Futabatei being a nihilist and his relations with a woman of the crudest social position.

I held out without cigarettes until lunch, but at last I went to Ikubundō with a copy of *Akogare* and two or three other books and sold them for fifteen sen.

"How much for this one?" I had said, pointing to *Akogare*.

"Five sen, I guess," replied the consumptive-looking shopkeeper. Ha, ha, ha.

Today again thoughts about going to the country. I spent the entire day thinking only of that. "How ought I to run a local newspaper? How ought I to edit it?" Only that!

Reduced to this state, I had spent an entire day thinking about such things without doing anything!

In bed at night as I was reading the *Shinshōsetsu*, I hit upon an idea.

It was *national life*.[35]

Monday, May 31

I spent two weeks doing practically nothing. I kept away from the office.

A letter from Shimizu's brother, but he hadn't enclosed any money.

Two or three times, letters from Iwamoto's father.

A letter also from Koyakko in Kushiro.

I didn't send any letters anywhere, not even to Hakodate.

I wrote and sent to the *Iwate Nippō* a five-installment essay, "Letters from a Dyspeptic." My aim: to awaken the people in Morioka from their lethargy. There *was* a response. The *Nippō* began a series called "Steps Toward Morioka's Prosperity."

This feeling as though waiting for execution! I actually used those words. I have been studying German every day. Besides that, I've been devising various models for editing a local newspaper. It really seemed best to take myself to some local sheet. Of course to do that I'd have to abandon literature.

Once Kanae Yamamoto, who paints in oil, dropped in. Discussion about a photographic news agency.

The last day of the month.

I couldn't remain in the house without saying anything about the rent, so I went out in the morning and pawning my *haori*, the only one I have, for seventy sen, I boarded the train from Ueno to Tabata without any destination in mind. I simply wanted to ride a train. At Tabata I roved about the paths through the fields and untiringly inhaled the odors of the earth.

After coming back, apologies to the landlord.

I had never seen Kindaichi's face as pitiable as it looked tonight.

Tuesday, June 1

By sending Iwamoto with a letter to the office in the afternoon, I got an advance of twenty-five yen on this month's salary. But as I had to pay five yen to Mr. Satō, my take-home pay was twenty yen.

I went to Iwamoto's lodging and paid about thirteen yen for his and Shimizu's last month's rent (for which they had already paid six yen). Then I went with Iwamoto to Asakusa, and after a movie we ate at a Western-style restaurant. I gave him a yen for spending money and left.

I slept with a naive young girl whose name slips me. Next I went to see that girl resembling Koyakko that I had once slept with, Hanako. I went with the old woman to that strange place.

She told me she was already sixty-nine. Finally Hanako arrived. We slept. So pleasant somehow, sleeping with this girl.

I returned around ten. I had bought several magazines. Only forty sen left.

Twenty Days

An account of my moving to the upstairs rooms of a barbershop c/o Arai (Kinotoko), 18, Yumichō 2-chōme, Hongō.

With my hair untrimmed and even my sparse moustache getting long, I looked so haggard that I felt disgusted with myself. A maid said I resembled a consumptive. I had been lying in my three-and-a-half-mat room until the morning of the tenth, ill from an overdose of laxatives. On no account could I bring myself to write. But an argument with Kindaichi served as an opportunity to put my various views on literature in order.

Iwamoto came spilling out his thanks for my kindness.

In bed on the morning of the tenth, I read the letters sent from Morioka by Miyazaki and Setsuko. They said they had left Hakodate on the seventh, my mother stopping at Nohechi, and Setsuko and Kyōko staying at Morioka with my friend Miyazaki. I thought: "And so at last!"

With the fifteen yen Miyazaki sent me, I rented two rooms from a barber named Arai at 18, Yumichō 2-chōme, Hongō. As for my present boardinghouse, they will receive a monthly installment of ten yen on the one hundred and nineteen yen I owe, Kindaichi acting as my guarantor. I sent word to my family to set off on the fifteenth.

I left the Gaiheikan that day. Putting only my bags in the rooms I had rented, I slept that night in Kindaichi's room. There was in us a strange feeling of farewell. Farewell!

On the morning of the sixteenth before the sun had risen, the three of us—Kindaichi, Iwamoto, and me—were on the platform at Ueno Station. The train arrived an hour late. My friend, my mother, my wife, and my child. We arrived at our new home by jinrikisha.

Notes

1. Five yen was a large sum in those days, especially for Takuboku, who rarely had that much in his purse.

2. The campus of Tokyo Imperial University.

3. Since early films were all imported—and silent, of course— someone had to explain them. Such a narrator was called a *benshi*, which means "orator." The *benshi* stood by the side of the screen, watching the movie and reading his script at the same time. The custom continued even when the Japanese produced their own silent movies. Some *benshi* enjoyed as much fame as today's popular singers, so much so that some fans went to the movies just to listen to their favorite commentator.

4. In those days, rooms in a boardinghouse were usually separated from the hallway by sliding paper screens (there was no actual wall), one of them serving as the door. Thus, a silhouette could easily be seen.

5. Italicized passages, other than titles of books, etc., represent Takuboku's own use of English words in the original.

6. A novel by Gorki entitled *Three Men* (1901). In a letter dated July 7, 1908, to Tadashi Iwasaki, one of the founders of the Bokushuku-sha in Hakodate, Takuboku writes: "I went to bed at two a.m. and read Gorki's *Three of Them* in bed. . . . Fine, very fine. I, who have surprised my friends by saying Turgenev is dated, am utterly impressed by Gorki. In the passage I read last night, the description of the psychology of the hero after he murdered someone on the spur of the moment and then stole the person's money was lifelike beyond description. There wasn't a trace of falsehood. I had become somewhat tired, but I was so engrossed in the book that when I put out the lamp, the light of dawn coming through chinks in the shutters formed whitish patches on the paper screen, and here and there clocks were striking four."

7. Mt. Iwate in Iwate Prefecture, the view of which was visible from Shibutami.

8. Takuboku was mimicking a yokel on his first trip to the big city.

9. The Pan Society was an organization founded by poets and artists in December 1908 to discuss new literary and artistic trends in Europe and Japan. The name "Pan" was taken from a similar group formed in Berlin. The Japanese police, however, thought that the Pan of Greek

123

fame meant "bread" (*pan* is "bread" in Japanese), so the group was under observation as a radical organization demanding food for the poor.

10. These were *henaburi*, a style of comic tanka. They were diametrically different from the romantic style of Akiko Yosano and her group; some of the members probably regarded them as an insult.

11. At one time, Japanese dandies liked creaking shoes. To help produce the sound, a thin layer of leather was inserted in the shoe.

12. When a parent writes to a son or daughter, *dono*, rather than *sama*, would normally be used in the greeting. Also, it is usual to use the given name instead of the family name. The salutation in this letter should thus be Hajime-dono, not Ishikawa-sama. (Today, such rules are becoming obsolete.)

13. *Hiragana* is one of two syllabaries, collectively called *kana*, which today consist of forty-six characters each. It is used for grammatical elements, such as inflections of verbs, which cannot be written in Chinese characters, or *kanji*. Any word in *kanji* can, of course, be spelled out in *hiragana*. This is what Takuboku's mother did, since she could not remember the more complex *kanji*.

14. A shutter-box is a storage place for sliding shutters, or *amado*, which are slid along the windowsill at night as protection from the elements.

15. No tidal waves had ever caused serious damage in Hakodate, so in his wild imaginings Takuboku may have been envisioning them washing away his family and thus releasing him from his heavy responsibilities.

16. In Japanese farm villages, babies were placed in rice-straw cribs for safety while their parents were working in the fields. The inside of the bowl-shaped crib was tolerably warm.

17. These stories are "Dysentery" (*Subaru*, no. 1, January 1909) and "Footsteps" (*Subaru*, no. 2, February 1909).

18. In a public bathhouse in Japan there is a stand at the entrance from which the attendant can watch both the men's and women's sides. A public bath is usually a single-family business, so male and female members of the family take turns being attendant, collecting the bath fee and guarding against theft. Bathers male and female do not mind disrobing before the attendant, who is treated as a non-person, so to speak. Male and female bathers cannot observe each other.

19. Teiko Ueki. Entries on this woman occupy more pages in Takuboku's diaries than any other female does. Takuboku first met her in 1904 when members of the Shinshi-sha gave theatricals. Takuboku had relations with her when she was nineteen, but later forsook her. She eventually became an Asakusa geisha.

20. This is Takuboku's own English, left uncorrected by the translators.

The last sentence of the first paragraph might mean something like, ". . . these great pains and deep sorrows of my physical struggle, but equally this rapture of a young nihilist."

A five-rin *dōkwa (dōka)* was a coin equal to one-half sen (there are one hundred sen to one yen), a very small amount of money even in those days.

The bizarre term "finger-bones" in the last paragraph probably means that other writers wrote without using their brains, that is, their work lacked substance. That they write with blood, an expression which can be interpreted as "they write enduring excruciating pain," is a reference to minor naturalist writers, who believed that a naked description of actual life, however ugly or shameful, would result in a work of art. (A G-pen was a popular nib of the day.)

The "green-coloured struggle" might refer to the green of nature, oppressive in a hot climate.

21. The expression "Too late, Yuranosuke!" is a translation of *"Osokarishi Yuranosuke,"* which comes from one of the most popular Kabuki plays, *Kanadehon Chūshingura.* A certain Lord Asano, who has been ordered to commit ritual disembowelment *(seppuku)*, is waiting impatiently for his chief retainer, Ōishi Yuranosuke, to entrust him with certain affairs. The official overseeing the rite waits as long as possible, but finally urges Lord Asano to carry out his suicide. Immediately after the lord thrusts the short sword into his belly, Yuranosuke appears, whereupon the dying lord utters, "Osokarishi Yuranosuke."

22. The May 1909 issue of *Subaru* was to be a tanka number, the editor's intention being to issue a manifesto on new trends in the genre. Takuboku contributed seventy tanka as specimens of this new direction, but with the subtitle "Don't Ask Me Again" to tell readers to figure out for themselves what was new in the poems.

23. A naval squadron with midshipmen aboard used to visit the United States or Britain as part of their training program.

24. A likely interpretation of this is ". . . when I am abandoned by everything."

25. In the May 1909 issue of *Subaru*, Tekkan Yosano published one hundred tanka under the title "One Hundred Sham Poems," which were mostly melancholy, self-pitying, and often cynical poems on past love affairs and marital discord. Among them we find the following: "Father beating them/Mother proposing divorce/Oh, my miserable kids!" "How unlovable a wife you have become!/To suggest divorce/In a fit of anger!" "Not a trace of that love/I trusted would endure—/For this is human life."

26. The Ryōunkaku (lit., "skyscraper"), a twelve-story tower, the highest structure in Tokyo at that time.

27. The translators conjecture that this was the name of a prostitute.

28. Carp streamers, one for each son, are hung on poles by Japanese families around the time of the Boys' Festival, May 5. Each streamer is a long tubular piece of cloth or paper shaped like a carp and painted red and black. The wind blowing through the streamers makes them extend horizontally their full length, so they look like big fish swimming in the sky.

29. Five rin equals one-half sen; one sen is 1/100 of a yen.

30. In the original, a *hyottoko*, a comical mask with one eye much smaller than the other and a pair of pouting lips.

31. The end of the previous entry, that is, "I slept as I was," probably refers to not changing into nightwear. The beginning of May is too cold to sleep without bedding, so Takuboku must have laid out the bed.

32. A short novel serialized in the Tokyo *Mainichi* from November 1, 1908, to the end of the year.

33. Probably the name of the shop where Takuboku bought the lamp, cigarettes, and other items.

34. Takuboku's first book of tanka of the same title was to be published in December 1910. This reference, though, appears to be the title of a story he had in mind at this time.

35. The expression "national life," in English in the original, is enigmatic, but Takuboku might have been hinting that the cause of his difficulties, of all difficulties, all evils, was the State, the structure of society. To the Japanese of his day, the State was all, and there was no clear notion of the people being the State. Takuboku's reference probably means that if the common people were to lead meaningful lives, the State would have to be changed.

Selected Allusions

Note: Many individuals close to Takuboku are mentioned in greater detail in the Introduction (to which the reader is referred); thus, only a brief mention of them is given in this list. Certain individuals mentioned in *Romaji Diary* seem not to have made names for themselves elsewhere; they are therefore not listed here.

Akiko: *See* Yosano, Akiko.

Akogare: Takuboku's first published volume of poems, dated May 3, 1905. The title means "yearning."

Asahikawa: A city in the center of Hokkaido.

Asakusa: An area of Tokyo in which are found Asakusa Park and Sensōji Temple. Many theatres, movie houses, and vaudeville halls were clustered there, as were numerous eating establishments serving substantial meals at moderate prices. Until World War II, it was by far the most popular amusement center for the common people. A bridge called Azumabashi spans the Sumida River there. On the opposite side of the river is Mukōjima, part of which is Kototoi, famed in poetry.

Chieko: *See* Tachibana, Chieko.

Chūōkōron: A famous Japanese journal, established in 1899. Its contents include politics, economics, philosophy, and literature.

Doppo: Doppo Kunikida. The penname of Tetsuo Kunikida (1871-1908). Doppo means "going my way." A well-known short story writer, Doppo was a precursor of the naturalist movement in Japanese literature. Some of his well-known stories are "Musashino," "Beef and Potato," and "The Diary of a Drunkard."

Evans, Miss: Anna Evans. A nurse and Anglican missionary with whom Takuboku's sister Mitsuko lived in Hakodate and Asahikawa, Hokkaido.

Futabatei Shimei: Penname of Tatsunosuke Hasegawa (1864-1909), coined from a slangy Tokyo dialectal phrase, "Kutabatte shimae!" (loosely translated, "Go to Hell!"). Although Futabatei was skeptical of his own literary talents, in the latter part of his career he joined the staff of the Osaka *Asahi* newspaper, in which he published two novels, *The Image* and *The Commonplace*. In 1908, he went to St. Petersburg as a reporter, but developed tuberculosis and died on his return voyage. Futabatei enjoys a solid position as a translator of Turgenev and as one of the pioneers of the modern novel in the Meiji era.

Gaiheikan: A boardinghouse near Tokyo Imperial University. Takuboku's room was at its branch house, a separate structure under the same ownership as that of the main house.

Gilyak: A Mongolian tribe living along the lower course of the Amur River, Mongolia, and in northern Sakhalin.

Hakodate: A port city on the southern coast of Hokkaido.

Hasegawa, Tatsunosuke: See Futabatei Shimei

Hiraide: Shū Hiraide (1878-1914). Lawyer, poet, and critic. Hiraide was counsel for the socialist Shūsui Kōtoku, several members of whose group participated in the alleged assassination attempt on Emperor Meiji in 1910 (see Introduction, p. 30).

Hirano: Banri Hirano (1855-1947). A romantic tankaist of the Myōjō school, one of the oldest members of the Shinshi-sha, and a co-founder with Takuboku and others of Subaru. He later broke with Takuboku over a dispute involving the handling of tanka in the magazine.

Hirayama, Yoshiko: The name taken by a young man whose real name was either Yoshitarō or Ryōtarō (the characters for his name can be pronounced in two ways). In November 1908, under the female name Yoshiko, Hirayama wrote to Takuboku, asking him to correct "her" tanka. Later he sent a photo, probably of a pretty young woman, which prompted Takuboku to write in his diary that he was surprised to find "her" so pretty. On January 15, 1909, Takuboku noted in his diary that he had found out that Yoshiko was actually a man. Yet on March 8 he wrote that he sent Subaru no. 3 to "Yoshiko Hirayama."

Hirosaki: A city in Aomori Prefecture.

Hotta, Hideko: (1885-1954). A colleague of Takuboku's at Shibutami Primary School towards whom Takuboku seems to have entertained friendly feelings. On May 3, 1907, when he was about to leave his job at the school to go to Hokkaido, he wrote in his diary: "In the evening I talked with Miss Hotta alone. It rained from time to time, and many frogs were croaking in the neighboring paddy fields. When I thought that this would probably be the last time I would sit with her in this room, my heart was full, and I could not give expression to my feelings. She didn't talk much either." Her name often appears in his diaries.

Isoko: Motoko Sasaki, a classmate of Takuboku's sister Mitsuko at Shibutami Primary School. In his diary entry for May 4, 1908, Takuboku wrote of a conversation with Kindaichi: ". . . we talked of home. Autumn flowers and songs of insects at Ibarajima were among the topics. I was so unutterably moved I shed tears. We fell into sleep talking about the woman of the firefly."

Iwamizawa: A city in Hokkaido. Takuboku's elder sister Sada (1876-1906) lived there.

Iwate Nippō: A local newspaper published in Morioka City, to which Takuboku contributed numerous articles.

Jinbo, Dr.: Dr. Kaku Jinbo (1883-1965). Philologist, professor at Tokyo Educational University. He was senior and apparently an advisor to Kindaichi.

Kadoebi: One of the most famous houses of prostitution in Yoshiwara. Its prestige was such that only the rich were able to frequent it.

Kanaya, Shin'ichirō: A friend from Takuboku's Shibutami days. He attended the same middle school as Takuboku and had a literary turn. His penname, Shūgen, appears frequently in Takuboku's early diaries.

Katsu: Katsu Ishikawa, née Kudō (1847-1912). Takuboku's mother.

Kindaichi: Kyōsuke Kindaichi (1882-1971). Takuboku's lifelong friend who introduced him to tanka during their Morioka school days. Kindaichi, two years Takuboku's senior, went on to become a student in the Literature Department of Tokyo Imperial University. His life's work was the study of the *Yukar*, the native epic of Japan's Ainu. In 1945 he was appointed a professor at Tokyo University; he was awarded the Order of Cultural Merit in 1954 for his work on the *Yukar*.

Kitahara: Ryūkichi (penname Hakushū) Kitahara (1885-1942). Poet. Published the book *Jashūmon* (The Heathens) in 1909. (Christians during the Tokugawa era were addressed as *jashūmon*.)

Koyakko: The geisha name of Jin Tsubo (1890-1965), with whom Takuboku had a brief romance.

Kunohe: An area in the northern part of Iwate Prefecture, facing the Pacific.

Kushiro: A city near the northeastern end of Hokkaido, where Takuboku found a job as chief editor of the *Kushiro Shinbun* (newspaper) and where he met Koyakko.

Kyōko: Kyōko Ishikawa (1906-1930). Takuboku's daughter. She appears in poems 70, 107, 127, and 153-162 of *Sad Toys*.

Mishina: Chōzaburō Mishina (1858-1936). A writer of stories for the *Asahi* newspaper. Today he is forgotten as a writer of fiction.

Mitsuko: Mitsuko Miura (1888-1968). Takuboku's younger sister. Wrote *Takuboku, My Sad Brother* (Hatsune Shobō, 1948).

Miyazaki: Daishirō (penname Ikuu) Miyazaki (1885-1962). Miyazaki was born in Niigata Prefecture and later moved to Hakodate, where he met Takuboku in 1907. Miyazaki wanted to marry Takuboku's sister Mitsuko, but dissuaded by the poet, eventually married Setsuko's sister Fukiko. He came to have a deep love and respect for Takuboku and repeatedly helped him and his family in their difficulties. In September 1911, however, Takuboku broke with his friend because of a misunderstanding about Miyazaki's sympathy toward the ailing Setsuko. Miyazaki published *The Sands of Hakodate: Takuboku's Tanka and Me* in 1960.

Mokichi: Mokichi Saitō (1882-1953). Psychiatrist and poet. The head of the Araragi school of tanka, he was one of the greatest tanka poets of the Taishō and Shōwa eras. His tanka were simple and strong after the manner of the *Man'yōshū*, the return to whose tanka principles he advocated. It was for this reason that Takuboku may have been opposed to his school.

Morioka: A city in Iwate Prefecture. Takuboku went to middle school and fell in love with Setsuko there.

Nakajima, Kotō: Penname of Moichi Nakajima (1878-1946). Novelist, critic, and translator. Nakajima was in charge of a column in *Shinshōsetsu* introducing movements in Western literature to Japanese readers. His translations of juvenile literature are still read.

Nakamura: Ō (penname Kokyō) Nakamura (1881-1952). A graduate of the English Department of Tokyo Imperial University and member of the foreign news section of the *Asahi* newspaper. He later went to a private medical college and became a practicing physician.

Namiki: Takeo (penname Hisui) Namiki. A shipping company employee whom Takuboku first met in Hakodate, in the Bokushuku-sha, a literary circle.

Nanase: Nanase Yosano. One of the twin daughters of Akiko and Tekkan Yosano.

naniwabushi: A kind of ballad recited to a particular tonal rhythm. Naniwa is an old name for Osaka; *bushi* (from *fushi*) means "tune."

Nohechi: A town in the eastern part of Aomori Prefecture. Takuboku's mother's elder brother was the incumbent of a temple there.

Numada, Seimin: One of the villagers who tried to help reinstate Takuboku's father after he lost his position as head of the temple in Shibutami.

Oideno: A field in Shibutami, Iwate Prefecture.

Orochi: A small Tungus tribe living near the mouth of the Amur River, Mongolia, and in eastern Sakhalin.

Ōta: Masao Ōta (1885-1945). A doctor who wrote poems, plays, stories, and critical pieces under the penname Mokutarō Kinoshita. His contributions to symbolic and impressionistic poetry in Japan are considerable.

Otaru: A port city on the west coast of Hokkaido, near Sapporo.

Ozaki: Yukio Ozaki (1858-1954). Orator and politician. Takuboku visited Ozaki in 1904 when the latter was mayor of Tokyo. He showed Ozaki the manuscript of *Akogare* and asked the mayor to introduce him to a publisher. Ozaki refused. Takuboku dedicated the book to Ozaki when it was published in 1905.

Reisō-sha: Possibly the name of some poetry association that published a small literary magazine.

Sakhalin: A large island north of Hokkaido. The portion south of the 50th parallel became Japanese government territory after the Russo-Japanese War (1904-1905). The Japanese government made various investigations in order to develop the area.

Sanshōdō: Takuboku's name for the publisher Sanseidō.

Satō, Isen: A reporter who worked on the staff of the *Kushiro Shinbun,* the newspaper that Takuboku edited for a time in Kushiro, Hokkaido.

Satō, Mr.: Shin'ichi Satō (1868-1914). Chief editor of the Tokyo *Asahi* newspaper, Satō was born in the same prefecture as Takuboku. Takuboku visited Satō and asked him to find him a job. Satō employed him. He did not fire the poet, even though the latter frequently neglected his duties. Satō was kind to Takuboku for the rest of the poet's life.

Sekishinkan: A boardinghouse near Tokyo Imperial University. Takuboku lived there before settling into the Gaiheikan.

Senzokumachi: The correct pronunciation is Senzokuchō. An area behind Asakusa Park in which were located many unlicensed brothels. The complicated procedure of finding a room described in the May 1 entry was typical.

Setsuko: Setsuko Ishikawa, née Horiai (1886-1913). Takuboku's wife.

shimada: A style of hairdo worn by unmarried women during the Tokugawa and Meiji eras. There are several varieties of which the tall style is worn today (in wig form) by brides. Geisha, too, wear a variation of this hairdo when in full dress.

shinnai: One of the many schools of *jōruri,* the music of the Bunraku puppet play. Its chief characteristic is pathos, its content mostly about double love-suicides. In red-light districts, itinerant *shinnai* singers used to perform to the accompaniment of their own samisen playing, waiting for restaurant customers to summon them inside to continue their presentation.

Shinshi-sha: A group of poets formed by Tekkan Yosano in November 1899.

Shinshōsetsu: A literary magazine published by Shun'yōdō. It featured short stories, novels, and criticism. It was established in 1889, folded a year later, but was revived from 1896 to 1926.

Subaru: A literary magazine established in 1909, lasting until 1913. Strongly influenced by Ōgai Mori, it was colored by anti-naturalism and aestheticism. Among the popular contributors were Hakushū Kitahara, Masao Ōta, and Isamu Yoshii. Takuboku contributed a short story entitled "Dysentery" to its first issue (January 1909). He was also the nominal publisher of that number.

Tabata: The fourth station to the north of Ueno on the National Railway line.

Tachibana, Chieko: (1889-1922). A teacher at a Hakodate primary school, where Takuboku met her in 1907.

Tengai: Tengai Kosugi (1865-1952). A writer of realistic novels before the days of naturalism, but later a writer of popular novels. In his *Star of a Millionaire,* a novel of the realistic genre, he informed his readers that he hoped to create a work which could not have been written by naturalists with their very narrow viewpoint, the naturalists writing only, he felt, their personal lives.

Tsubo, Jinko: See Koyakko.

Tsugaru, Sea of: More properly known as the Tsugaru Strait. The body of water between Hokkaido and Honshu.

Ueda, Bin: (1874-1916). Poet and translator, professor at Kyoto University. He was an anti-naturalist.

Ueno: An area of Tokyo, comprising Kurumazaka, Ikenohata ("pond's edge"), and Hirokōji. There were, and still are, a zoo, museums, temples, and a park there.

Yachigashira: A part of Hakodate, Hokkaido.

Yamakawa, Tomiko: (1878-1909). Poet and friend of Akiko Yosano's. An ardent follower of the Shinshi-sha, she, like Akiko, loved Tekkan, the group's founder. The following tanka by Yamakawa gives her blessing to Tekkan and Akiko's future: "Leaving all the red flowers/For my friend/And crying without her knowledge,/I gather/Flowers of forgetfulness." She died of tuberculosis at the age of twenty-nine, at which time Tekkan composed twelve poems of tribute to her. Akiko did not immediately write anything, but later the following tanka by her appeared: "That secret/We sealed in a jar,/The three of us,/My husband, myself,/And the dead one." (See the Introduction to our *Tangled Hair,* Purdue University Press, 1971.)

Yamamoto, Kanae: (1882-1946). Painter, woodblock artist, and a contributor to art education in school curricula. As an advocate of free drawing in primary school, he liberated schoolchildren from the copying of model drawings and paintings.

Yano, Ryūkei: (1850-1931). Penname of Fumio Yano. A famous journalist who, because of his intense interest in politics, wrote novels about Greek politicians.

Yasukuni Shrine: A shrine situated in Kudan in Tokyo, founded in the Meiji era as a place sacred to the spirits of the war dead. In the precincts many open-air stalls and show tents were set up.

Yatsuo: Yatsuo Yosano. One of the twin daughters of Akiko and Tekkan Yosano.

Yoichi: A city near Otaru, Hokkaido.

Yosano, Akiko: (1878-1942). One of the most famous tankaists of the Meiji and Taishō eras. Wife of Tekkan Yosano. She is most well known for her tanka cycle *Midaregami* (1901), a collection of bold poems asserting female individuality: "Softly I pushed open/That door/We call a mystery/These full breasts/Held in both my hands." "After my bath/At the hot spring,/These clothes/As rough to my skin/As the world!" (See our *Tangled Hair,* Purdue University Press, 1971).

Yosano, Tekkan (Mr. Yosano): (1873-1935). With his wife, Akiko, one of the most famous tankaists of his day. He founded the Shinshi-sha in 1899 and the literary magazine *Myōjō.* He was known as "Tekkan the Tiger" and was the founder of the "tiger-and-sword" style, so named because his poems were so masculine: "Rubbing my sword/In the autumn wind/Over these Korean/Hills—/Oh this thrill in my heart!" "They say tigers roar/In these Korean hills,/Yet I hear/Only the desolate wind/Of autumn . . ."

Yoshii: Isamu Yoshii (1886-1960). A tanka poet, well known for his fondness for saké as well as for his poems.

Yoshiwara: The licensed quarter in Takuboku's time, a red-light district of the highest class, situated to the north of Asakusa. Poorer men could not afford to visit the elegant restaurants, etc., in the area, but were content to lounge about the quarter and stare at the beautiful women.

Sad Toys

Our attempt in *Sad Toys* has been to translate these poems in the spirit of Takuboku, preserving wherever possible his mixture of the formal and colloquial. Sometimes we omit the names of places or plants or other terminology too weighty for poetry. We have avoided syllabic count and rhyme in order to preserve the spontaneity, naturalness, and simplicity of tanka, and as Takuboku himself wrote these poems in three lines, we have created three-line tanka but without following Takuboku's experiment on indentation. He also experimented with punctuation, and at times we follow his, but the tone and nuance of English have dictated our own use of punctuation.

1

When I breathe,
This sound in my chest
Lonelier than the winter wind

2

Though I closed my eyes,
Nothing crossed my mind ...
Only this emptiness on opening them again

3

That whim on the way
And again I took the day off
To roam the river's edge

3
途中にてふと氣が戀り、
つとめ先を休みて、今日も
河岸をさまよへり。

2
眼閉づれど
心にうかぶ何もなし。
さびしくもまた眼をあけるかな

1
呼吸すれば、
胸の中にて鳴る音あり。
凩よりもさびしきその音！

4

Throat parched
I went hunting for fruit stalls
Late this autumn night

5

My child not yet returned from playing somewhere
I take out the toy train
And run it myself

6

"I want to buy books! I want to buy books!"
These words to my wife
But not to rebuke, not to wound!

6
本を買ひたし、本を買ひたしと、
妻に言ひてみる。
あてつけのつもりではなけれど、

5
遊びに出て子供かへらず、
取り出して
走らせて見る玩具の機關車。

4
咽喉がかわき、
まだ起きてゐる果物屋を探しに行きぬ。
秋の夜ふけに。

7

Husband's mind on travel!
The wife scolding, the child in tears!
O this table in the morning!

8

For five blocks after I left home,
I walked like a man
With something to do, someplace to go—

9

Hand pressed against my painful tooth,
I notice the sun rising
Blood-red in winter fog . . .

9

痛む歯をおさへつつ、
日が赤赤と
冬の靄の中にのぼるを見たり。

8

家を出て五町ばかりは
用のある人のごとくに
歩いてみたれど――

7

旅を思ふ夫の心！
叱り、泣く、妻子の心！
朝の食卓！

10

Suddenly felt
As if I had to walk without end
Along these midnight streets

11

How precious the winter morning!
Soft against my face,
Steam from the hot water in this bowl ...

12

Somehow, this morning,
Things don't seem so bad—
I trim my nails.

10

いつまでも歩いてゐねばならぬごとき

思ひ湧き來ぬ、

深夜の町町。

11

なつかしき冬の朝かな。

湯をのめば、

湯氣がやはらかに顔にかかれり

12

何となく、

今朝は少しくわが心明るきごとし。

手の爪を切る。

13

Absorbed
By the illustrations in this book—
Smoke from my cigarette blown their way

14

Too late to transfer to another car,
I felt like crying—
And what's more, the rain!

15

Every third night
About one a.m. I climbed this slope
To earn my bread

15
二晩おきに
夜の一時頃に切通の坂を上りしも──
勤めなればかな。

14
途中にて乗換の電車なくなりしに
泣かうかと思ひき。
雨も降りてゐき。

13
うつとりと
本の挿繪に眺め入り、
煙草の煙吹きかけてみる。

16

Going home—
And my brain itself so steeped in this smell of wine
And weighted down down

17

Saké again today!
How well I know this nausea
From booze!

18

At least thinking
I mumbled something now,
Close my eyes to taste this drunken state!

<table>
<tr><td>

18

何事か今我（われ）つぶやけり。
かく思（おも）ひ、
目をうちつぶり、酔（ゑ）ひを味（あぢ）ふ。

</td><td>

17

今日（けふ）もまた酒（さけ）ののめるかな――
酒（さけ）のめば
胸（むね）のむかつく癖（くせ）を知（し）りつつ。

</td><td>

16

しつとりと
酒（さけ）のかをりにひたりたる
脳（なう）の重（おも）みを感（かん）じて帰（かへ）る。

</td></tr>
</table>

19

Midnight awakening!
And so refreshed, so sober!
Begin making ink . . .

20

Midnight,
And through the bay window in this narrow room
Fingertips cooled against the wooden railing's frost!

21

O this secret desperation nowadays
As if to say
Let Fate do what it will!

21
どうなりと勝手になれといふごとき
わがこのごろを
ひとり恐るる。

20
眞夜中の出窓に出でて、
欄干の霜に
手先を冷やしけるかな。

19
すつきりと酔ひのさめたる心地よさよ
夜中に起きて、
墨を磨るかな。

22

As if these hands, these feet, were scattered—
O this sluggish waking!
This sad waking!

23

This morning's sorrow:
Spreading out the shabby paper from back home
And scouting for misprints

24

Wish someone
Would rebuke me and rebuke me again!
That's the kind of mind I have!

24
誰か我を
思ふ存分叱りつくる人あれと思ふ。
何の心ぞ。

23
みすぼらしき郷里の新聞ひろげつつ、
誤植ひろへり。
今朝のかなしみ。

22
手も足もはなればなれにあるごとき
ものうき寂覚！
かなしき寂覚！

25

Morning after morning
The sorrow on rubbing
The numbness from this thigh after a night of sleep

26

Like some train across a wild waste
This agony
Now and then through my mind!

27

Somehow
It's like visiting the grave of a first love,
This being in the suburbs ...

27

何がなく
初恋人のおくつきに詣づるごとし。
郊外に來ぬ。

26

噉野ゆく汽車のごとくに、
このなやみ、
ときどき我の心を通る。

25

朝な朝な
撫でてかなしむ、
下にして痲た方の腿のかろきしびれを。

28

Like returning to one's precious town—
That's how I felt
Riding a train at long last!

29

"I believe a new dawn's coming!"
Say these words in earnest
And still—

30

Thought about the things I really wanted
And yet it all boiled down to none—
I polish my long-stemmed Japanese pipe!

30
考へれば、
ほんとに欲しと思ふこと有るやうで無し。
煙管をみがく。

29
新しき明日の來るを信ずといふ
自分の言葉に
嘘はなけれど—

28
なつかしき
故郷にかへる思ひあり、
久し振りにて汽車に乗りしに。

31

I stare at these soiled hands—
Just like
My mind these days!

32

When I washed these dirty hands—
My scant satisfaction
For the day . . .

33

Yearning suddenly for my hill,
I came out today—
O where's that rock I sat on last year!

31
よごれたる手をみる——
ちやうど
この頃の自分の心に對ふがごとし。

32
よごれたる手を洗ひし時の
かすかなる滿足が
今日の滿足なりき。

33
今日ひよいと山が戀ひしくて
山に來ぬ。
去年腰掛けし石をさがすかな。

34

Overslept
And again unable to scan the news—
How like some monetary debt it feels!

35

So relaxed this New Year's Day,
Mind vacant
As if all my past erased!

36

This alert mind
From morning to night—
Until yesterday I tried to keep it up.

36　**35**　**34**

忘あ昨<ruby>日<rt>き</rt></ruby>の<ruby>朝<rt>あさ</rt></ruby>から<ruby>晩<rt>ばん</rt></ruby>まで<ruby>張<rt>は</rt></ruby>りつめし
れのこころもち、

<ruby>年明<rt>としあ</rt></ruby>けてゆるめる<ruby>心<rt>こころ</rt></ruby>—
うつとりと
<ruby>來<rt>こ</rt></ruby>し<ruby>方<rt>かた</rt></ruby>をすべて<ruby>忘<rt>わす</rt></ruby>れしごとし。

<ruby>朝寐<rt>あさね</rt></ruby>して<ruby>新聞讀<rt>しんぶんよ</rt></ruby>む<ruby>間<rt>ま</rt></ruby>なかりしを
<ruby>負債<rt>ふさい</rt></ruby>のごとく
<ruby>今日<rt>けふ</rt></ruby>も<ruby>感<rt>かん</rt></ruby>ずる。

37

Just like last New Year—
Outside the sound of battledore and shuttlecock
And laughter too . . .

38

Feel somehow
As if this will be my year—
O this clear, windless dawn on the first!

39

From deep in my guts the urge to yawn,
And so it came—a long long roar
This New Year day!

39

腹の底より欠伸もよほし
ながながと欠伸してみぬ、
今年の元日。

38

何となく、
今年はよい事あるごとし。
元日の朝晴れて風無し。

37

戸の面には羽根つく音す。
笑ふ聲す。
去年の正月にかへれるごとし。

40

Much the same each year
My friend's two or three poems
On his New Year card

41

On the fourth
At last
His once-a-year card

42

My brain
Concocting only the impossible in this world!—
Will the coming year be the same?

42
世におこなひがたき事のみ考へる
われの頭よ！
今年もしかるか。

41
正月の四日になりて
あの人の
年に一度の葉書も來にけり。

40
いつの年も、
似たよな歌を二つ三つ
年賀の文に書いてよこす友。

43

All these people
Going in the same direction—
And *me*, watching them from the side

44

Fed up with this framed tablet
Across my wall,
How long will I let it hang!

45

Slowly inch by inch
Like a candle burning down,
This last day of the year has finally passed!

43
人がみな
同じ方角に向いて行く。
それを横より見てゐる心。

44
いつまでか、
この見飽きたる懸額を
このまま懸けておくことやらむ。

45
ちりちりと、
蠟燭の燃えつくるごとく、
夜となりたる大晦日かな。

46

Leaning on this blue-glazed brazier
And closing my eyes and opening them again,
I begrudge the passing of time . . .

47

Scolding myself
For somehow counting on tomorrow's luck,
I went to bed.

48

Is this fatigue the accumulation of a year?
New Year's Day
And yet so sleepy, so drowsy . . .

48

過ぎゆける一年のつかれ出しものか、
元日といふに
うとうと眠し。

47

何となく明日はよき事あるごとく
思ふ心を
叱りて眠る。

46

青塗の瀬戸の火鉢によりかかり、
眼閉ぢ、眼を開け、
時を惜めり。

49

New Year afternoon
And sad somehow
Knowing the cause of this drowsy mind ...

50

Helpless
Motionless
I stare at my nails stained from an orange

51

This irritation nowadays
Like the irritation of hands that clap
And wait forever until some sleepy voice replies!

51

手を打ちて
眠氣の返事きくまでの
そのもどかしさに似たるもどかしさ！

50

ぢつとして、
蜜柑のつゆに染まりたる爪を見つむる
心もとなさ！

49

それとなく
その由るところ悲しまる、
元日の午後の眠たき心。

52

That single cachou I took on the way—
Came back,
My important errand forgotten

53

Bedding completely over my head,
Legs drawn up—
It's at no one in particular I stick out my tongue!

54

Gone all too soon
The New Year days,
And again the same old rut . . .

54

いつしかに正月も過ぎて、
わが生活がまたもとの道にはまり來れり。

53

すつぽりと蒲團をかぶり、
足をちぢめ、
舌を出してみぬ、誰にともなしに。

52

やみがた
き用を忘れ來ぬ
途中にて口に入れたる
ゼムのためなりし。

55

In the morning about four days ago—
O that dream
In which I argued with a god and cried!

56

Just waiting
For the time to return home—
Today, too, I worked.

57

Unable to guess
The thoughts of these men—
Again, today, I went quietly about my work . . .

<table>
<tr><td>57</td><td>56</td><td>55</td></tr>
</table>

いろいろの人の思はく
はかりかねて、
今日もおとなしく暮らしたるかな。

家にかへる時間となるを、
ただ一つの待つことにして、
今日も働けり。

神様と議論して泣きし――
あの夢よ！
四日ばかりも前の朝なりし。

58

O those many things
I once thought I'd do—
Had I been editor of this sheet!

59

This butter
From a farm bride
In the distant north!

60

So similar that voice!
Midnight, and I stop to listen,
Chin buried in the collar of my great coat ...

60
外套の襟に頤を埋め、
夜ふけに立どまりて聞く。
よく似た聲かな。

59
石狩の空知郡の
牧場のお嫁さんより送り來し
バタかな。

58
おれが若しこの新聞の主筆ならば
やらむ──と思ひし
いろいろの事！

61

Here and there in my old diary
The initial Y—
It stood for *him*.

62

Hear most of the peasants had to lay off drink—
If more hard up,
What'll they lay off next?

63

O this mind just after waking!
That item on some old man deserting his home
Brought tears to my eyes . . .

63
目さまして直ぐの心よ！
年よりの家出の記事にも
涙出でたり。

62
百姓の多くは酒をやめしといふ。
もつと困らば、
何をやめるらむ。

61
Yといふ符牒
古日記の處處にあり――
Yとはあの人の事なりしかな

64

This *self*
Incapable of acting with others:
My thought on waking

65

Somehow,
Feel more people than I expected
Think as I do . . .

66

Exhausted
Talking big half a day
To some younger guy!

66
自分よりも年若き人に
何となく、
半日も氣焰を吐きて、
つかれし心！

65
案外に多き氣もせらる、
自分と同じこと思ふ人。

64
人とともに事をはかるに
遇せざる
わが性格を思ふ寐覺かな。

67

Rare these tears today
In cursing the Diet—
But the joy I felt!

68

Trying to force the blooms in one night,
Warmed the potted plum on the brazier—
Failed after all

69

That accident with the teacup
And again this morning the thought—
O the joy of destruction!

<table>
<tr><th>69</th><th>68</th><th>67</th></tr>
</table>

あやまちて茶碗をこはし、
物をこはす氣持のよさを
今朝も思へる。

ひと晩に咲かせてみむと、
梅の鉢を火に焙りしが、
咲かざりしかな。

珍らしく、今日は、
議會を罵りつつ涙出でたり。
うれしと思ふ。

70

Pulling the ear of the cat
And hearing its cry—
O the startled face, the happy face, of my child!

71

Scolding my weakness again and again
And miserable wondering about the *why* of this me,
I went out to borrow ...

72

That day she failed to come
Though I waited and waited
Was the day I put my desk here ...

70

猫の耳を引つぱりてみて、
にやと啼けば、
びつくりして喜ぶ子供の顔かな。

71

何故かうかとなさけなくなり、
弱い心を何度も叱り、
金かりに行く。

72

待てど、待てど、
來る筈の人の來ぬ日なりき、
机の位置を此處に變へしは。

73

An old newspaper!
Why, they're praising my poems—
Though only in two lines or three . . .

74

At my feet the morning I moved—
A snapshot of a woman!
A snapshot I'd forgotten!

75

At that time so many misspellings
Slipped my notice
In these old love-letters!

75
その頃は氣もつかざりし
假名ちがひの多きことかな、
昔の戀文！

74
引越しの朝の足もとに落ちてゐぬ、
女の寫眞！
忘れゐし寫眞！

73
古新聞！
おやここにおれの歌の事を賞めて書いてあり
二三行なれど。

76

That bundle of letters from my wife
Eight years ago—
Keep wondering where I put it!

77

Miserable insomniac!
The least bit sleepy
And I rush to bed—

78

Felt like laughing but couldn't—
That knife I searched for so long
Was in my hand . . .

78

笑ふにも笑はれざりき――
長いこと捜したナイフの
手の中にありしに。

77

眠られぬ癖のかなしさよ！
すこしでも
眠氣がさせば、うろたへて寝る。

76

八年前の
今のわが妻の手紙の束、
何處に藏ひしかと氣にかかるかな。

79

These last four years or five
Not once to look skyward—
Can a *man* change this much?

80

Convinced you can't put characters
On unlined paper—
O this innocence of my kid!

81

Somehow managed to get through these thirty days—
No other desire in me
This last night of the month

81

暗<ruby>昨<rt>きの</rt></ruby>日の晩かな。
外<ruby>外<rt>ほか</rt></ruby>に欲<ruby>欲<rt>ほ</rt></ruby>もなき
どうか、かうか、今月<ruby>月<rt>げつ</rt></ruby>も無事<ruby>事<rt>ぶじ</rt></ruby>に暮らしたりと、

80

字を書かぬものと、
<ruby>原稿紙<rt>げんかうし</rt></ruby>にでなくては
かたく信<ruby>信<rt>しん</rt></ruby>ずる我<ruby>我<rt>わ</rt></ruby>が兒<ruby>兒<rt>こ</rt></ruby>のあどけなさ!

79

この<ruby>四五<rt>しご</rt></ruby>年<ruby>年<rt>ねん</rt></ruby>
空<ruby>空<rt>そら</rt></ruby>を仰<ruby>仰<rt>あふ</rt></ruby>ぐといふことが<ruby>一度<rt>いちど</rt></ruby>もなかりき。
かうもなるものか?

82

In those days I often lied,
And lied with ease—
O this sweat for that shame!

83

His old letters!
Was I so thick with that type
Just five years ago?

84

What was his given name?
Suzuki his last—
What's he doing now and where?

84
名は何と言ひけむ。
姓は鈴木なりき。
今はどうして何處にゐるらむ。

83
古手紙よ！
あの男とも、
五年前は、
かほど親しく交はりしかな。

82
あの頃はよく嘘を言ひき。
平氣にてよく嘘を言ひき。
汗が出づるかな。

85

Reading his card about the birth—
And for some time
How my face brightened!

86

Just as I predicted!
Even *he* could produce a child—
Felt satisfied somehow and went to bed . . .

87

"That poor fellow Ishikawa!"
Sometimes with such words
I indulge my sorrow

87
「石川はふびんな奴だ。」
ときにかう自分で言ひて
かなしみてみる。

86
そうれみろ、
あの人も子をこしらへたと、
何か氣の濟む心地にて寐る。

85
生れたといふ葉書みて、
ひとしきり、
顏をはれやかにしてゐたるかな。

88

A push of the door and one step—
How endless to the eyes of a patient
This long corridor

89

O the feeling
On this hospital bed
As if a load had tumbled from my back!

90

"Then you do not wish to live?"—
How the doctor's words
Silenced this inner me!

90
そんならば生命が欲しくないのかと、
醫者に言はれて、
だまりし心！

89
重い荷を下したやうな
氣持なりき、
この寢臺の上に來ていねしとき。

88
ドア推してひと足出れば、
病人の目にはてもなき
長廊下かな。

91

Suddenly waking at midnight
And wanting to cry for no reason at all—
I pull this quilt over my head!

92

No reply from the next bed . . .
I looked,
Found him in tears.

93

O this joy
In leaning out a window in my ward
And seeing a cop after so long a time!

93

病室の窓にもたれて、
久しぶりに巡査を見たりと
よろこべるかな。

92

話しかけて返事のなきに
よくみれば
泣いてゐたりき、隣りの患者。

91

眞夜中にふと目がさめて
わけもなく泣きたくなりて
蒲團をかぶれる。

94

One of the sorrows of a fine day—
Enjoying a smoke
Leaning out a window in my ward!

95

The bustle in some room late at night—
This breathless wondering
If a man has died

96

That nurse's hand taking my pulse—
Some days warm and gentle,
Some days cold and hard ...

94
晴れし日のかなしみの一つ！
病室の窓にもたれて
煙草を味ふ。

95
夜おそく何處やらの室の騷がしきは
人や死にたらむと、
息をひそむる。

96
脉をとる看護婦の手の
あたたかき日あり
つめたく堅き日もあり

97

Immediately asleep
My first night at the hospital—
O this feeling of something missed!

98

Somehow
Thought myself important—
O this childish me!

99

Hand on my swollen belly—
O this sorrow
Alone on a hospital bed . . .

99
ふくれたる腹を撫でつつ、
病院の寝臺に、ひとり、
かなしみてあり。

98
何となく自分をえらい人のやうに
思ひてゐたりき。
子供なりしかな。

97
病院に入りて初めての夜といふに
すぐ寐入りしが、
物足らぬかな。

100

Waking,
Unable to move, my body in pain—
I'm almost in tears waiting for dawn

101

Dawn:
Drenched with night sweat
I feel, even half awake, the weight of this sorrow

102

With nightfall
A vague sorrow
Steals upon this hospital bed

100

目さませば、からだ痛くて
動かれず。
泣きたくなりて夜明くるを待つ。

101

びつしよりと盗汗出てゐる
あけがたの
まだ覺めやらぬ重きかなしみ。

102

ぼんやりとした悲しみが、
夜となれば、
寢臺の上にそつと來て乘る。

103

Leaning against this hospital window,
I watch
The vigorous walk of other kinds of men

104

"Now I see through you completely!"
O those words of my mother
In that dream!

105

Recoiling
From a stethoscope—
As if some hidden thought were being pried loose

103
病院の窓によりつつ、
いろいろの人の
元氣に歩くを眺む。

104
もうお前の心底をよく見届けたと、
夢に母來て
泣いてゆきしかな。

105
思ふこと盗みきかるる如くにて、
つと胸を引きぬ—
聽診器より。

106

My secret wish:
May this illness worsen
And some nurse watch me through the night!

107

In this hospital
I regain my love of wife and child,
I regain my true self . . .

108

Resolved only this morning
"No more lies"—
O the one I told just now!

106
看護婦が徹夜するまで、
わが病ひ、
わるくなれともひそかに願へる。

107
病院に來て、
妻や子をいつくしむ
まことの我にかへりけるかな。

108
もう嘘をいはじと思ひき——
それは今朝——
今また一つ嘘をいへるかな。

109

Somehow
Feeling as if I were a pack of lies,
I clamp these eyes shut!

110

All my past unreal, invented, made up—
Even that pretense
Gives no comfort to this mind!

111

"I'll be a soldier!"
It was long long ago
I troubled my parents with these words

111
軍人になると言ひ出して、
父母に
苦労させたる昔の我かな。

110
今までのことを
みな嘘にしてみれど、
心すこしも慰まざりき。

109
何となく、
自分を嘘のかたまりの如く思ひて、
目をばつぶれる。

112

O that rapture
Picturing myself on a horse,
A sword at my side!

113

As if he were my kid brother—
That's how much I cried for
Fujisawa, the M.P.

114

O this feeling
To commit some great crime
And look on unconcerned!

112
うつとりとなりて、
剣をさげ、馬にのれる己が姿を
胸に描ける。

113
藤沢といふ代議士を
弟のごとく思ひて、
泣いてやりしかな。

114
何か一つ
大いなる悪事しておいて、
知らぬ顔してゐたき気持かな。

115

"Be good and stay in bed"—
My doctor's word for the day
As if to a kid!

116

Eyes glaring
Under an icebag,
I hated *man* this sleepless night!

117

These feverish eyes
Look mournfully
At this flurry of spring snow

117
春の雪みだれて降るを
熱のある目に
かなしくも眺め入りたる。

116
氷嚢の下より
まなこを光らせて、
寐られぬ夜は人をにくめる。

115
ちつとして寐ていらつしやいと
子供にでもいふがごとくに
醫者のいふ日かな。

118

—This,
Man's greatest sorrow,
And I shut my eyes . . .

119

How slow the doctor's rounds!
Hand on this chest in pain,
I shut my eyes tight.

120

Chest pains on the increase,
Nothing to fix this gaze on today
Except my doctor's face . . .

120

醫者の顔色をちつと見し外に
何も見ざりき――
胸の痛み募る日。

119

廻診の醫者の遅さよ！
痛みある胸に手をおきて
かたく眼をとづ。

118

人間のその最大のかなしみが
これかと
ふつと目をばつぶれる。

121

How MAN weakens once he's ill!
A cluster of numberless thoughts
And the desire to cry . . .

122

Resting these hands
Weary from holding a book in bed . . .
O this tangle of thought

123

How come
More than once today
I wanted a gold watch?

123　　　　　　122　　　　　　121

今日は、なぜか、　　　寝つつ讀む本の重さに　　　病みてあれば心も弱るらむ！
二度も、三度も、　　　手を休めては、　　　　　さまざまの
金側の時計を一つ欲しと思へり。　つかれたる　　　　　泣きたきことが胸にあつまる。
　　　　　　　　　　　物を思へり。

124

Telling my wife
About the book I'd definitely publish someday,
About its cover and everything else!

125

Chest pains
On this day of spring sleet—
Doubled over choking from medicine, I close my eyes

126

Delightful
The color of *salade*!
Chopsticks in hand and yet—

126
あたらしきサラドの色の
うれしさに
箸とりあげて見は見つれども——

125
胸いたみ、
春の霙の降る日なり。
薬に噎せて伏して眼をとづ。

124
いつか、是非、出さんと思ふ本のこと、
表紙のことなど
妻に語れる。

127

O that feeling when I scolded our child!
Think of it not, dear wife,
Only as habit on days of high fever . . .

128

Awakened at midnight
And wondering if Fate rode me—
O the heaviness of this quilt!

129

Unbearable my thirst
And yet too weary this day
To reach for an apple

129　　　　128　　　　127

たへがたき渇き覺ゆれど、
手をのべて
林檎とるだにものうき日かな。

運命の來て乘れるかと
うたがひぬ――
蒲團の重き夜半の寐覺めに。

子を叱る、あはれ、この心よ。
熱高き日の癖とのみ
妻よ、思ふな。

130

Suddenly awake—
The ice melted, the bag warm,
And in every muscle *pain*!

131

Just now in my dream, the cuckoo—
How sad
Not to have forgotten its song!

132

Five years since I left home
And now, sick in bed,
I hear that cuckoo in dreams!

132

ふるさとを出でて五年、
病をえて、
かの閑古鳥を夢にきけるかな。

131

いま、夢に閑古鳥を聞けり。
閑古鳥を忘れざりしが
かなしくあるかな。

130

氷嚢のとけて温めば、
おのづから目がさめ來り、
からだ痛める。

133

O cuckoo!
This yearning for dawn
In the forest round my mountain home!

134

O the cuckoo
That sang on high
In the cypress by the temple of my home!

135

How sad
To feel it tremble on my pulse—
The hand of that young nurse given a doctor's rebuke!

135
脈をとる手のふるひこそ
かなしけれ——
醫者に叱られし若き看護婦——

134
ふるさとの寺の畔の
ひばの木の
いただきに來て啼きし閑古鳥——

133
閑古鳥！
遊民村の山莊をめぐる林の
あかつきなつかし。

136

This memory which crept in unawares—
That nurse called F
And her cold hand . . .

137

That long hospital corridor!
How I wanted
Just once to walk to its very end!

138

That moment I left my bed
Only to feel compelled to lie down—
O the tulip I adored with these tired eyes!

136
いつとなく、記憶に殘りぬ——
Ｆといふ看護婦の手の
つめたさなども。

137
はづれまで一度ゆきたしと
思ひぬし
かの病院の長廊下かな。

138
起きてみて、
また直ぐ寐たくなる時の
力なき眼に愛でしチュリップ！

139

These poor thin hands
Without power
To grasp and grasp hard!

140

Pondering my sickness,
So deep and so remote its ground, its cause—
I have to shut these eyes to think!

141

How sad to have a mind
Without desire to recover from disease—
O the *why* of this mind!

141
かなしくも、
病いゆるを
願はざる心我に在り。
何の心ぞ。

140
わが病の
その因るところ深く且つ遠きを思ふ。
目をとちて思ふ。

139
堅く握るだけの力も無くなりし
やせし我が手の
いとほしさかな。

142

O for a new body—
The thought I had
Rubbing this operation scar . . .

143

Sick for so long—
O this vague delight
In forgetting to take my pill

144

That Russian name Borodin—
For no reason at all
Again and again on my mind today . . .

新しきからだを欲しと思ひけり、
手術の傷の
痕を撫でつつ。

藥のむことを忘るるを、
それとなく、
たのしみに思ふ長病かな。

ボロオデンといふ露西亞名が、
何故ともなく、
幾度も思ひ出さるる日なり。

145

O these men,
All too soon coming upon me to clasp my hand
And all too soon slipping away!

146

How sad they seem, my friend, my wife—
For even in sickness
This talk of revolution I cannot suppress!

147

Thought it somewhat alien to me,
The terrorist's sad heart—
But some days how close it feels!

147　　146　　145

やや遠きものに思ひし
テリストの悲しき心も——
近づく日のあり。

友も、妻も、かなしと思ふらし——
病みても猶、
革命のこと口に絶たねば。

いつとなく我にあゆみ寄り、
手を握り、
またいつとなく去りゆく人人——

148

So many times
Have I faced this plight!
Now, whatever comes I will let be . . .

149

On thirty yen a month
To live some rustic life of ease—
My thought of a moment

150

Again pains in my chest today . . .
If die I must,
In my village let it be

150

今日もまた胸に痛みあり。
死ぬならば
ふるさとに行きて死なむと思ふ。

149

月に三十圓もあれば、田舍にては
樂に暮らせると——
ひよつと思へる。

148

かかる目に
すでに幾度會へることぞ！
成るがままに成れと今は思ふなり。

151

Summer came on unawares—
How kind to a convalescent's eyes
The *light* from this rain!

152

Four months in bed!
How wistful to remember now
The taste of medicine that changed from time to time . . .

153

Four months of illness—
O this sadness in seeing my child
So much taller even in that time

151
いつしかに夏となれりけり。
やみあがりの目にこころよき
雨の明るさ！

152
病みて四月—
そのときどきに變りたる
くすりの味もなつかしきかな。

153
病みて四月—
その間にも、猶、目に見えて、
わが子の脊丈のびしかなしみ。

154

Why this sadness each day
In seeing the healthy growth
Of my child?

155

Bidding my child come sit by my bed,
I stared straight into her face—
O how she scampered away!

156

Always
I thought the child a bother—
And now my kid is five ...

156
いつも、子を
うるさきものに思ひゐし間に、
その子、五歳になれり。

155
まくら辺に子を坐らせて、
まじまじとその顔を見れば、
逃げてゆきしかな。

154
すこやかに
脊丈のびゆく子を見つつ、
われの日毎にさびしきは何ぞ。

157

May you never resemble your father,
Nor your father's father!
Thus thinks your father, my child.

158

What saddens me
(For I was that way too)
My kid, scolded or spanked, never cries ...

159

Picking up words
Like "Workers!" "Revolution!"—
O my five-year-old!

159

「労働者」「革命」などといふ言葉を
聞きおぼえたる
五歳の子かな。

158

かなしきは、
（われもしかりき）
叱れども、打てども泣かぬ兒の心なる。

157

その親にも、
親の親にも似るなかれ——
かく汝が父は思へるぞ、子よ。

160

Once in a while
Praising my kid
Singing at the top of her voice!

161

What prompted her—
Flinging aside that toy—
To gently come and sit by me?

162

So absorbed upstairs
Watching passers-by along the street,
My kid forgot the time for sweets!

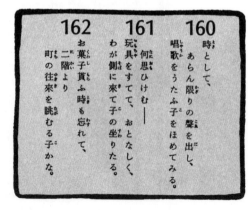

162　　　　　161　　　　160

お菓子貰ふ時も忘れて、　　玩具をすてて、おとなしく、　　時として、
二階より　　　　わが側に來て子の坐りたる。　　あらん限りの聲を出し、
町の往來を眺むる子かな。　　何思ひけむ――　　　唱歌をうたふ子をほめてみる。

163

Sad the way these eyes smart
From the smell of fresh ink—
And all too soon the garden into a world of green . . .

164

My thought
As I gazed at a point on the mats—
Is that what you want to be told, dear wife?

165

Those dark glasses worn in late spring
During the year of that infection in my eye—
Were they lost? Were they broken?

165

あの年のゆく春のころ、
眼をやみてかけし黒眼鏡、
こはしやしにけむ。

164

ひとところ、畳を見つめてありし間の
その思ひを、
妻よ、語れといふか。

163

新しきインクの匂ひ、
目に沁むもかなしや。
いつか庭の青めり。

166

How joyful after so long a time
To be scolded by my mother
For failing to take this pill!

167

Gazing up at the sky,
The sliding screens by my bed opened for me—
O this habit formed during long illness!

168

Like some meek domesticated beast—
Helpless
On this day of high fever

168
おとなしき家畜のごとき
心となる、
熱ややや高き日のたよりなさ。

167
枕辺の障子あけさせて、
空を見る癖もつけるかな——
長き病に。

166
薬のむことを忘れて、
ひさしぶりに、
母に叱られしをうれしと思へる。

169

Urged on by something nameless,
I pick up my pen—
O this morning with fresh flowers in a vase!

170

On this day in which my wife behaves
Like a woman unleashed,
I gaze at these dahlias ...

171

Another day spent
Forever lying in bed, forever getting up—
O this feeling as if waiting for a windfall I know will never come!

171

あてのなき金などを待つ思ひかな。
寐つ、起きつして、
今日も暮したり。

170

放たれし女のごとく、
わが妻の、
ダリヤを見入る。
振舞ふ日なり。

169

何か、かう、書いてみたくなりて、
ペンを取りぬ—
花活の花あたらしき朝。

172

This feeling
Of disgust for everything!—
Even my smoking's occasional!

173

That story of an affair
My friend claims he had in some town
Contains, alas, lies

174

Rare
This sudden burst of laughter—
That fly wringing its hands!

何もかもいやになりゆく
この氣持よ。
思ひ出しては煙草を吸ふなり。

或る市にゐし頃の事として、
友の語る
戀がたりに嘘の交るかなしさ。

ひさしぶりに、
ふと聲を出して笑ひてみぬ──
蠅の両手を揉むが可笑しさに。

175

Like the butt of a delicious cigarette,
Even the sorrow of a day with pains in my chest
Not wholly to be flung aside!

176

The pity I feel for this self
That a moment ago
Longed to create some terrible row

177

O this pleasure I feel
In ridiculously giving my five-year-old
The Russian name Sonia!

胸いたむ日のかなしみも、
かをりよき煙草の如く、
棄てがたきかな。

何か一つ騒ぎを起してみたかりし、
先刻の我を
いとしと思へる。

五つになる子に、何故ともなく
ソニヤといふ露西亜名をつけて、
呼びてはよろこぶ。

178

Placed in the midst
Of a discord impossible to dispel—
Sadly I spent another day in anger

179

If I keep a cat,
That too will sow some seed of strife—
O my miserable home!

180

Today too
Almost tempted to say,
"Let me live by myself in some boardinghouse room!"

180

俺
ひとり下宿屋にやりてくれぬかと、
今日も、あやふく、
いひ出でしかな。

179

猫を飼はば、
その猫がまた争ひの種となるらむ。
かなしき我が家。

178

解けがたき
不和のあひだに身を處して、
ひとりかなしく今日も怒れり

181

Suddenly forgetting my illness one day,
I bellowed forth that imitation of a cow!—
My wife and child out . . .

182

How pathetic my poor father!
Again bored with today's paper
And playing with ants in the garden

183

Their only son
Grown up to this!
How sad my parents must be!

183
ただ一人の
をとこの子なる我はかく育てり。
父母もかなしかるらむ。

182
かなしきは我が父！
今日も新聞を讀みあきて
庭に小蟻とあそべり。

181
ある日、ふと、やまひを忘れ、
牛の啼く眞似をしてみぬ——
妻子の留守に。

184

My mother who gave up tea
To pray for my recovery—
Why so angry again today?

185

Felt like playing with the neighborhood kids today,
But no one came when called—
Unfathomable, the mind of another!

186

Not cured
And still not dying—
This bitterness more and more each day these last several
months!

186

死なず、
やまひ癒えず、
日毎にこころのみ險しくなれる七八月かな。

185

今日ひよつと近所の子等と遊びたくなり
呼べど來らず。
こころむづかし。

184

茶まで断ちて、
わが平復を祈りたまふ
母の今日また何か怒れる。

187

That money order
On the morning my medicine gave out—
O this sadness over the kindness of a friend!

188

Scolded,
My kid cried herself to sleep—
I touched her face, her lips slightly apart

189

Awake and feeling somehow
As if these lungs had shrunk,
O this morning so close to fall!

189
肺が小さくなれる如く思ひて起きぬ—
何がなしに
秋近き朝。

188
兒を叱れば、
泣いて、寐入りぬ。
口すこしあけし寐顔にさはりてみるかな。

187
買ひおきし
藥つきたる朝に來し
友のなさけの爲替のかなしさ。

190

Autumn is near!
O the comfort of these fingers warmed
Against this electric bulb!

191

Setting the doll I bought for my child
By her bed where she naps,
I enjoy myself alone.

192

At my words "Christ was a man,"
The sorrow I felt
Seeing my sister's eyes pitying *me*.

192

クリストを人なりといへば、
妹の眼がかなしくも
われをあはれむ。

191

ひる寐せし兒の枕邊に
人形を買ひ來てかざり、
ひとり樂しむ。

190

秋近し！
電燈の球のぬくもりの
さはれば指の皮膚に親しき

193

Lying on a pillow I had them bring to the verandah,
I gaze lovingly at this evening sky
Seen after a long long time.

194

A white dog outside the garden.
I look back
And ask my wife about having one.

194

庭にのそとを白き犬ゆけり。
ふりむきて、
犬を飼はむと妻にはかれる。

193

縁先にまくら出させて、
ひさしぶりに、
ゆふべの空にしたしめるかな。

Romaji Renderings

In our translations of the tanka of *Sad Toys*, we have not followed Takuboku's indentations of various lines, nor have we followed his punctuation for the most part. However, in these Romaji renderings we have observed the punctuation and indentation of the Iwanami Bunko edition of *Sad Toys* (see Note 24). Only in tanka 136 and 165 did we not follow the edition—we indented the third line of tanka 136 because it is indented in the gray notebook and in the first edition of *Sad Toys*; we omitted one comma in tanka 165 because, as in tanka 108, 152, and 153, Takuboku never uses a comma between a noun and the dash following it. In our Romaji renderings we indicate first-line indentations by appropriate spacing from the tanka number; second-line and third-line indentations are spaced appropriately from the diagonal (/).

1 Iki sureba,/ Mune no uchi nite naru oto ari./   Kogarashi yorimo sabishiki sono oto!

2 Me tozuredo/ Kokoro ni ukabu nani mo nashi./   Sabishiku mo mata me o akeru kana

3 Tochū nite futo ki ga kawari,/ Tsutomesaki o yasumite, kyō mo/ Kashi o samayoeri.

4 Nodo ga kawaki,/ Mada okite iru kudamonoya o sagashi ni yukinu./ Aki no yofuke ni.

5 Asobi ni dete kodomo kaerazu,/ Toridashite/ Hashirasete miru omocha no kikansha.

6 Hon o kaitashi, hon o kaitashi to,/ Atetsuke no tsumori dewa nakeredo,/ Tsuma ni iite miru.

7 Tabi o omou otto no kokoro!/ Shikari, naku, tsumako no kokoro!/ Asa no shokutaku!

8 Ie o dete gochō bakari wa/ Yō no aru hito no gotoku ni/ Aruite mitaredo—

9 Itamu ha o osaetsutsu,/ Hi ga aka aka to/ Fuyu no moya no naka ni noboru o mitari.

10 Itsu made mo aruite ineba naranu gotoki/ Omoi wakikinu,/ Shin'ya no machi-machi.

11 Natsukashiki fuyu no asa kana./ Yu o nomeba,/ Yuge ga
yawaraka ni kao ni kakareri.

12 Nan to naku,/ Kesa wa sukoshiku waga kokoro akaruki gotoshi./
Te no tsume o kiru.

13 Uttorito/ Hon no sashie ni nagameiri,/ Tabako no kemuri
fukikakete miru.

14 Tochū nite norikae no densha nakunarishini/ Nakōka to
omoiki./ Ame mo furite iki.

15 Futaban-oki ni/ Yo no ichijigoro ni Kiridōshi no saka o noborishi
mo—/ Tsutome nareba kana.

16 Shittori to/ Sake no kaori ni hitaritaru/ Nō no omomi o
kanjite kaeru.

17 Kyō mo mata sake nomeru kana!/ Sake nomeba/ Mune no
mukatsuku kuse o shiritsutsu.

18 Nanigoto ka ima ware tsubuyakeri./ Kaku omoi,/ Me o
uchitsuburi, ei o ajiwau.

19 Sukkiri to ei no sametaru kokochiyosa yo!/ Yonaka ni okite,/
Sumi o suru kana.

20 Mayonaka no demado ni idete,/ Rankan no shimo ni/ Tesaki o
hiyashikeru kana.

21 Dōnari to katte ni nare to yū gotoki/ Waga konogoro o/
Hitori osoruru.

22 Te mo ashi mo hanarebanare ni aru gotoki/ Monouki nezame!/
Kanashiki nezame!

23 Misuborashiki kuni no shinbun hirogetsutsu,/ Goshoku hiroeri./
Kesa no kanashimi.

24 Tare ka ware o/ Omou zonbun shikaritsukuru hito are to
omou./ Nan no kokoro zo.

25 Asana asana/ Nadete kanashimu,/ Shita ni shite neta hō no
momo no karoki shibire o.

26 Arano yuku kisha no gotokuni,/ Kono nayami,/ Tokidoki ware
no kokoro o tōru.

27 Naniganaku/ Hatsukoibito no okutsuki ni mōzuru gotoshi./
Kōgai ni kinu.

28 Natsukashiki/ Furusato ni kaeru omoi ari,/ Hisashiburi nite kisha
ni norishi ni.

29 Atarashiki asu no kitaru o shinzu to yū/ Jibun no kotoba ni/ Uso
wa nakeredo—

30 Kangaereba,/ Honto ni hoshi to omou koto aruyō de nashi./
Kiseru o migaku.

31 Yogoretaru te o miru—/ Chōdo/ Konogoro no jibun no kokoro
ni mukō ga gotoshi.

32 Yogoretaru te o araishi toki no/ Kasukanaru manzoku ga/ Kyō
no manzoku nariki.

33 Kyō hyoi to yama ga koishikute/ Yama ni kinu./ Kyonen
koshikakeshi ishi o sagasu kana.

34 Asane shite shinbun yomu ma nakarishi o/ Fusai no gotoku/
Kyō mo kanzuru.

35 Toshi akete yurumeru kokoro!/ Uttori to/ Koshikata o subete
wasureshi gotoshi.

36 Kinō made asa kara ban made haritsumeshi/ Ano kokoromochi,/
Wasureji to omoedo.

37 Tonomo niwa hane tsuku oto su./ Warau koe su./ Kyonen no
shōgatsu ni kaereru gotoshi.

38 Nantonaku,/ Kotoshi wa yoi koto aru gotoshi./ Ganjitsu no asa
harete kaze nashi.

39 Hara no soko yori akubi moyōshi/ Naganaga to akubi shite
minu,/ Kotoshi no ganjitsu.

40 Itsu no toshi mo,/ Nitayona uta o futatsumitsu/ Nenga no fumi
ni kaite yokosu tomo.

41 Shōgatsu no yokka ni narite/ Ano hito no/ Nen ni ichido no
hagaki mo kinikeri.

42 Yo ni okonaigataki koto nomi kangaeru/ Ware no atama yo!/
Kotoshi mo shikaru ka.

43 Hito ga mina/ Onaji hōgaku ni muite yuku./ Sore o yoko yori
mite iru kokoro.

44 Itsu made ka,/ Kono miakitaru kakegaku o/ Kono mama kakete
oku koto yaran.

45 Jirijiri to,/ Rōsoku no moetsukuru gotoku,/ Yoru to naritaru
ōmisoka kana.

46 Aonuri no seto no hibachi ni yorikakari,/ Me toji, me o ake,/
Toki o oshimeri.

47 Nantonaku asu wa yoki koto aru gotoku/ Omou kokoro o/
Shikarite nemuru.

48 Sugiyukeru ichinen no tsukare deshimono ka,/ Ganjitsu to yū
ni/ Utouto nemushi.

49 Sore to naku/ Sono yoru tokoro kanashimaru,/ Ganjitsu no
gogo no nemutaki kokoro.

50 Jitto shite,/ Mikan no tsuyu ni somaritaru tsume o mitsumuru/
Kokoromotonasa!

51 Te o uchite/ Nemuge no henji kiku made no/ Sono modokashisa
ni nitaru modokashisa!

52 Yamigataki yō o wasurekinu—/ Tochū nite kuchi ni iretaru/
Zemu no tame narishi.

53 Suppori to futon o kaburi,/ Ashi o chijime,/ Shita o dashite
minu, tare ni tomo nashini.

54 Itsushika ni shōgatsu mo sugite,/ Waga kurashi ga/ Mata moto
no michi ni hamarikitareri.

55 Kamisama to giron shite nakishi—/ Ano yume yo!/ Yokka bakari
mo mae no asa narishi.

56 Ie ni kaeru jikan to naru o,/ Tada hitotsu no matsu koto ni
shite,/ Kyō mo hatarakeri.

57 Iroiro no hito no omowaku/ Hakarikanete,/ Kyō mo otonashiku
kurashitaru kana.

58 Ore ga moshi kono shinbun no shuhitsu naraba/ Yaran—to
omoishi/ Iroiro no koto!

59 Ishikari no Sorachi-gōri no/ Bokujō no oyomesan yori okurikishi/
Bata kana.

60 Gaitō no eri ni ago o uzume,/ Yofuke ni tachidomarite kiku./
Yoku nita koe kana.

61 Y to yū fuchō/ Furu-nikki no shosho ni ari—/ Y towa ano hito
no koto narishi kana.

62 Hyakushō no ōku wa sake o yameshi to yū./ Motto komaraba,/
Nani o yameruran.

63 Me samashite sugu no kokoro yo!/ Toshiyori no iede no kiji
nimo/ Namida idetari.

64 Hito to tomo ni koto o hakaru ni/ Tekisezaru/ Waga seikaku o
omou nezame kana.

65 Nani to naku,/ Angai ni ōki ki mo seraru,/ Jibun to onaji koto
omou hito.

66 Jibun yorimo toshi wakaki hito ni/ Hannichi mo kien o hakite,/
Tsukareshi kokoro!

67 Mezurashiku, kyō wa,/ Gikai o nonoshiritsutsu namida idetari./
Ureshi to omou.

68 Hitoban ni sakasete min to,/ Ume no hachi o hi ni aburishiga,/
Sakazarishi kana.

69 Ayamachite chawan o kowashi,/ Mono o kowasu kimochi no
yosa o/ Kesa mo omoeru.

70 Neko no mimi o hipparite mite,/ Nya to nakeba,/ Bikkuri shite
yorokobu kodomo no kao kana.

71 Naze kōka to nasakenaku nari,/ Yowai kokoro o nando mo
shikari,/ Kane kari ni yuku.

72 Matedo, matedo,/ Kuru hazu no hito no konu hi nariki,/ Tsukue
no ichi o koko ni kaeshi wa.

73 Furu-shinbun!/ Oya koko ni ore no uta no koto o homete kaite
ari/ Nisangyō naredo.

74 Hikkoshi no asa no ashimoto ni ochite inu,/ Onna no shashin!/
Wasureishi shashin!

75 Sono koro wa ki mo tsukazarishi/ Kanachigai no ōki koto kana,/
Mukashi no koibumi!

76 Hachinen-mae no/ Ima no waga tsuma no tegami no taba,/
Doko ni shimaishi ka to ki ni kakaru kana.

77 Nemurarenu kuse no kanashisa yo!/ Sukoshi demo/ Nemuke ga
saseba, urotaete neru.

78 Warau nimo warawarezariki—/ Nagaikoto sagashita naifu no/
Te no uchi ni arishi ni.

79 Kono shigonen,/ Sora o aogu to yū koto ga ichido mo nakariki./
Kō mo naru mono ka?

80 Genkōshi ni de nakutewa/ Ji o kakanu mono to,/ Kataku
shinzuru waga ko no adokenasa!

81 Dōka, kōka, kongetsu mo buji ni kurashitari to,/ Hoka ni yoku
mo naki/ Misoka no ban kana.

82 Ano koro wa yoku uso o iiki./ Heiki nite yoku uso o iiki./ Ase
ga izuru kana.

83 Furu-tegami yo!/ Ano otoko to mo, gonen-mae wa,/ Kahodo
shitashiku majiwarishi kana.

84 Na wa nan to iiken./ Sei wa Suzuki nariki./ Ima wa dōshite doko
ni iruran.

85 Umareta to yū hagaki mite,/ Hitoshikiri,/ Kao o hareyaka ni
shite itaru kana.

86 Sōre miro,/ Ano hito mo ko o koshiraeta to,/ Nani ka ki no
sumu kokochi nite neru.

87 "Ishikawa wa fubin na yatsu da."/ Toki ni kō jibun de iite/
Kanashimite miru.

88 Doa oshite hitoashi dereba,/ Byōnin no me ni hate mo naki/
Naga-rōka kana.

89 Omoi ni o oroshita yōna/ Kimochi nariki,/ Kono nedai no ue ni
kite ineshi toki.

90 Sonnaraba inochi ga hoshiku nainoka to,/ Isha ni iwarete,/
Damarishi kokoro!

91 Mayonaka ni futo me ga samete/ Wake mo naku nakitaku
narite/ Futon o kabureru.

92 Hanashikakete henji no naki ni/ Yoku mireba/ Naite itariki,
tonari no kanja.

93 Byōshitsu no mado ni motarete,/ Hisashiburi ni junsa o mitari
to/ Yorokoberu kana.

94 Hareshi hi no kanashimi no hitotsu!/ Byōshitsu no mado ni
motarete/ Tabako o ajiwau.

95 Yoru osoku dokoyara no shitsu no sawagashiki wa/ Hito ya
shinitaran to,/ Iki o hisomuru.

96 Myaku o toru kangofu no te no/ Atatakaki hi ari/ Tsumetaku
kataki hi mo ari.

97 Byōin ni irite hajimete no yo to yū ni/ Sugu neirishi ga,/
Monotaranu kana.

98 Nan to naku jibun o erai hito no yō ni/ Omoite itariki./
Kodomo narishi kana.

99 Fukuretaru hara o nadetsutsu,/ Byōin no nedai ni, hitori,/
Kanashimite ari.

100 Me samaseba, karada itakute/ Ugokarezu./ Nakitaku narite yo
akuru o matsu.

101 Bisshori to ne'ase dete iru/ Akegata no/ Mada sameyaranu
omoki kanashimi.

102 Bon'yari to shita kanashimi ga,/ Yo to nareba,/ Nedai no ue ni
sotto kite noru.

103 Byōin no mado ni yoritsutsu,/ Iroiro no hito no/ Genki ni aruku
o nagamu.

104 Mō omae no shintei o yoku mitodoketa to,/ Yume ni haha kite/
Naite yukishi kana.

105 Omou koto nusumikikaruru gotoku nite,/ Tsu to mune o
hikinu—/ Chōshinki yori.

106 Kangofu ga tetsuya suru made,/ Waga yamai,/ Waruku nare
tomo hisoka ni negaeru.

107 Byōin ni kite,/ Tsuma ya ko o itsukushimu/ Makoto no ware ni
kaerikeru kana.

108 Mō uso o iwaji to omoiki—/ Sore wa kesa—/ Ima mata hitotsu
uso o ieru kana.

109 Nan to naku,/ Jibun o uso no katamari no gotoku omoite,/ Me
oba tsubureru.

110 Ima made no koto o/ Mina uso ni shite miredo,/ Kokoro
sukoshimo nagusamazariki.

111 Gunjin ni naru to iidashite,/ Chichi haha ni/ Kurō sasetaru
mukashi no ware kana.

112 Uttori to narite,/ Ken o sage, uma ni noreru ono ga sugata o/
Mune ni egakeru.

113 Fujisawa to yū daigishi o/ Otōto no gotoku omoite,/ Naite
yarishi kana.

114 Nani ka hitotsu/ Ōi naru akuji shite oite,/ Shiranu kao shite itaki
kimochi kana.

115 Jitto shite nete irasshai to/   Kodomo ni demo yū ga gotoku ni/
Isha no yū hi kana.

116 Hyōnō no shita yori/ Manako o hikarasete,/   Nerarenu yoru
wa hito o nikumeru.

117 Haru no yuki midarete furu o/   Netsu no aru me ni/
Kanashiku mo nagameiritaru.

118 Ningen no sono saidai no kanashimi ga/   Kore ka to/ Futto me
oba tsubureru.

119   Kaishin no isha no ososa yo!/ Itami aru mune ni te o okite/
Kataku me o tozu.

120 Isha no kaoiro o jitto mishi hoka ni/ Nani mo mizariki—/
Mune no itami tsunoru hi.

121 Yamite areba kokoro mo yowaruran!/ Samazama no/
Nakitaki koto ga mune ni atsumaru.

122 Netsutsu yomu hon no omosa ni/ Tsukaretaru/ Te o yasumete
wa, mono o omoeri.

123 Kyō wa, naze ka,/ Nido mo, sando mo,/ Kinkawa no tokei
o hitotsu hoshi to omoeri.

124 Itsu ka, zehi, dasan to omou hon no koto,/ Hyōshi no koto
nado/ Tsuma ni katareru.

125 Mune itami,/ Haru no mizore no furu hi nari./ Kusuri ni
musete fushite me o tozu.

126 Atarashiki sarado no iro no/ Ureshisa ni/ Hashi toriagete mi
wa mitsuredomo—

127 Ko o shikaru, aware, kono kokoro yo./ Netsu takaki hi no
kuse to nomi/ Tsuma yo, omouna.

128 Unmei no kite noreruka to/ Utagainu—/ Futon no omoki
yowa no nezame ni.

129 Taegataki kawaki oboyuredo,/ Te o nobete/ Ringo toru
dani monouki hi kana.

130 Hyōnō no tokete nurumeba,/ Onozukara me ga same kitari,/
Karada itameru.

131 Ima, yume ni kankodori o kikeri./ Kankodori o wasurezarishi
ga/ Kanashiku aru kana.

132 Furusato o idete itsutose,/ Yamai o ete,/ Kano kankodori o
yume ni kikeru kana.

133 Kankodori!/ Shibutamimura no sansō o meguru hayashi no/
Akatsuki natsukashi.

134 Furusato no tera no hotori no/ Hiba no ki no/ Itadaki ni kite
nakishi kankodori!

135 Myaku o toru te no furui koso/ Kanashikere—/ Isha ni
shikarareshi wakaki kangofu!

136 Itsu to naku, kioku ni nokorinu—/ F to yū kangofu no te no/
Tsumetasa nado mo.

137 Hazure made ichido yukitashi to/ Omoi ishi/ Kano byōin no
nagarōka kana.

138 Okite mite,/ Mata sugu netaku naru toki no/ Chikara naki me
ni medeshi chūrippu!

139 Kataku nigiru dake no chikara mo nakunarishi/ Yaseshi waga te
no/ Itōshisa kana.

140 Waga yamai no/ Sono yoru tokoro fukaku katsu tōki o
omou./ Me o tojite omou.

141 Kanashiku mo,/ Yamai iyuru o negawazaru kokoro ware ni
ari./ Nan no kokoro zo.

142 Atarashiki karada o hoshi to omoikeri,/ Shujutsu no kizu no/
Ato o nadetsutsu.

143 Kusuri nomu koto o wasururu o,/   Sore to naku,/ Tanoshimi ni omou nagayamai kana.

144 Borōjin to yū roshia na ga,/   Naze tomo naku,/ Ikudo mo omoidasaruru hi nari.

145 Itsu to naku ware ni ayumiyori,/   Te o nigiri,/ Mata itsu to naku sariyuku hitobito!

146 Tomo mo, tsuma mo, kanashi to omourashi—/   Yamite mo nao,/   Kakumei no koto kuchi ni tataneba.

147 Yaya tōki mono ni omoishi/ Terorisuto no kanashiki kokoro mo—/   Chikazuku hi no ari.

148 Kakaru me ni/   Sudeni ikutabi aeru koto zo!/ Naru ga mama ni nare to ima wa omounari.

149 Tsuki ni sanjūen mo areba, inaka nitewa/ Raku ni kuraseru to—/   Hyotto omoeru.

150 Kyō mo mata mune ni itami ari./   Shinu naraba/   Furusato ni yukite shinan to omou.

151 Itsushika ni natsu to narerikeri./   Yamiagari no me ni kokoroyoki/   Ame no akarusa!

152 Yamite yotsuki—/   Sono tokidoki ni kawaritaru/   Kusuri no aji mo natsukashiki kana.

153 Yamite yotsuki—/   Sono ma nimo, nao, me ni miete,/   Waga ko no setake nobishi kanashimi.

154 Sukoyaka ni/ Setake nobiyuku ko o mitsutsu,/   Ware no higoto ni sabishiki wa nazo.

155 Makurabe ni ko o suwarasete,/ Majimaji to sono kao o mireba,/   Nigete yukishi kana.

156 Itsumo, ko o/   Urusaki mono ni omoiishi aida ni,/ Sono ko, itsutsu ni nareri.

157 Sono oya nimo,/   Oya no oya nimo nirunakare—/ Kaku na ga chichi wa omoeruzo, ko yo.

158 Kanashiki wa—/   (Ware mo shikariki)/   Shikaredomo, utedomo nakanu ko no kokoro naru.

159 "Rōdōsha" "kakumei" nado to yū kotoba o/   Kikioboetaru/ Itsutsu no ko kana.

160 Toki to shite,/   Aran kagiri no koe o dashi,/ Shōka o utau ko o homete miru.

161   Nani omoiken—/ Omocha o sutete, otonashiku,/ Waga soba ni kite ko no suwaritaru.

162 Okashi morau toki mo wasurete,/   Nikai yori/   Machi no yukiki o nagamuru ko kana.

163 Atarashiki inku no nioi,/ Me ni shimu mo kanashi ya./   Itsu ka niwa no aomeri.

164 Hitotokoro, tatami o mitsumete arishi ma no/   Sono omoi o,/ Tsuma yo, katare to yū ka.

165 Ano toshi no yuku haru no koro,/ Me o yamite kakeshi
kuromegane—/   Kowashi ya shiniken.

166 Kusuri nomu koto o wasurete,/   Hisashiburi ni,/ Haha ni
shikarareshi o ureshi to omoeru.

167 Makurabe no shōji akesasete,/ Sora o miru kuse mo tsukeru
kana—/   Nagaki yamai ni.

168 Otonashiki kachiku no gotoki/   Kokoro to naru,/ Netsu yaya
takaki hi no tayorinasa.

169 Nani ka, kō, kaite mitaku narite,/   Pen o torinu—/ Hanaike no
hana atarashiki asa.

170 Hanatareshi onna no gotoku,/ Waga tsuma no, furumau hi nari./
   Dariya o miiru.

171 Ate no naki kane nado o matsu omoi kana./   Netsu, okitsu
shite,/   Kyō mo kurashitari.

172 Nani mo ka mo iya ni nariyuku/ Kono kimochi yo./
   Omoidashite wa tabako o suu nari.

173 Aru machi ni ishi koro no koto to shite,/   Tomo no kataru/
Koigatari ni uso no majiru kanashisa.

174 Hisashiburi ni,/   Futo koe o dashite waraite minu—/ Hae no
ryōte o momu ga okashisa ni.

175 Mune itamu hi no kanashimi mo,/   Kaori yoki tabako no
gotoku,/   Sutegataki kana.

176 Nani ka hitotsu sawagi o okoshite mitakarishi,/   Sakki no ware
o/   Itoshi to omoeru.

177 Itsutsu ni naru ko ni, naze tomo naku/ Soniya to yū roshia na o
tsukete,/   Yobite wa yorokobu.

178 Tokegataki/ Fuwa no aida ni mi o shoshite,/   Hitori kanashiku
kyō mo ikareri.

179 Neko o kawaba,/ Sono neko ga mata arasoi no tane to naruran./
   Kanashiki waga ie.

180 Ore hitori geshukuya ni yarite kurenu ka to,/   Kyō mo,
ayauku,/   Iideshi kana.

181 Aru hi, futo, yamai o wasure,/ Ushi no naku mane o shite
minu—/   Tsumako no rusu ni.

182 Kanashiki wa waga chichi!/   Kyō mo shinbun o yomiakite,/
   Niwa ni koari to asoberi.

183 Tada hitori no/ Otoko no ko naru ware wa kaku sodateri./
   Fubo mo kanashikaruran.

184 Cha made tachite,/ Waga heifuku o inoritamō/   Haha no kyō
mata nani ka ikareru.

185 Kyō hyotto kinjo no kora to asobitaku nari/ Yobedo kitarazu./
   Kokoro muzukashi.

186 Yamai iezu,/ Shinazu,/   Higoto ni kokoro nomi kewashiku
nareru nanayatsuki kana.

187 Kaiokishi/ Kusuri tsukitaru asa ni kishi/   Tomo no nasake no
kawase no kanashisa.

188 Ko o shikareba,/ Naite, neirinu./   Kuchi sukoshi akeshi negao
ni sawarite miru kana.

189 Nani ga nashi ni/ Hai ga chiisaku nareru gotoku omoite
okinu—/   Aki chikaki asa.

190 Aki chikashi!/   Dentō no tama no nukumori no/   Sawareba
yubi no hifu ni shitashiki.

191 Hirune seshi ko no makurabe ni/ Ningyō o kaikite kazari,/
Hitori tanoshimu.

192 Kurisuto o hito nari to ieba,/   Imōto no me ga kanashiku mo/
Ware o awaremu.

193 Ensaki ni makura dasasete,/   Hisashiburi ni,/   Yūbe no sora
ni shitashimeru kana.

194 Niwa no soto o shiroki inu yukeri./   Furimukite,/   Inu o
kawan to tsuma ni hakareru.

Notes

1. In his postscript to *Sad Toys*, Aika Toki (b. 1885), Takuboku's friend who advocated replacing Chinese and Japanese characters with Roman letters and whose creation of tanka in three lines influenced Takuboku, writes: "... concerning the text [of *Sad Toys*], I meticulously followed the 'dismal-looking' notebook. The order of the poems, punctuation, division into lines, and indentation—all are as they were in the notebook. The first two poems, however, were not in the notebook, but I included them. I found them written on a piece of paper." Tanka 1 and 2 are the poems referred to.

The "sound" Takuboku feels is one familiar to tuberculosis or asthmatic patients, the patient himself able to hear it. It occurs in the chest, probably caused by mucus in the bronchial tubes. At this stage of his illness, Takuboku perhaps realized he had tuberculósis, so this poem may have been written near the end of his life. Tuberculosis was incurable in those days. Rich men at least were able to go to a better climate, rest, and take nutritious food, but such possibilities were closed to Takuboku.

The word *kogarashi* is a combination of *ki* (tree) and *garashi* (from *karasu*, to make dry, to sear). *Kogarashi*, a cliché in Japanese poetry, refers to a strong cold wind that blows at the end of autumn. *Kogarashi* suggests loneliness and coldness.

2. Perhaps the speaker was writing a poem or story, so he closed his eyes to summon up some image but failed. *Sabishi* usually means "lonely," yet in this situation the emotion aroused is more of disappointment. Feeling momentarily inadequate, the speaker suffers from a sense of void.

Most of the language in this tanka is formal. *Me tozuredo*, if written in colloquial form, would be *me o tojita ga* or *me o tojita keredomo*.

3. A markedly diary-like poem. We may wonder if this selection deserves the name poetry. Still it does evoke many associations with Takuboku's life. The office of the *Asahi* newspaper, where Takuboku worked from March 1909 to the end of his life, was near the famous Sumida River. At the end of the Ginza, Tokyo's Fifth Avenue, there used to be a creek leading to the Sumida. The distance from Takuboku's office to the creek or river was not great. Takuboku's job consisted mainly of proofreading, so we can understand his occasional reluctance to report for duty.

The Japanese in this tanka is markedly colloquial. The first line, except for the formal *nite* instead of *de*, is actually conversational Japanese.

4. Though *Sad Toys* is a continuation of Takuboku's earlier tanka collection *A Handful of Sand* (December 1910), there are marked differences between the two volumes. In *Sad Toys*, Takuboku is more liberal in his use of the colloquial. Generally he adheres to the traditional rhythm of 5-7-5-7-7, but irregular rhythms occur more frequently in this last volume.

The whimsical mood in this tanka and others (for example, 2, 3, 8, and 10) is an indication of Takuboku's restlessness and irritation. Some of these tanka must involve recollections from his recent past. He had obtained his position as proofreader with the *Asahi* in March 1909, but he had incurred considerable debts since coming to Tokyo the previous spring. His wife and mother had expected he would send for them, but he could not afford the traveling expenses, nor could he rent a house to accommodate them. He was himself in arrears with his own lodging expenses. His *Romaji Diary* contains a copy of the pathetic letter his mother sent him pleading with him to allow her to come to Tokyo as soon as possible (see April 13). Other entries show his humiliation over the snubbing he had to endure at the boardinghouse (see April 18 and 19).

The whimsy of this tanka is in its illogicality. If we are thirsty and have no money, water may have to do. But the poet perversely goes out. Yet the hour is quite late, and certainly no fruit stores *(kuda-monoya)* would be open then. Such *kudamonoya* were very rare in Meiji Japan. Fruit was often sold at a vegetable shop, but the poet was searching for a store specializing in fruit. The whimsy, then, may be an indication of irritation and frustration. The poverty-stricken often have an urge to spend the little money they have.

Kudamonoya is a new word in tanka; it created a fresh sensation in the traditional tanka form. *Yukinu* is an older word, but "mada okite iru" is quite conversational.

5. The child in this poem is Kyōko, a daughter born in 1906, but the toy locomotive, a new creation in Meiji Japan, was bought for Takuboku's short-lived son Shin'ichi, born in 1910 but dead in less than a month. Takuboku sold the manuscript of *A Handful of Sand* for twenty yen in anticipation of the expenses for the child's birth. The train was probably bought soon after the boy's birth with some of the funds received from the publisher. The odd choice of a toy locomotive for his daughter in this tanka may be explained with this background in mind and adds a further element of pathos to the poem. In the December 1910 issue of *Subaru*, Takuboku published a series of twelve poems entitled "Death," all of them concerning the death of his son. The third poem in the series, printed in one line, *Ko no tame ni kaishi omocha no kikansha o moteasobitaru asa no hitotoki* translates as follows: "For a while in the morning I played with the toy locomotive I had bought for my child." That the speaker plays alone with the toy underscores the loneliness of the event.

This tanka must have been written after Takuboku's family came to live with him in Tokyo in June 1909. We can imagine the life the poet was then leading: the family was not happily united, and the bickering between his wife and mother was painful.

Poems 3 through 114 have no indentation. Takuboku used indentation to give emphasis to certain lines and to show connections between the parts of a poem. It is impossible to translate tanka so that the order of the lines is identical; as a result, the translators have followed neither the punctuation for the most part nor the indentation.

This tanka is once more a mixture of literary and colloquial styles. *Kaerazu* is literary; the second and third lines in the Japanese are colloquial. This mixture does not seem incongruous to the Japanese, especially since Meiji was a transitional period in which older Japanese forms were being replaced by modern ones. Even the letters of Sōseki Natsume (1867-1916), the famous novelist, reveal the change in style, his earlier letters in the traditional *sōrōbun* style, the later letters mostly colloquial.

6. The speaker has no money with which to buy books. If he had money, it ought to be spent on household goods. The wife knows there is no money, so if her husband keeps repeating his desire to buy books, she will be hurt. Yet he so much desired to make these purchases that he could not help telling her about his hopes. The husband's continual lament on this one occasion may be taken by the wife as an indirect way of criticizing her for using money on less important items and for not understanding his real needs. But the speaker does not intend any such criticism or innuendo. He is exasperated and cannot contain himself; he has to say these words even if they hurt his wife's feelings.

From another point of view, though, we may feel the speaker is presuming upon his wife's love for him. The situation in this tanka presupposes that the man is confident of his wife's love and that she is tolerant towards him. Otherwise, his words would directly lead to bickering and recrimination. But he is certain this will not happen. In uttering the words to give vent to his exasperation, he is playing the part of a spoiled child pressing its mother to buy something beyond her means. Takuboku is availing himself of his wife's tolerance and love to release these pent-up feelings of frustration. Since Takuboku views himself in this negative way, it is wrong to account for his conduct in terms of mere egoism.

7. An unbearable anguish in this tanka. The husband and wife who once loved each other are responding at different levels; there is no communication. The family is poor, yet the husband dreams of travel. The wife's scolding of the child is an outlet for her marital frustrations.

Overwhelmed by the heavy responsibility of supporting his family through literary works which the world did not appreciate, Takuboku sometimes thought of death. Sometimes he wanted to be ill, simply to be relieved of the family burdens. He dreamed of going on trips, as if escaping from Tokyo meant escaping these responsibilities.

A tanka in this form was quite rare in the history of tanka poetry. The three lines are fragments, each line containing a noun preceded by a qualifier.

8. The anguish of the first line in the Japanese is memorable. The person in the poem had no place to go, but he did not want others to feel he was loafing. Takuboku probably wished to absent himself from the office at the *Asahi*, or perhaps he had no special work to do that day but had to escape from his home. Usually a man writes at home, but if he has money, he rents a room at an inn or a hotel in which to do his creative efforts. Yasunari Kawabata (1899-1972), the Nobel Prize winner, had such a hotel room. If one's house is large, the writer may be able to isolate himself in some special part of his home.

The second and third lines in the Japanese represent one line of prose, but the syllables are arranged in the tanka tradition. The dash which breaks off the sentence of this prose-like poem makes the real point of the tanka moment; the conflict and tension are unstated.

9. It is early morning, and the man is going out after a night of work. Perhaps the speaker was writing through the night, so his toothache was caused by overwork.

10. Whether the speaker has been drinking or not is unimportant. He had to walk at midnight because of anxiety. It is a compulsive yet necessary walking. Perhaps he could not write, his creative powers having failed him. Perhaps he needed money or had quarreled with someone. At any rate, the speaker was too overwrought, so he tried to walk it off. But as he was walking, the anxiety returned, and he felt driven to continue onward. As he walks ahead like the Flying Dutchman, he cannot make the return. To walk eternally suggests he is unhappy at home.

The first two lines in the Japanese are formed as if they were a single line of prose, but the lines contain the traditional number of tanka syllables.

11. Takuboku's poems are usually filled with sadness, irritation, or anger. But this tanka sings of a rare precious moment, the poet in a peaceful mood.

In Japanese homes hot water was poured into the rice bowl at the end of a meal and drunk. This custom originated from the practice of Zen priests who after each meal drink the same water they use for cleaning dishes and utensils. This action is symbolic of Zen's refusal to waste. Since Zen priests did not eat fish, everything on each dish could be completely consumed.

The custom of drinking boiled water after a meal is becoming obsolete. In Takuboku's day, however, many people drank hot water, and in the countryside this was the rule.

Natsukashiki is a difficult word in Japanese, for its meaning is broad and its nuance varied. To think of an old friend or of one's childhood is *natsukashii*. Takuboku may have been remembering the winter mornings at Shibutami village when he drank a bowl of hot water after breakfast. In this tanka the winter morning is lovable or precious or dear.

In the January 1911 issue of the magazine *Shusai Bundan*, in which this tanka first appeared, the last line reads *Yuge yawaraka ni kao ni kakareru*. The difference in lines suggests that Takuboku polished the poem by adding the particle *ga* after the word *yuge* when he wrote the poem in his notebook with the intention of publishing it as a volume. By adding *ga*, Takuboku made the rhythm less conventional and more colloquial, that is, more familiar. With *ga* the verb became *kakareri*.

12. If the speaker were worried or irritated, he would not have time to cut his fingernails. Clipping his nails suggests the quiet, peaceful mood the speaker suddenly felt one morning—a fragmentary, ephemeral, tanka-like moment.

13. Always worried about debts and other family matters, Takuboku must have found real enjoyment in the peaceful interludes of this tanka and the preceding two. We can imagine his pleasure in tanka 13 in which he tries to prolong the experience in order to find temporary relief. The mood is whimsical yet quiet.

The speaker may be smoking a cigarette or the traditional Japanese *kiseru* (pipe) with its long thin stem made either of metal or bamboo, the attached firebowl of metal with just enough tobacco for a few puffs.

Usually popular novels (those involving love affairs) had many illustrations—colored ones at the beginning and many black and white inside. Even novels of real merit had at least one illustration at the front. In this tanka the poet is apparently enjoying a popular novel.

14. A feeble cry of pain in a moment of sheer misery. Ordinary Japanese would not express their feelings in this way, though a woman would not hesitate to cry. Certainly such feelings expressed publicly by a man are rare. Takuboku was probably returning from night duty or some unsuccessful negotiation. At times he sinks into helpless despair and abject self-pity, many entries in the *Romaji Diary* testifying to this aspect of Takuboku's character.

The hour in this tanka is quite late, perhaps past midnight. There are no more streetcars running, and the speaker has no money for an expensive jinrikisha ride; besides, he would have to find a rickshaw station, for rickshaw men do not run along the streets in search of customers. Western readers may be surprised that the man in this tanka may be wearing a *hakama* (the traditional Japanese skirt) over his dark kimono. If he was returning from his office, he most probably wore a *hakama*, for most professions it was an indispensable part of office apparel. He may or may not have worn *tabi* (socks), for he was not a regular reporter. If he wore *tabi*, these would be blue-black ones, not the white ones worn by people of higher rank. He wore wooden *geta*, (wooden clogs), and there were no raincoats to be worn over kimono of this kind. So walking in the rain in such attire was by no means easy. It is true that some businessmen and government employees wore Western apparel, but those of lower status did not. In those days newspaper reporters preferred kimono.

15. Takuboku was employed by the Tokyo *Asahi* newspaper at a beginning salary of twenty-five yen per month. For each night of work he received an extra yen, his night duty consisting of proofreading the early morning edition. We can imagine the poet's weariness as he walked up Kiridōshi Slope in the very early morning hours after such tedious work, the slope connecting Ueno Avenue and Yumichō, where Takuboku lived. He took the last streetcar as far as Ueno and then walked about a mile to get to his house.

One of Takuboku's weaknesses is self-pity. Unlike the typical Japanese, he does not hesitate to express this type of emotion. This tanka itself is not too effective, for going up a slope at night is not unusual—many workers do so every night. Takuboku felt his work did not deserve him; he felt he was above such menial labor.

16. A unique, clever tanka. When one drinks too much, the head becomes heavy, but Takuboku feels this heaviness in his brain comes from the odor of the sake itself that has immersed itself in the brain to make it heavy. When one drinks excessively, one smells from alcohol, but Takuboku felt his own brain smelled of sake. At this moment the speaker is satiated, sick of sake.

Takuboku might drink alone or attend a drinking party and then continue drinking by himself afterward. From this poem we do not know the actual situation. Because he was poor, he drank either at cheap restaurants or bars.

17. The poet who drinks is traditional in China (for example, Li Po [701-762]) and Japan. The *Man'yō-shū* (ca. 759) contains poems on the pleasures of alcohol. Ōtomo no Tabito (665-731) writes:

Rather than indulge in futile worries,
How much better to drink a cup of unrefined sake!

(Shirushi naki mono o omowazuwa hitotsuki no/
Nigoreru sake o nomubeku arurashi)

Rather than say clever things,
How much better to drink and sob!

(Sakashimi to mono yū yori wa sake nomite/
Einaki surushi masaritarurashi)

But in Takuboku's poem the drinking is not the pleasure it should be; he reveals only his remorse and self-hatred because of his physical weakness.

The sake in this tanka is the traditional Japanese drink of fermented rice. Before the Tokugawa era (1600-1867), sake, as noted in Ōtomo no Tabito's poem, was not as clear as it is today. Beer was brewed in Japan during Takuboku's time, but it was not a common drink because it was too costly and most Japanese were not used to its bitterness. Only a few could afford the expense of whiskey. *Shōchū* is a very strong ill-tasting liquor mostly distilled from sake lees or potatoes— *shōchū* the cheapest sake. We can imagine the poverty-stricken Takuboku asking for an advance in salary in order to spend it for drinking and whoring. A small bottle of sake at a cheap bar or restaurant would have been fifteen to twenty sen; one *shō* (two quarts) would have cost about a yen in those days.

Once more this tanka is a mixture of the literary and colloquial, *sake nomeru kana* and *shiritsutsu* literary.

18. The reverse of tanka 17. When we are quite far gone in drink, this experience is typical. The poet is not certain if he actually spoke and, if so, what the words were. But as he was deeply and happily drunk and unable to resolve the dilemma, he closed his eyes, the better to enjoy his inebriation. Sometimes a Japanese will close his eyes in order to concentrate on the taste of the food he is eating.

Me o tsuburu means "to close one's eyes." The *"uchi"* of *uchitsuburi* slightly intensifies the verb without changing its meaning. The prefix *uchi* comes from the verb *utsu* (to strike). In very early Japanese usage, it retained something of the meaning of the original verb, adding to the following verb the adverbial meanings of "suddenly," "energetically," "slightly," but from about the thirteenth century on, *uchi* became in many cases a mere formal prefix without meaning. Sometimes it slightly intensifies the meaning of the verb, as in this tanka, but it is most often added to adjust the number of syllables.

19. A drunken person falls asleep quickly, but once awake he finds it difficult to sleep again. Usually he feels sick on awakening, but in this instance the poet woke up refreshed. Of course he felt like writing tanka then. In Takuboku's day many writers used the traditional brush and Chinese ink, though pen and ink were also in use. One rubs the ink stick on the *suzuri* (inkstone). The fresh feeling of awakening suggests the enthusiasm with which the poet prepared his Chinese ink. Takuboku often wrote at night.

20. We can imagine various situations in this poem, but most likely the poet has been feverishly writing tanka in his room. In tanka 19, he prepared the Chinese ink; in tanka 20, he must rest his feverish, tingling fingers on the frost of the wooden railing that acts as a kind of safeguard for the *demado*, a window projecting out from the wall in narrow Japanese rooms. This type of window sometimes has a paper sliding screen in front of the glass. When there is no space for a corridor lined with windows, some Japanese have this kind of window built into the room.

In this tanka we feel the separate life led by a man of literature. What ordinary men are doing at this late hour the poet does not do.

21. The poet in this tanka fears his own desperate mood. He is aware he is becoming desperate and knows he ought not to be, but he cannot help feeling this way.

When we think of Takuboku's circumstances, it is not unnatural that he should have become desperate at times. This poem was probably written in 1911. At the beginning of the year he witnessed an event which showed how formidable the ruling power-structure was; he realized how difficult it was for the socialist movement to make even a slight advance. The impasse must have seemed to him hopeless. His health, which had been undermined, could not be regained; he always had a slight fever, which at times rose drastically to disable him. His poverty was so chronic that it caused him intense aggravation, and this added to the depletion of his strength. A crisis between him and his wife, Setsuko, occurred in June. Later in the summer Setsuko was found to have tuberculosis. All the members of the immediate family except his daughter Kyōko were invalids, and Takuboku's sister Mitsuko had to be sent for to help maintain the household. Further trouble between Takuboku's parents led to the father's desertion of the family. The magazine *Jumoku to Kajitsu (The Tree and the Fruit)*, on which Takuboku had spent a great deal of energy, failed to materialize. What supported him in such circumstances must have been his desire to live as a socialist, as a writer, and as a decent human being. But sometimes he found even these aspirations too demanding.

Once more we find this tanka a mixture of literary and colloquial styles. *Dōnari to katte ni nare* is definitely colloquial, but the rest of the poem is formal.

22. The grammar in this tanka is unusual. A tanka usually forms one or two sentences, but here we have only fragments. The first line in the Japanese qualifies *nezame*, so the structure is a noun with an adjective qualified by a clause, but the same noun is repeated with a different adjective.

The speaker is in ill health. He feels at his most anguished just at the moment of awakening. When he is tired and is sleeping restlessly, he feels as if his arms and legs have become disjointed.

23. Takuboku was employed by the Tokyo *Asahi* as a proofreader, so the habit had become ingrained, and before he realized it, he was proofreading even his own hometown paper from Iwate Prefecture. Of course local newspapers were inferior in paper, printing, and style. Local papers had only a small circulation, for most people who read newspapers subscribed to such great ones as the *Asahi, Mainichi, Yomiuri, Jiji, Hōchi,* and *Yorozuchōhō*. Takuboku may have subscribed to his hometown paper while he lived in Tokyo, for he sometimes published his tanka and articles in it (in Japan, local papers send authors the newspapers in which their works are printed), or possibly someone whose poem had appeared in the paper had sent it to Takuboku for comment.

In the first published edition of *Sad Toys*, this tanka is 25; tanka 24 is 26, tanka 25 is 23, and tanka 26 is 24. On each page of the first edition, two poems were printed. In the course of printing galley proofs, the printer inadvertently disturbed the order of the sheets; the proofreader did not notice this error until it was too late to correct it. But we have followed the Iwanami edition of *Sad Toys* which is based on the facsimile edition of Takuboku's notebook. According to Saburō Saitō, editor of the Iwanami text, the first edition contains a considerable number of typographical errors, and some of the *furigana* (phonetic syllabary printed at the right side of a Chinese character) were added by someone other than Takuboku's friend Toki, whose responsibility it had been to get the publisher to accept the manuscript.

24. This tanka is about an enfeebled and tired mind which knows it is exactly that but at the same time knows it should not be. Obviously the speaker is dissatisfied with his present condition. He wants to be scolded, for he feels vaguely that he has not been doing the right thing. Perhaps he is wondering about his own lack of independence. He realizes he is doing what he should not be doing, so a good scolding by someone might help; yet he should actually scold himself and stop doing foolish things instead of waiting for someone else to remind him of his responsibilities. Of course, Takuboku drank, whored, borrowed money, and wished to avoid family responsibilities, but the last line *(Nan no kokoro zo)* shows the ambiguity of these feelings.

Many editions of Takuboku's *Sad Toys* exist. The Iwanami Bunko edition (1946) follows the facsimile edition of Takuboku's notebook, though we know the notebook was not Takuboku's final draft, that Takuboku himself wished to make some alterations before sending the poems to the publisher (see the postscript to *Sad Toys*). The Kadokawa edition (1967) follows the first edition of *Sad Toys*, but according to the editor of the Iwanami edition, that first printing had many typographical errors. We have chosen mainly to follow the Iwanami text for our Romaji renderings, but occasionally we have preferred the Kadokawa. The Kadokawa edition cites the third line of this tanka as "Nan no kokoro zo," while the Iwanami edition cites the line *Nani no kokoro zo*. In the more formal *kanbun* style (Chinese classics read in Japanese style pronunciation—the extremely literary style), the Chinese character is usually read *nan* and not *nani*. This last line in the Japanese makes the style more formal and at the same time more forceful.

25. Those who have had long illnesses can appreciate this poem. Perpetual numbness is a sign of ill health, the disturbance in the circulation of the blood a foreshadowing of illness, especially in a person as young as the poet was. This tanka was published in the January 1911 issue of *Waseda Bungaku* magazine, and Takuboku was hospitalized in February of the same year. Tanka 22 also reveals symptoms of illness.

Though Takuboku was honest, he lacked Japanese stoicism, and it is characteristic of him, as in this tanka, to feel self-pity.

In his diary entry for February 22, 1911, he writes: "The numbness in my thigh, which I had forgotten about since my abdomen became bloated, has recurred."

The first line, *Asana asana*, is very formal; the second line and the last half of the third line are formal; *Shita ni shite neta hō no* is colloquial.

26. There were no trains before the Meiji period, so the subject was quite new for tanka. Because of the simile Takuboku uses, the pain the poet feels must have been overpowering. In those days even though locomotives were slow, they were symbols of superlative power. We feel as if the poet has been experiencing in his mind the power of an onrushing train. The speaker does not specify the pain, but loneliness is part of every wasteland, so there is the impact of the poignancy of agony and its power and the loneliness accompanying it.

The cleverness in this tanka consists in the turn of the usual Japanese expression *kisha ga tōru* (the train goes through) to what would be equivalent to saying *nayami ga tōru* (the agony goes through), an expression the Japanese do not use.

27. This tanka seems un-Takubokian because the moment is less actual than it is imagined. On the other hand, we feel the honesty of this psychological moment, for the poet was longing to return to nature. Takuboku was living in a boardinghouse in Tokyo and yearning, despite the beautiful landscapes in Tokyo in those days, to escape to more natural settings. When the poet came to the outskirts of the city, his thirst for nature was alleviated. The joy he felt perhaps reminded him of something lost, probably the views of nature found in his native place, Shibutami, which he so dearly loved; consequently, the suburb he visited offered him only a semblance of what he could see in his village. The mingled feeling of love and regret probably called forth the simile.

28. The poet had boarded a train simply for the pleasure of the experience. The trip would have been very short. During his Tokyo days, Takuboku had no need to ride trains. He went from home to office and back by streetcar. Of course, travel was a luxury at that time. A main railway line went from Tokyo to Aomori Prefecture.

A series of poems in *A Handful of Sand* may be cited on Shibutami village, one of which follows: "So dear Shibutami village,/ I remember its hills!/ I remember its river!" We also find the following poem about Ueno Station: "How dear my native dialect!/ Only to hear it/ Did I go among the station crowds!"

29. But the writer does not think he will live to see the new age he has predicted. This tanka shows Takuboku's limitations as a revolutionary: he really does believe in a new Japan and thinks about revolution and change, yet he knows the transformation will take too long. Theoretically he believes, but actually he doubts if the "new dawn" will come in the near future. It does not matter if the revolution occurs before his death or after—it is still too remote a possibility for him. Critics today make much of Takuboku's socialist inclinations, but he could not have joined the movement—he lacked strength and persistence, qualities necessary for the true radical. Takuboku was, in fact, old-fashioned in his daily life. To his wife he was a typically Japanese husband-tyrant.

The first line is a standard socialist cry, but in those days such an utterance must have struck the Japanese as new and even alarming. An expression like "a new dawn" was all right, but Takuboku would have risked a confrontation with the authorities if he had written, "I believe in revolution."

This tanka serves as a further illustration that Takuboku revised a number of these tanka before he set them down in his gray notebook. When this poem was first published in the January 1911 issue of *Waseda Bungaku* magazine, Takuboku used as the last word in the first line *chō* instead of *to yū*, the former being an older literary form.

30. A diary-like poem. When one is poor, as Takuboku was, there is a hunger for possessions. At this moment of polishing his metal *kiseru*, the poet thought deeply about the necessities and discovered he desired only a few things. Immediately before this key moment, the poet had felt the urge of wanting much more than he actually had, but the polishing of his pipe quieted him down. A rare moment of contentment, the polishing of the pipe a simple need.

The *kiseru* in this tanka might have had a middle section of bamboo instead of being an all-metal one. The length of a *kiseru* may vary from four inches to fifteen. The polishing is done by rubbing the brass with a piece of cloth.

This tanka is generally colloquial, only slightly mixed with formal elements. We find *hoshi to* formal; *aruyō de nashi* is a mixture of colloquial and formal. To make the latter totally colloquial, the expression would be *aru yō de nai*.

Another instance of Takuboku's revising some of the poems before he set them down in his notebook, for when this poem was first published in the January 1911 issue of *Waseda Bungaku* magazine, the poet had used *kaerimireba*, a decidedly archaic literary expression, instead of the more modern and colloquial *kangaereba*.

31. The Occidental is likely to think of "dirty mind" as relating only to the erotic, but this expression in Japanese *(kitanai kokoro)* refers in colloquial usage to the mean, sordid, or degraded. Takuboku must have been referring to his drinking, his visits to bawdy houses, and his irresponsibility toward his family. Such outbursts of self-abhorrence appear frequently in his *Romaji Diary* as he gives vent to them after a night of dissipation, after his attempts at playing the clown to conceal his despair, and after thinking about his financial incompetence.

This tanka is 33 in the first edition.

32. In tanka 31 and 32, the poet's dissatisfaction with his present life is a common theme. In tanka 31, however, he is dissatisfied with his own moral degradation; in tanka 32, he is disgruntled about his life and the world in general. In this tanka Takuboku's discontent with the world and with his own helplessness is more pronounced than his moral reflection on the state of his mind. That the slight satisfaction he felt when he washed his hands was his one satisfaction for the day is an ironic expression of his discontent.

Sad Toys was published in 1912, but about 120 of these tanka had appeared earlier in such literary magazines as *Sōsaku*, *Bunshō Sekai*, *Waseda Bungaku*, and *Shiika*, two of these tanka appearing in a letter to Takuboku's friend Kindaichi. Some were published in the Tokyo *Asahi*. Later Takuboku gathered these poems into the sequence he preferred in his notebook. Thus a number of these tanka are companion pieces, for example 31 and 32. Nevertheless, tanka 32 is listed as 34 in the first edition. Tanka 31 and 32 as arranged in our volume appeared in *Waseda Bungaku*, no. 62, January 1911 (Meiji 44).

33. Takuboku had written tanka about Mount Iwate in his home district: "When I face the mountain of my native land,/I have nothing to say—/Only gratitude I feel" *(A Handful of Sand)*; but the *yama* in this poem is different. After 1910, he was not able physically or financially to visit Shibutami village. Possibly he may have visited a hill near Tokyo; more probably this tanka is imaginary. Atagoyama is a hill in Tokyo near Shiba Park, and it could have easily been reached by streetcar. Once more we feel Takuboku's whimsical nature: a sudden yearning and he goes out to locate a rock. The memory of that earlier time was pleasant, so he wanted to recapture it.

Sometimes *yama* in Japanese means a high mountain or a small hill; *oka* usually refers to low hills, but it too can refer to something majestic. Even *koyama* (a low hill with an elevation of one hundred feet or so) may be designated as *yama*.

Tanka 33 and 31 appear in reversed positions in the first edition.

34. Though Takuboku was only a proofreader for the Tokyo *Asahi*, he must have felt obligated to read the morning edition before going to the office. The irony of the poem is that he was not a regular reporter, but more important is the fact that a poet or writer ought not to feel this way. Before Takuboku was aware of it, he had taken on the psychology of a regular reporter. There is a kind of self-scorn in having sunk to this level because formerly not reading the paper before he went to work did not bother him. Now it is as troublesome as the money he owes, *fusai* referring only to monetary debts.

Tanka 34 and 32 appear in reverse order in the first edition.

35. Tanka 35 through 49 deal with the New Year holidays in Japan. We feel the poems must relate to the New Year of 1911, for in that of 1912 Takuboku was extremely ill. During the latter period he had a fever of 100 degrees, sometimes more.

This tanka is typically Japanese. The problem of poverty-stricken Japanese is how to tide over the last days of the old year. Debts must of course be paid, but no one will come to ask for money once the temple bells are being struck at midnight on the thirty-first. In Meiji Japan, debts were settled in mid-July and at the end of the year. A *senryū* (a satiric haiku): *Ganjitsu ya/ Kinō no oni ga/ Rei ni kuru* (On New Year's Day/ Last night's devil/ Comes to offer greetings).

On New Year's Day the Japanese wish to forget their unpleasant experiences of the past. Superstition has it that if one is fortunate on the first day of the year, he will have a lucky year. At this moment in tanka 35, Takuboku seems to have found some respite.

36. Tanka as diary. Once more Takuboku feels a respite from tension. The tension does not necessarily reflect Takuboku's concern over financial matters. Perhaps he was determined to work hard, to save money, to avoid the old mistakes, a whole catalogue of good intent possible. But it is the New Year holiday, and he lets his anxieties go and merely feels relaxed.

Again a mixture of formal and colloquial language: *Kinō made asa kara ban made* is colloquial, the rest of the first line formal; the second line is colloquial, the third formal.

37. The poet was comparatively peaceful and happy during the New Year holidays of the previous year, but this year he is not that contented. Still, for a moment the poet relaxed.

The game *hanetsuki* (battledore and shuttlecock) derives from Tokugawa Japan (beginning 1600). The origin of the game of battledore is not clear. What appears to be the game turns up in an old chronicle of 1342. The word *hagoita*, the bat or racket used in the game, is listed in a dictionary published in 1444. Sometimes the *hagoita* was purely ornamental, hung on a wall or displayed in an alcove. One side of such *hagoita* had the face of a famous Kabuki actor represented in a well-known role, or occasionally the face of a popular geisha was the design. But the portrait was padded to give a three-dimensional effect; as a result, it looked like a colored high relief made of silk alone. Only the face itself was painted on silk, but real hair (or thin silk threads dyed black) and pieces of actual silk were also used to represent the portrait's hair and kimono. In actual play, smaller rackets are used.

During the New Year holidays, the Japanese play this game and others, for example, kite-flying and a kind of backgammon. One of the most famous games is the *hyakunin isshu* (poems of one hundred poets). These one hundred poems representing one hundred famous poets are said to have been selected by Fujiwara no Teika (1162-1241), one of the most widely known poets of his time. As he lived at Ogurayama, this selection of poems is known by the name *Ogura Hyakunin Isshu*. A reader recites the upper half of a tanka (the 5-7-5, the *kami no ku*), and the players, each with a share of the one hundred cards face up, try to find the card corresponding to the second half of the tanka (the 7-7, the *shimo no ku*). Sometimes only the first syllable by the reader is enough to identify the poem. The player identifying the most poems, that is, grabbing the most cards with the 7-7 lines, wins. Other card games are played during the New Year holidays as well.

38. The Japanese want January 1 to be weather-perfect. The climate of Tokyo, while not warm, is nevertheless fairly pleasant. The Japanese wish the three festival days of the New Year to be quiet and bright. This tanka is a good example of traditional feeling on the New Year.

Tanka 38 maintains its tanka rhythm while being exceedingly colloquial except for *aru gotoshi* and *nashi*.

39. A yawn is an unusual subject for tanka. The poet is quiet and relaxed, but the yawn is free, unrestrained. New Year's Day in Japan is usually boring. All one can do is eat and drink. In the morning, a special kind of sake flavored with herbs is served. The drink is considered medicinal, and it is drunk or sipped after the participant prays for longevity. Some Japanese pay calls; some get up late after perhaps having worked at bill-collecting until midnight or having gone to a shrine. Homage to the shrine is offered for two years in this one visit which occurs shortly before midnight and lasts until after the midnight hour.

Most people have worked hard on New Year's Eve bustling about, getting ready, paying off debts. Housewives are quite busy at the year-end, cleaning the house for the New Year, decorating the guest and living rooms, cooking New Year dishes. To compensate for this labor and for their year-long household chores, the three days of the New Year are a real holiday for them. It is taboo to clean the house or launder on New Year's Day. Dishes prepared at the year-end are served during the three-day interval, though warmed if necessary—all to give rest to the housewife. This food for three days is placed in the *jūbako*, a lacquered, tiered box beautifully decorated. The well-cooked food has had extra salt and sugar added as preservatives.

40. The *uta* in this humorous New Year poem are tanka. The humor is difficult to catch in the English, for in order to make the first half of the second line in Japanese into seven syllables *(Nitayona uta o)*, Takuboku wrote the *yo* in *nitayōna* short instead of long. The added punch is revealed by the fact that in popular songs, in which rhythm is all-important, *yō* was shortened to *yo* to form a line of seven syllables, usually composed of words of four and three syllables, a frequent combination in Japanese. Thus the implication is that the tanka of Takuboku's friend were dull, commonplace.

The custom of sending greeting cards instead of making the traditional New Year visit became quite popular from Taishō on (beginning 1912). In a diary entry for January 1911, Takuboku writes: "I received 20 New Year letters, sent three." On January 4, he received fifteen cards; on January 5, eight. During the Meiji period, fewer cards were sent; nowadays the greeting card industry is booming. Postmen deliver thick bundles of New Year cards on the morning of January 1. Today few people compose poems on these cards.

41. The simplicity, brevity, and humor of this tanka appeal, yet a serious element is also suggested. While most New Year cards are now neatly tied in large bundles for postal delivery to individual families on the morning of January 1, letters and cards continue to trickle in for over a week during this period. Many of these New Year cards serve as once-a-year greetings. While it is true that the sending of these cards is a formality, many Japanese write them to inform friends of being alive and well, in addition to apologizing for a long silence. When the expected cards are in the pack, the recipient feels reassured, but when he misses some, he worries and speculates.

42. In this pessimistic poem, the speaker knows his weakness. Most Japanese reflect on the past year and then make New Year resolutions. Takuboku realizes it is too late for him to change his impractical ways. The question posed is mostly rhetorical.

43. A figurative tanka. It is characteristic of the Japanese to conform and to obey the authorities, represented earlier by the emperor and today by the government and, in some cases, unions or political parties. In one sense, Takuboku ridicules such mass automatism, but the tanka also suggests the sorrow of the outsider. The satire is not completely genuine, mixed as it is with a kind of inferiority complex which the speaker has. On another level, however, poets usually feel they are outside the main current.

To make Takuboku's first line (which is quite colloquial) formal, the line would have to read *Hito no mina* or *Hito wa mina*. The second line is also colloquial. *Yoko yori* in the third line is formal; *Yoko kara* would make the expression colloquial.

44. In Japanese homes, drawings and calligraphy are hung on walls for decoration. These decorations are mounted on silk or paper. If they are scrolls and hung vertically, they are called *kakemono*. The place to hang these *kakemono* is the *tokonoma* (alcove), though today any convenient spot on the wall is used because alcoves take up too much space. Sometimes the calligraphy or mounted pictures have lacquered frames and are hung horizontally (usually facing east or south) on the walls above the level of the lintel. These horizontal decorations are called *kakegaku* or simply *gaku*. *Kakemono* and *kakegaku* contain drawings or calligraphy or both, but, comparatively speaking, *kakemono* are more often drawings and *kakegaku* calligraphy. The texts of calligraphy are sometimes taken from contemporary poets, but usually from Chinese and Japanese classics.

The *kakemono* is usually changed seasonally, especially so at the time of the New Year, the drawing in a *kakemono* matching the season. The *gaku* is not so easy to change; in most houses the same *gaku* remains on the wall throughout the year. The *gaku* have increased the Japanese fascination for calligraphy.

This tanka is the poet's indirect way of criticizing himself. It is a poem of self-scorn. The *gaku*, which the poet has grown tired of observing, is an indication of his lazy mind. He is bored with the written text, yet he does not take down the *gaku*. The moment is symbolic of the poet's laziness and dull routine, which, in spite of realizing he must change at this season of the New Year, he does not attempt to alter.

45. The poet had been irritated, for he wanted the New Year to start. The day preceding January 1 is one of tremendous anxiety, especially for the man in debt. When we look at a candle, we do not notice the wax is decreasing, but after some time we realize how much shorter the candle has become. The *kana* exclamation shows the poet's relief after what seemed an endless wait. Takuboku probably could not gain the necessary funds to pay off his debts. His habit of asking for his salary in advance made this New Year commitment an impossibility. So he must have felt an enormous relief once the midnight temple bells were heard, for no more dunning occurs after that period. Still, the feeling of impatience expressed in this tanka is complex. On one level, the poet is impatiently waiting for the passing of the day. On another, he is impatient with himself who, shiftless in money matters, can do nothing but sit at home. On still another level, he is angry he has to spend the day wastefully without doing any literary work.

The word *jirijiri* is effective. One meaning of the word is "slowly but steadily" (the way a candle burns); the other meaning is "impatient." The Japanese call New Year's Eve *ōmisoka*: *ō* means "big" or "great"; *misoka*, "thirtieth day" or "end of the month."

46. If this poem was written on New Year's Eve, as seems likely, the poet apparently had nothing to do. The moment of quiet came unexpectedly, and he was enjoying it. For a short interlude he regretted that time would move on, unable to stand still. If such a quiet moment could last forever, the poet's mind would remain tranquil, but he knows time's wingèd chariot.

Japanese blue *(ao)* is sometimes greenish-blue. The Japanese word for the green traffic light is, for example, *ao-shingō*.

The *hibachi* of blue porcelain referred to in the poem is not too expensive. Takuboku's brazier, in which charcoal is fired to keep a person's hands warm, was the popular kind, its shape round. Elegant braziers are made of glazed white porcelain or bronze or fine wood, for example *kiri* (paulownia).

47. This poem does not necessarily refer to the New Year, but the feeling it expresses is apt to occur on this day when the mind is relaxed. During the New Year holidays, all Japanese try to feel relaxed. The poet knows, however, that he cannot expect his luck to change. It is foolish to hope; he must work, make an effort, distrust his dreams. He must begin to work seriously the very next day. That his problems will take care of themselves is facile and unrealistic.

48. It is New Year's Day, and the poet can spend it without doing any work. Yet he feels quite drowsy. So he wonders if the drowsiness is due to the accumulated fatigue of the past year. Actually, however, it is because he is liberated from tension. On New Year's Day, many Japanese remain at home—they eat and drink and play a few games. The relaxation of the day itself makes one feel drowsy; the *toso* (sake with herbs thought to be medicinal) also causes one to feel sleepy. But the poet realizes his exhaustion is greater than that of the average person. His attempt to account for his drowsiness makes him wonder if it is due to the exhaustion that has piled up during the year. But the sleepiness is probably due to the pressures at the end of the year. The line of thought that his drowsiness may be due to the accumulated fatigue of the past year rather than from the relaxation of the poet makes us realize how hard-pressed Takuboku was at the end of the year.

49. The poet realizes his drowsiness is somewhat different from that of most people, that it is due to the mental fatigue of the past year. At the back of his mind is the thought that he should be lively and energetic at the beginning of the New Year. He is irritated not to be doing something significant, but he has been in ill health and his economic difficulties have exhausted him. Much of his exhaustion came from the pressures of knowing he had to pay his debts by midnight of December 31, debts he was probably unable to erase. Instead of the fresh start he anticipated, he perhaps felt deadlocked by a lack of creative power.

50. The *mikan* in the poem is the Japanese tangerine. In those days it was eaten from early winter to the beginning of February, so this tanka may rightly belong among the New Year poems of *Sad Toys*.

The poet thinks he ought to be doing something, but his poverty prevents him from doing anything. Though Takuboku wanted to ease the situation between his mother and wife, he could not. In the poignant moment of this tanka, he is totally helpless and despondent. His staring at his nails signifies his utter helplessness.

Patients confined to their beds a long time are apt to look at their fingers and nails. They try to guess the state of their health from the color and gloss of the skin and nails or from the size of the crescent-shaped white part at the root of the nail. A patient near death may frequently look at his hands.

51. In earlier times a Japanese clapped his hands to summon a servant at home or at a restaurant or inn, a custom which is today obsolete. Often no one appeared for a long time, but finally a tired voice responded. The long wait, however, often caused one to feel irritated.

Takuboku felt this same kind of impatience with his life. He wanted to write poems and stories, but ill health and the struggle for a livelihood gnawed at him and kept him from his creative tasks.

The key word in this tanka is *modokashisa* (irritation or impatience). This last word in the tanka is preceded by the long simile that makes up the rest of the poem, the word *modokashisa* repeated in the simile itself. It is a rather awkward word to pronounce, so repeating the word in the same line makes the rhythm stagnant and enhances the effect of irritation.

52. The *Zemu* in this tanka was a kind of fragrant and refreshing pill sold for breath and heartburn (during Meiji and Taishō). *Zemu* means "gem." Today the Japanese use *Jintan* for this purpose, a very small pearl-like pellet silver in color.

A strange tanka. Perhaps subconsciously the poet did not want to perform the important task he had set out to do. Because of the breath pellet he claims he forgot the important errand he was on the way to perform. The tanka reveals Takuboku's restlessness in those days. Usually taking a pill does not make one forget some important task. Something trivial, however, made him forget something essential because the poet's mind at this moment was unstable. The errand must have been a delicate one so that he had to summon up courage to perform it. Subconsciously he wanted to escape the task, so he perhaps felt uneasy and irritable. To calm himself, he put the pellet into his mouth and was diverted. He tried to justify his forgetfulness because of the *Zemu*, but it is difficult to believe he was not aware of his reluctance to proceed.

53. Takuboku was conscious of the weakness in his personality. In his *Romaji Diary* for Saturday, April 10, 1909, he writes: "I'm a weakling. I'm a weakling even though I have a sword sharper than anybody else's." The solitary antic described in this tanka must have been performed during a moment of desperation. The action was a kind of escape. Another form of escape was to wear a mask figuratively, to wear it at those moments he acutely felt the pain of humiliation. As he was in arrears with his board and lodging, the servants at the boardinghouse he stayed at in Tokyo snubbed him. On these occasions he almost never revealed anger but offered a smile without saying anything.

In his *Romaji Diary* entry for Thursday, April 8, he writes that it was not his generosity that kept him from showing his anger; rather his silence actually hid what he felt was a cruel desire. On the same day he accidentally met a friend on a streetcar. His friend was dressed in a brand-new Western-style suit. Takuboku himself was in a threadbare kimono with frayed sleeves. He was acutely conscious of the contrast, and he was unable to ignore it. Characteristically he affably accosted his friend but uttered an irony which he knew his friend would not catch. Moreover, Takuboku said rude things about old women, his voice loud enough for some elderly women to hear as they sat across the aisle from him, the action done merely to embarrass his friend.

Alone at home, Takuboku could show his defiance of the world, his despair and derision. The psychology in this tanka is morbid, but there is more pathos in the childlike figure huddling and performing a kind of futile revenge. One finds in Takuboku an inordinate pride combined with an inferiority complex. In this tanka that rings with the psychology of the underdog, the grown man's childish act is understandable and moving when done in private.

The poem is mostly colloquial except for the formal *dashite minu*. *Futon* means the mattress and quilts, but obviously only the latter are referred to in this tanka.

54. In a diary entry for January 4, 1911, Takuboku writes: "I have returned to my routine. This was what I felt today. I went to the office as usual and came back as usual."

This tanka reveals the poet's reluctance and dissatisfaction. He suddenly realizes the holidays are over, and he now has to return to the rut of earning a living. During the New Year period he was freed from monetary worries and could devote his mind to other matters which he considered more worthy, at this time (January 18) to the inquiry into the sensational trial of Kōtoku and his comrades. But with the holidays ended, Takuboku has first to consider the support of his family, so he must return to the routine of a job which does not satisfy him. Of course, most Japanese gird themselves after the New Year holidays to return to the necessary routines, but not so with the speaker in this tanka.

Itsushika is the old-style diction for "before one realizes it," today's expression being *itsunomanika*. While the Japanese usually take three days off for the New Year period, it is actually a seven-day affair, especially in the villages. The official holiday is three days, but during the *nanakusa* (the seven-day period from January 1), the New Year mood continues.

55. In one of Takuboku's letters dated March 2, 1911, while he was in the hospital, he wrote to Miyazaki, who had married Setsuko's sister:

> This was a poem I wrote before I was hospitalized. The dream was one of numberless ones which my disgruntled internal organs, suffering under pressure since my abdomen began to swell, brewed every night. It went something like this: A crowd of police suddenly surrounded my house and hauled me before a god. The god, who was like an aged Ainu, had a long white beard reaching to his kness. Standing on a platform, he ordered me to do something, a shining rod wielded in his hand. I didn't understand what I had been ordered to do. Someone by me said, "Now that things have come to this, you'd better accept his order obediently." The man seemed to be one of my intimate friends,

but it wasn't clear to me who he was. I didn't answer the god, but shedding hot tears, I argued with him. I kept protesting for a long time. At last the god, who'd been listening to me with folded arms, stood up and coming to me patted me on the head and said like a primary school teacher, "There! There! Stop crying." When I woke up, I was in a sweat. I clearly remembered the words I kept telling him: "What I seek is a rational life—a life in which nothing but reason has the right to give orders!"

A famous proverb in Japanese: *Yume wa go-zō no tsukare* (Dreams come from the fatigue of the five internal organs). *Yume* in this proverb chiefly refers to unpleasant dreams. That is, we have unpleasant dreams when there is some internal disorder in the body; in good health one does not dream such dreams. According to old Chinese medicine, there are five internal organs: the heart, the liver, the kidney, the lungs, and the spleen. The stomach, together with the great intestine, the small intestine, the gall, the bladder, and the *sansho*, for which we have no corresponding name today, forms the *roppu* (the six *fu* or entrails).

56. Though Takuboku liked choosing poems for his tanka column in the Tokyo *Asahi*, he sometimes disliked his dull job of proofreading. *Kaeru* usually means "to go back home," but for Takuboku the pleasures of family life were quite limited.

Naru o is formal, as is *hatarakeri*. Their colloquial forms are *Naru no o* and *hataraita*.

57. At this time in his life Takuboku's ideas on socialism became stronger, but in those days such an ideology was dangerous, so he had to be careful. Takuboku was certainly a loner, an outsider, as he sat with the older men who did proofreading for the *Asahi*. These men, while learned in Chinese characters, were prosaic individuals; at least Takuboku refers to them in this way in his diary. All the people in his section, with the exception of the office boys, were his superiors since he was the youngest; furthermore, his job required little talent. Sometimes he was unable to fathom what these elderly proofreaders thought about him, nor did he know the attitudes of reporters and other employees, so he played it safe or he might have lost his job. It must have been trying for a proud and bellicose man like Takuboku to subordinate himself.

58. Takuboku is not thinking of monetary gain but of newspaper policy. He would probably have progressive opinions on the editorial page, and he would perhaps reevaluate the literary section. He might have been concerned about the question of formal and/or colloquial styles.

The choice of the pronoun *ore* is significant. The use of *I* is not a polite or neutral choice, for it has some connotation of swaggering. In Meiji Japan, journalists had a great deal of pride in considering themselves leaders of public opinion. In many cases they had something of the braggart about them. In the moment referred to in this tanka, Takuboku's self-confidence as an editor must have been revived. For a short time he had been the successful editor of the *Kushiro Shinbun* (see Introduction). While working as a proofreader, he must have sometimes looked at the *Asahi* with a critic's eye and dreamed of the many changes he would have liked to make. Now that he is nearly overwhelmed by poverty and poor health, he recalls somewhat bitterly his former ambitions.

59. An entry from Takuboku's diary of January 16, 1911: "The butter sent from Chieko-*san* in Sorachi arrived." Chieko Kitamura, née Tachibana, was at the time the happy bride of a dairy farmer in Hokkaido. Takuboku had met her as a colleague in 1907 when he was appointed a substitute teacher at Yayoi Primary School in Hakodate. A pretty girl of eighteen, she was loved by her colleagues for her gentleness and good nature. Takuboku seems to have conceived a platonic love for her, but he had few opportunities to talk to her. When he was leaving Hakodate for Sapporo, he visited her for the first time and gave her a copy of his first book of poems, *Akogare*, on the title page of which he wrote, "On parting, the author dedicates this to Miss Tachibana. September 12, 1907." *A Handful of Sand* has a series of twenty-two love poems obviously written with her in mind. A few examples follow:

> The memory of my love—
> Soft spring sunshine
> On cool clean marble

> Were I to confess
> I wished to see you before I died,
> Would you give me the slightest nod?

> O the years have increased
> Since we parted,
> Yet the dearer you are with each spring.

Butter is not only an unusual subject for tanka, but butter itself was not as appealing in those days as it is today. It was salty and had a pungent odor in the cans it was packed in. Obviously the butter in this tanka was quite fresh, sent as it had been in the winter months from Sorachi, a district in Hokkaido.

During the Meiji period, Japan was divided into one *dō* (Hokkaido), three *fu* (Tokyofu, Kyotofu, and Osakafu), and forty-three *ken* (prefectures). The *dō* and *fu* and *ken* were subdivided into *gun* or *kōri*. Next in order came city, town, and village, the difference among these latter being chiefly one of population. *Gun* does not exist today as an administrative unit, but persists as a geographical unit. *Sorachi-gōri* in this tanka is in the central and western part of Hokkaido facing the Sea of Japan.

The simple flowing rhythm of the Japanese in this tanka is memorable. The naive quality of this poem, without flourish or sentimentality, comes from the nature of Takuboku's feelings about this girl. He once wrote to a friend: "But, mind you . . . I don't want carnal relations with a woman if I love her ever so slightly. Not only that. I want us to love one another in secret, without confessing our love to each other, talking only about ordinary things when we meet. I'd like to be loved until I die without being told of that love ..." (July 7, 1911). To have received Chieko's gift when he was ill must have given rise to the simple flowing rhythm of this tanka.

60. A kind of diary moment. Along a midnight street in winter the poet stopped, thinking the voice he heard (not necessarily a woman's) resembled that of someone he knew. The experience is common and typical, but Takuboku created a poetic atmosphere.

Most probably the poet was in kimono, and the cloak was a *tonbi*, a Japanese version of the Inverness coat which could be worn over a kimono. The cloak was called *tonbi* (kite) because the flaps on both sides looked like the wings of a kite. This modified inverness coat could be worn over a kimono. In Meiji and Taishō, there were many kinds of modified Western coats, but the type varied according to class and occupation. Students liked mantles; the cloaks worn by some shop-keepers and some workers had square sleeves fitted to the kimono shape; *tonbi*, however, were worn mostly by professional people and rich men dressed in kimono.

61. Some of Takuboku's diaries are lost, but of those extant no entries contain, as far as we know, the initial Y. Takuboku rarely used initials, so this person must have had some important connection to him.

The words *ano hito* create something of a problem. Should the initial Y stand for a man or a woman? *Ano hito*—literally "that person" —when used for a man connotes slight respect or some aloofness. If the man is younger than the speaker or writer or if the man is a friend, the term *ano hito* would not be used, for *ano otoko* would. *Ano hito* might be used for a woman, though the words suggest some kind of familiarity. On the other hand, she might be a woman for whom the speaker once cherished some affection. In using this expression for a woman, the man reveals a kind of aloofness—he may like her, though no love for her is intended, or she might have once been an object of his love, though she is no longer. However, some slight degree of respect is hinted at. Certainly the woman is not a geisha, for in speaking of her, the man would say *ano ko* or *ano onna*. We conclude with two possibilities for the Y of this tanka: the person was older than the poet and was a man the poet respected or was not very familiar with; on the other hand, Takuboku might have been referring to a woman for whom he once had tender feelings. In his diaries Takuboku always wrote names in full, so the initial implies Takuboku did not want to reveal the identity of the person he had undoubtedly mentioned in a diary.

62. Many critics cite this bleak tanka as one of Takuboku's socialist poems. The tanka may be interpreted as showing his love for the peasants of any place and his sympathy for the poor. Clearly, beneath his sympathy for the hard lot of the peasants, there is anger at the inequality existing in the world. But whether he related the poverty of the peasants to the policy of the government is not clear from the poem itself. To the Japanese peasants sake used to be just about the only consolation in their hard lives. In the Tōhoku district (which includes Iwate Prefecture of Takuboku's early years), farming was especially rigorous. The climate was cold, and rice required tropical temperatures, as it still does. Because of the geographical location of the region, its inhabitants frequently had a bad crop in those days, and even today crop failures are not rare. Only technological advances have enabled the peasants to grow rice in this district.

Farmers had to buy sake—it was against the law to ferment it themselves. Because of their difficult life and the severe cold of winter, these peasants were especially hard drinkers. Indirectly Takuboku may be venting his wrath against the government and society for permitting such poverty.

63. The poet had thought he was inured to the miseries of the world, but the item in the newspaper brought tears to his eyes. Takuboku had been sensitive to the miseries of mankind, but while living a life of poverty in Tokyo, he thought he had lost some of his sensitivity toward the poor and wretched, absorbed as he was in his own economic distress and unhappy home life. Yet at this moment of waking, his mind was fresh, not tired. His old sympathy for the downtrodden was momentarily revived. To feel sympathy for other men was a rare experience for him in those days, so this tanka reveals his joy over this "terrible" event. The poem suggests Takuboku's inward fear that the life he was leading was eroding his humanity.

We remember, too, that Takuboku's father deserted the family.

64. This tanka complements tanka 63. In the previous tanka the poet refers to his state of mind after he woke and looked at the newspaper. In tanka 64, the poet has awakened early and has time, therefore, to reflect on his own character, his life. Self-reflection had been a marked characteristic of the poet, yet this tanka shows that such moments of self-reflection had become rare due to his daily struggle against poverty and ill health.

The word *hito* in this tanka does not refer to one's family members but to others. If Takuboku were referring to his family, he would use such words as *tsuma* (wife), *oya* (parent), or *ko* (child).

This tanka offers another instance of Takuboku's revising many of the poems before he set them down in his notebook. This poem had appeared earlier in the February 1911 issue of *Sōsaku* at which time the second line was *Tsugō waruki* (inconvenient) instead of his final choice *Tekisezaru*, the latter expression more literary, closer to the more complicated formal style; the earlier choice is colloquial usage made slightly literary by its ending.

65. A casual, diary-like poem, though completely formal. Perhaps the poet was reading an article in a newspaper or magazine and felt a momentary reassurance that his ideas were not as eccentric as he had thought. The psychology in this almost-too-trivial poem is nevertheless honest and accurate and universal.

66. Another tanka of Takuboku's self-scorn. He is disgusted with himself because it is foolish to exhaust oneself by "talking big" half a day, especially since the listener was a younger man. That the listener was younger is the key implication for a Japanese. An older man ought to know better, of course. Age is an especially important element in Oriental culture. It is easy for an older man to talk big to a younger. The young man must listen more out of respect for age than for any other reason. Should the young man talk big to his elders, that at least would be a sign of courage, of boldness, of contempt for tradition. But it was the older Takuboku who followed the usual pattern of age, forgetting perhaps that it was equally foolhardy to devote so much energy to a younger man forced by convention and courtesy to listen.

67. The psychology of this tanka is similar to that of tanka 63. For the historical event to which this tanka may be connected, see note 113. Takuboku is once more glad he can really be socially serious, that he can feel for others.

Today the Japanese Diet is divided into two houses—the House of Representatives and the House of Councillors (in Takuboku's time the Diet consisted of the House of Representatives and the House of Peers). The prime minister must appear in both houses to conduct government business and debate.

68. A humorous tanka. The miniature plum tree is usually placed in the alcove during the New Year holidays. If the *bonsai* blooms on New Year's Day, the Japanese are delighted. Takuboku tried to hurry the process but failed. The naiveté of the poem is intentional. One can see beneath the humor the philosophy of Orientals—knowledge of the futility of going against nature.

The plum tree *(prunus mume)* comes from China. It is a symbol of nobility, for it blossoms in the very cold season and its smell is considered pure. Cherry blossoms have no real odor, but that of plum blossoms, especially in the dark, is one any Japanese would immediately recognize and delight in. Usually plum trees blossom in Tokyo in February, but greenhouse *bonsai* can bloom in January in time for the holidays.

Pink plum blossoms are considered feminine and slightly erotic, the smell not so strong. White plum blossoms are masculine and pure.

Akiko Yosano's poems on plum blossoms in *Midaregami*:

> In the darkling
> Bamboo grass
> Around the graves of my lover's parents,
> Immaculate
> My offering of white plum.

> Pink morning mist
> Over the valley
> Of blossoming plum,
> O the beauty of those hills,
> O this beautiful me!
> [See *Tangled Hair*, tanka 69 and 143]

69. To a man of Takuboku's disposition, this trivial event is especially meaningful. For a long time the speaker had thought about destruction

—his life style, his reactions to society, and his lack of literary success made him feel frustrated, dissatisfied, and he could do nothing to change his situation. One morning he accidentally broke his teacup or rice bowl (*chawan* can be either), and he suddenly realized how pleasant it was to destroy something, anything, even an article as small and valueless as a *chawan*. The psychology here is not too far removed from Dostoyevsky's underground man or Yukio Mishima's destructive acolyte in *The Temple of the Golden Pavilion*.

70. A humorous and innocent tanka. The child, of course, is Takuboku's daughter, Kyōko.

In English cats "meow," in Japanese *nyan*, but to get the right number of syllables, Takuboku wrote *nya*. The tanka is mostly colloquial, *Bikkuri shite yorokobu* markedly so. *Hipparite* is partly colloquial, the stem that and the ending formal. The purely colloquial form is *hippatte*, the purely formal *hikite*. That the grammar of our translation is not correct adds, we hope, to the childish and innocent quality.

71. A poem of self-disgust. The poet needed money but was reluctant to go out to borrow some, so he chided himself for his weakness, for his reluctance. On the surface this tanka deals with the speaker's inability to act. But the deeper layer of meaning lies in the poet's use of *Naze kōka*. This expression is vague, yet characteristically Japanese. To the Japanese mind this vague expression (literally "Why am I like this?") is perfectly clear. The situation is of course vague (the poet may have wasted his money and now needs it for rent or other household expenses—he would not reprimand himself if he hesitated because he wanted to borrow funds to meet a prostitute), but the emotional reaction is clear. The poet knows he is basically incompetent in money matters, in being responsible, in following his best interests. We feel in this moving moment of self-realization the lament of a man who is saddened by what he is, what he has become. Takuboku did not ask *Naze kō yowai ka?* (Why am I afraid to borrow?) That would have made the tanka too simple, too restricted. He wanted some deeper meaning with which to question his entire personality and inner world.

72. A bittersweet moment of remembrance. The poet noticed his desk and recalled a crucial day in his past. Though *hito* can mean a man or a woman (see note 61), it seems more natural to think the person the poet expected was a woman. Did the poet change the position of his desk while waiting or after he had waited an excessively long time and had realized the woman would not turn up? Or did he change its position before the appointed hour? It seems he changed it much later during the interval of his waiting. He was disappointed and irritated, so much so that he could not read or create any poems; consequently, to change his mood and refresh his mind, he moved his desk.

Western readers may be surprised to learn that a Japanese desk is very small, its top not too far from the straw mats of the room. The desk is light and can easily be carried to any part of the room. Often, though, it is placed near a window. A Chinese saying is *Meisō jōki* (Light window, tidy desk). Desks were made from hardwood or paulownia. The desk did not have to be large, for earlier Japanese books were thin and lightweight, several easily encased in a small cardboard box which was sometimes bound with cloth.

Here is an example of Takuboku's revision even of punctuation before he entered these tanka in his gray notebook; in the *Waseda Bungaku* magazine of March 1911, in which this tanka first appeared, a dash was used at the end of the second line.

73. The Japanese usually save newspapers to wrap things in, and on one such occasion the poet was wrapping something in an old newspaper when he suddenly noticed his name in the poetry column (newspapers in those days had a column on literature [*bungeiran*] which reviewed the stories and poems published during the month). In this tanka we feel the poet's pride, though a sensitive pride. The poet treats the discovery as trivial and casual, but actually he is proud his tanka were praised, if even in a few lines. The psychology is that despite the fact that he is now poor and despised by others as a poet and man, he had once been praised.

Furu-shinbun refers to old newspapers, not clippings *(kiri-nuki)*.

In this tanka Takuboku uses *ji-amari* (more than the traditional thirty-one syllables). He deliberately broke the rhythm to achieve a more casual or colloquial flavor. Only *naredo* (instead of *dakeredo*) and *ari* are formal in the last two lines. The use of the exclamation mark was new in tanka—as was Takuboku's occasional use of the dash. In *A Handful of Sand*, he did not use such marks. This tanka is a good example of the mixture of old and new forms.

In the *Waseda Bungaku* of March 1911, where this tanka first appeared, Takuboku used a comma after *Oya* in the second line and a dash at the end of this line, another illustration of Takuboku's punctuation revision before entering these poems in his gray notebook.

74. Tanka as diary. Perhaps tanka 73 was part of the same moving-day (Takuboku first moved in June 1909 from his lodging house in Tokyo to two rooms upstairs over a barbershop; then, on August 7, 1911, to a small rented house). Since the photograph was suddenly discovered at his feet, he may have remembered an actual situation of a woman throwing herself at his feet. Since he had forgotten the photograph (one the woman herself may have sent him), she was probably not so important to him. The poet is only slightly nostalgic—casual in spite of the surprise of discovery.

It is startling for us to think that Takuboku during this period of writing these tanka was a young man in his twenties. Tanka 74 seems to suggest the poet is middle-aged. In the Meiji period, of course, a thirty-year-old man was considered just that.

75. There is no regret here. Formerly the poet was so caught up in his romance he had not noticed the *kanachigai* in the woman's love letters or possibly even in those letters he himself may have written to his wife, Setsuko. These *kanachigai* are misspellings due to dialectal pronunciation or to insufficient training in writing *kana* (the Japanese syllabaries). The letters were probably not from Koyakko, the geisha Takuboku met in Kushiro in 1908. The word *mukashi* suggests the letters were from a much earlier period. During those days when Takuboku was in love, he did not mind the errors, possibly not even noticing them, but now that he is older and more mature, he does notice them. The change in his awareness reveals the change in his feelings. The more one lives in Tokyo, the more one becomes aware of the importance of standard Japanese.

We may ask if these letters were actually Takuboku's or Setsuko's. The following diary entry for December 26, 1906 (during this period Setsuko had gone to Morioka as her delivery was near) is relevant:

> I went to bed about midnight, but I couldn't sleep.
>
> I happened to remember that in a bamboo trunk in a corner of the room there was a bundle of letters I had written Setsuko during the past five years. When I remembered it, I felt as if I had been lit up by the spring moon in a dark forest....
>
> I took out the bundle of a hundred and few score letters. They are the eternal symbol of my youthful blood and tears, the story of my first love, no, of the only love in my life, the love between Setsuko and me!
>
> Reading them, I saw the colors and scents of the past days revive. It was a picture scroll alternating with tears of happiness and sorrow. Our love so rich in vicissitudes would make a good novel.
>
> Setsuko, Setsuko. I cry for you.
>
> You were my saviour. If I have anything I can be proud of, I owe it to you. Wasn't it because I had you as my love that I live today, and live with joy, I who twice tried to commit suicide? To me you are the loveliest, the dearest, and the most valuable.
>
> Marriage is said to be the graveyard of love. Let them say so who want to. But we were and are lovers. This love will continue until I die....

76. Takuboku married Setsuko in 1905, their relationship having begun several years before. Biographer Iwaki cites the May 26, 1928, issue of the *Iwate Nippō* newspaper which introduces reminiscences by a friend of Takuboku who stated that in the spring of 1901, Takuboku showed him a long love letter written by Setsuko that covered five to six sheets of Japanese *hanshi*, equivalent in space to double the number of pages of ordinary letter paper. Takuboku must have kept her letters as cherished mementos. But their relationship was strained at the time tanka 76 was written. Takuboku's not remembering where the letters are is symbolic of the fading of his love for her. Perhaps at the moment he was trying to find them in order to reread them. But why? It might not be a totally wild conjecture to suppose that he was doing so in an attempt to regain his old feelings toward Setsuko.

77. Those who have suffered from insomnia can appreciate this tanka. They try every means to get to sleep. The least bit tired, as the speaker is in this tanka, and the insomniac scampers off to bed, though of course ultimately he cannot sleep. The tanka is comical to the outsider but not to the insomniac. Young people are especially troubled by insomnia—older people expect it.

Occasionally Takuboku mentions insomnia in his diaries: "I have formed the habit of sleeplessness" (March 29, 1911). "Sleepless again" (March 30, 1911). Generally speaking, however, he does not refer to insomnia in his diaries. Having stayed up late to write, drink, or indulge his sexual appetites, he often slept until ten or eleven in the morning.

Yo! at the end of the first line is formal, the poem mostly colloquial.

78. A diary-like tanka. The situation is comical to an observer but not to the performer, so Takuboku was disgusted with himself.

The "knife" in this instance is not for eating. In those days forks and knives were used only in some restaurants. Takuboku would never have used one at home. This knife is for cutting paper or sharpening pencils.

The first and third lines in the Japanese are formal; the second line is colloquial.

79. In Takuboku's younger days he lived in the country and enjoyed the world of nature. But his hard existence in Tokyo narrowed his awareness—he lost his earlier freedom. This tanka laments his degeneration—financial concerns made him into a mean, constricted person. When a man is worried about the "petty worries of the mundane world" (literally *jinrō*), he does not have time to look at the sky.

The expression *Kō mo naru mono ka?* is vague yet perfectly comprehensible ("That I should become so"—that is, such a narrow, mean, contemptible man).

For this volume we have followed the Iwanami Bunko edition of Takuboku's *Sad Toys,* but we prefer to use a comma after the first line in our Romaji rendering in order to emphasize the importance of that line. Takuboku used a comma in this instance when the poem appeared in *Wadeda Bungaku* in March 1911, though no comma appears after the first line in the Iwanami. A comparison of the first lines of tanka 44 and 50, which have a comma at the end of the line, with those of tanka 49 and 41, which have not, will show the difference in emphasis.

80. Most of this tanka is in colloquial Japanese, especially the first line.

Takuboku's daughter, Kyōko, is referred to in this diary-like poem of childhood innocence. She always saw her father writing, so she thought Chinese characters and the *kana* could only be written on special paper. The *genkōshi* is writing paper in which the entire sheet is ruled into squares—one character fitting into each box. Usually the writing proceeds from the right, moving vertically down each column.

81. The end of the month was a difficult time for poor people. Modern-day Japanese use cash, but in those days people bought almost everything on credit. Bills were paid by the month, so the *misoka* (the last day of the month) was the time for tradesmen to come for payment. In the country, bills were often paid only twice a year, in August at Obon (the season of the Festival for the Dead) and in December. Even in Tokyo, bills were paid at the end of the month. We can imagine Takuboku asking for an extension or having just enough to meet his payments. The poet in this tanka is satisfied he has managed to get through the month—indirectly the poem underscores his difficulties. The economic problems he faced occupied him, so he had no room to consider other desires at that moment. On the other hand, something of the Buddhist recognition of the limitation of desire also comes through in this appealing moment.

82. It is the remembrance of lies past that causes the poet to break out into a sweat now. When younger, he felt irresponsible, but now that he is older and has more time for reflection, his conscience pricks him. To lie is not considered so immoral because of the social complexities, but at this "late" moment in Takuboku's life, he reconsiders his past with regret.

In *Ase ga izuru,* "*izuru*" is formal, "*ase ga*" colloquial. To make the expression fully formal, Takuboku would have had to write "*Ase izuru*"; to make the expression fully colloquial, it would have to be written "*Ase ga deru.*" When the Japanese feel ashamed, they say, "I perspire" or "Cold sweat comes out under the arms." The same expressions are used when a narrow escape from danger has occurred.

83. The poet discovered a bundle of letters from a former friend. Having read through them, Takuboku is startled he could have been so intimate with a man he now thinks of contemptuously. The tone of the letters revealed the close relationship between the two. This tanka is typical of Takuboku's connections with men. One after another he severed these relationships. A man of strong pride with the egotism of an artist, Takuboku must have been a difficult companion. He abandoned even Kindaichi (see note 85), his good friend who had been a constant source of help to him. Takuboku's petulance was due partly to illness, partly to economic distress, and partly to a kind of Buddhistic outlook on ephemerality, mutability, and human limitation. Love, friendship, health, even art—all decay. The April 12 entry in the *Romaji Diary* reveals the poet's explicit feelings in this regard.

84. A very casual, very momentary tanka. We feel the persons in tanka 83 and 84 are different, for a letter (as in tanka 83) would have been written first with the family name followed by the given name. Shirō Suzuki (1880-1953), the person referred to in tanka 84, worked for a short period of time under Takuboku when the poet was city editor of the *Otaru Nippō.* Suzuki was born in Aomori Prefecture. While he was employed as a cook in Sapporo, he turned socialist and joined a cooperative farm. At the time this poem was written, he earned his living as a postman in addition to working on the farm where he had once lived.

Standard tanka focus on some strong emotion, some psychological conflict, but this tanka, a type Takuboku often favored, is so casual as to be almost trivial. Interestingly enough, this tanka is mostly in the formal style.

85. Tanka 85 and 86 were included in a note to Takuboku's friend Kyōsuke Kindaichi (1882-1971) dated January 29, 1911. Kindaichi had been Takuboku's senior by two years at Morioka Middle School. In those days Kindaichi wrote tanka in the style of the circle of poets connected to the *Myōjō* magazine (April 1900 to November 1908); their poems were romantic and characterized by gorgeous fantasy and pictorial elements. Kindaichi used a pseudonym and contributed poems to various magazines. He was one of the persons who initiated Takuboku into the literary arts. The *Myōjō* magazine Takuboku borrowed from Kindaichi opened the former's eyes to tanka. Living in the same Tokyo boardinghouse, the two continued their earlier friendship, Kindaichi helping the other over many financial difficulties. We often come across Kindaichi's name in the *Romaji Diary*. Kindaichi was a serious student with sober habits. It was Kindaichi who persuaded Setsuko to return home after she had run away from Takuboku. But toward the end of Takuboku's life, the poet's friendship with Kindaichi cooled. The following entry appears in a memo on important events in 1910 attached to Takuboku's diary for 1911: "One change was the cooling of my friendship with Kindaichi . . . I dedicated *A Handful of Sand* to him and Miyazaki [Setsuko's sister's husband] as a token of gratitude for their friendship and help in the past. But Kindaichi did not even send a note that he had received the book." In a diary reference for January 3, 1911, Takuboku writes: "In my absence Kindaichi came to offer his New Year greeting. He returned very much embarrassed, I was told." Takuboku does not specifically give the reason for their estrangement. Later Kindaichi became a professor of linguistics at Tokyo University. His special interest was the Ainu language.

The Japanese often omit the subject in a sentence, a tendency which proves confusing if the context is not known. In this tanka we do not specifically know whose child was born or who was reading the postcard that the new father had sent as an announcement. But since tanka are poems about the poet's life in all its fleeting moments, we can easily supply the grammatical subject and fill in the situation. Usually the Japanese let friends know about the birth of a child by forwarding the information on handwritten postcards.

In the Meiji and Taishō eras and even before, people were fond of creating occasional poems of congratulation or condolence enclosed in letters. These poems were mostly in tanka form, but some were haiku. Today most Japanese are too busy to write such poems.

As a poem of congratulation to his friend Kindaichi, Takuboku's tanka is nevertheless unusual for the situation because of its Takubokian personal reference. The poet had been in a bleak mood that day when suddenly Kindaichi's postcard arrived. For a moment the poet's mood changed and he was glad, but only for a moment. Thus, *Hitoshikiri* (for a while), which is set off by commas, is the key word in this tanka.

The words *hagaki mite* are formal. In colloquial Japanese the particle *o* is usually put after *hagaki*.

86. See note 85 for the background on Kindaichi in relation to this tanka as well. That the friendship of the two men had not completely cooled is revealed in Takuboku's diary reference for January 27, 1911: "On returning from the office, I found Kindaichi, who had not come to see me for some time. He said his wife had been in labor since morning."

This poem, whose first two lines (especially the slangy *Sōre miro*) are colloquial, is unconventional as a poem of congratulation. While the content suggests the intimacy between the two men, it also shows something of the barrier Takuboku had felt. That is, he felt inferior to his friend, a man of sober habits. Kindaichi had seemed more like a demigod than a man with earthly desires. He was a serious scholar and a hard worker whose conduct was usually beyond reproach. Such a man in regard to sexual matters and other areas is called *kinchoku*—moral, upright, scrupulous, conscientious. Takuboku was glad to realize his friend had indulged the passions, that he too was not above sexual appetite. Reading the poem, Kindaichi would have smiled at the humor, but on another level there are serious undertones. That he was not impervious to the pleasure quarters is obvious in the *Romaji Diary* entry for April 25 (p. 101).

87. This tanka was created in a moment of self-pity. But instead of using the expression "What a poor fellow I am!" Takuboku objectified his sadness by writing "That poor fellow Ishikawa!" There are of course many ways of expressing one's sadness, but Takuboku let his imagination objectify his sorrow. He put himself in the position of a friend or acquaintance who is using those very words Takuboku would at times say aloud to himself. And the objectification deepened the feeling of sadness. There is also an element of whimsy in objectifying that state, but the sorrow of the poet does not become any the less shallow for it.

Takuboku's contemporaries would have been quite startled by the first line of the poem. It is perfectly prosaic, perfectly flat, but the prose is elevated to poetry by what follows. The entire poem is in fact colloquial except for two syllables, and these two syllables (we might call them "letters" in English) completely change the colloquial quality into the mixture of colloquial and traditional elements Takuboku is so fond of using. Thus the formal *iite* and the formal *Kanashimite miru* might have been colloquial if Takuboku had written *itte* and *kanashinde miru* respectively.

Miru is the same verb as that common one meaning "to see," but it has another meaning, "to try." For instance, the expression *aji o miru* means "to try the taste." From this meaning a new use has developed in attaching *miru* to various verbs and thus adding the meaning "by way of experiment" or "for trial." *Kite miru*, for example, means "to try on," while the verb *kiru* simply means "to put on." The difference between *taberu* and *tabete miru* lies in the former meaning the act of eating while the latter connotes "to eat by way of experiment" and suggests that the item of food is new to the eater or that the eater is not certain whether it tastes good or not. In the same way, *itte miru* does not simply mean "to go" but has the connotation of venturing forth. A comparison of the last line of this tanka with that of tanka 99 may prove revealing. In the latter a state of sorrow is meant; that is, the poet is in sorrow rubbing his swollen belly. But in this tanka the sorrow is not lasting; the poet tries to experience a new feeling of sorrow by the use of these words.

88. Tanka 88 through 107 may be called "hospital poems." On February 4, 1911, Takuboku was hospitalized for what was supposedly chronic peritonitis (see note 97). He remained until March 15. When he returned home, he underwent medical treatment there, for already complications of pulmonary tuberculosis had developed.

The hospital of the Medical School of Tokyo Imperial University had many patients in its one-story wooden building with long dark corridors.

In this tanka *dereba* is the only colloquialism.

89. It seems that life in the hospital was something of a respite for Takuboku. For a while at least, he was in a peaceful mood, relieved of financial worries and feeling no great pain. In his diaries he often refers to the easygoing life at the hospital, but he also notes its ennui.

Takuboku did not realize the nature of his disease at this time in the hospital, or he would not have been in the mood this tanka creates.

Takuboku was admitted free of charge to the hospital attached to Tokyo Imperial University, which was considered the best hospital in those days. All hospitals of government schools had an appropriation for receiving patients without charge. In return for the free service, these patients were obligated to cooperate in medical research by undergoing experimental treatment. These obligations were mostly nominal, but sometimes the patients were taken to lecture halls as specimen cases. In those days any of these free patients who died had to have an autopsy. Today, because of medical insurance, this system has become obsolete, but even now we hear of patients who are treated free of charge as "experimental cases." Actually Takuboku was better off financially during his hospitalization than he had been before, mainly because the *Asahi* continued to pay his salary.

The first line in the Japanese is colloquial, the second and third lines traditional. *Nedai* means a Western-style bed, which was just coming into use in those days. Today *shindai* is the word for this kind of bed. The *futon* or *toko* is the traditional Japanese bed laid out on the *tatami* mats each night and put away in closets in the morning.

90. The poet had asked his doctor at the hospital, "Can I work?" or "Can I get dressed and leave?" The doctor said, "If you do, then you'll die. If you want to live, you must rest." It was at this moment that Takuboku realized the seriousness of his illness. The doctor's words silenced him, and he knew the doctor was right, but he felt the pathos of being reduced to such a state. All the creative urgency he felt, all the desperate necessity of earning a living, all that had to wait. This poem implies Takuboku wanted to live.

There are two kinds of tuberculosis. One type is called "open," the patient's bacilli contagious. The other type is different because the bacilli are contained or controlled. But the seriousness of the disease is not directly commensurate with its "open" or "contained" state. Takuboku was first put in the tuberculosis ward, and that meant his disease was considered infectious, but later he was moved to a ward having patients with various diseases. Thus his tuberculosis was not yet considered contagious. In this tanka, however, Takuboku expresses his sudden awareness of the seriousness of his illness.

91. The poet is in a room in the hospital, a dark light kept on as complete darkness would be too dangerous. The poet's urge to cry at this poignant moment is not necessarily merely self-pity, for all patients with a serious illness have such psychological interludes. According to Takuboku's diary entry for February 4, 1911, he was in Room 18 with two other young men.

The first line in the Japanese is colloquial, and the rest of the tanka is formal, though *Wake mo naku* is both colloquial and formal.

A distinct feature of *Sad Toys* is that Takuboku attempted to break with some of the traditions of tanka in a much more thoroughgoing way than he had in his earlier tanka collection, *A Handful of Sand*. In the latter volume the division of each tanka into three lines gave a fresh visual effect, but for the most part his rhythms were traditional. In *Sad Toys*, however, Takuboku consciously tried to depart from traditional rhythms by bringing those rhythms closer to speech. He also experimented with punctuation. He had earlier written this tanka with commas at the end of each of the first two lines (March 1911 issue of *Bunshō Sekai*), but since the resulting rhythm was awkward with the commas, he eliminated these in his gray notebook; at least we conjecture this to be the case.

92. Many of these hospital tanka represent diary-like moments. In Japanese there is the expression *dōbyō ai awaremu* (patients of the same disease pity each other). Takuboku's pathetic realization in this tanka is that each patient has his own inner torment. All patients have individual illnesses and circumstances, but in common they share illness, the inability to work, and the fear of death. What makes a man cry, though, is probably not the fear of death but his fear concerning the survival of his family, especially if the patient is the breadwinner.

93. Only at first was Takuboku confined to his bed because of the necessity for absolute rest. This tanka is perfectly understandable to anyone who has been hospitalized for a considerable period of time, the enforced rest through hospitalization making the commonplace in the outside world seem fresh.

The first eight words in Romaji are colloquial, the last five formal.

94. A diary entry for February 10, 1911: "The man in the next bed complained to the nurse that he coughs because of cigarette smoke, so I have been obliged to stop smoking in the room. Towards evening I could no longer restrain myself, and going out to the corridor, I smoked one cigarette....In a Hakodate newspaper there was an article about one of the condemned anarchists who, after smoking three cigarettes in succession before execution, said, 'Now I am satisfied.' O tobacco!"

On February 11: "Many times I went out into the corridor and smoked."

On February 12: "... smoked with my head out the window."

On a fine day a patient is sad because he cannot go outside—the good weather makes him feel even sadder. Apparently Takuboku was not prohibited from smoking, though his doctor must have advised him not to.

Takuboku used the line *Byōshitsu no mado ni motarete* (leaning against a hospital window) in tanka 93 and 94. In tanka 103, the line reads *Byōin no mado ni yoritsutsu.* *Yoritsutsu* and *motarete* are synonyms, but the former is formal, the latter colloquial.

95. A common hospital experience. Someone died, and there was a stir in the corridors and the victim's room. In the old-type hospital building, noises in the corridor were clearly audible in the patients' rooms. This tanka underscores the poet's wish to live; he is so shocked by the death of another sick person that Takuboku thinks about his own life and possible death. Usually patients about to die are removed from their wards and put into private rooms. Hospital personnel endeavor to perform the necessary procedures as quietly as possible in order to avoid distressing the other patients. But many of the inmates know of the death because of the hurried footsteps of doctors and nurses and whispered orders.

Hito ya shinitaran in this formal tanka is especially formal. Colloquially one would say, *Dare ka shinda no darō.* The *to* in the second line implies *to omotte* (thinking, wondering).

96. Was the nurse the same one? *Kangofu no te* in Japanese can mean one nurse's hand(s) or nurses' hands. We prefer to translate the reference as singular. If the hands are different, the situation is not as interesting. The poem is mainly an observation with no criticism intended. The patient, in this instance the poet, is an observer of men and women, of human nature. Outwardly nurses look impersonal, but once some contact is made, in this situation feeling the pulse, differences begin to emerge and nurses take on a personal quality.

97. Takuboku's diary entry for February 4, 1911: "I decided to be hospitalized at once. After going home to pack my things, I went to the university hospital at half past two and entered Room 18, Aoyama Internal Department [the Department of Internal Medicine had two divisions: one presided over by a Dr. Aoyama, the other by Dr. Miura]. Two other roommates. Towards evening, examination by Dr. Arima. I had an ordinary meal for dinner.

"My first night in the hospital was lonely. I felt as if I had been thrust far out of the world. The life I had thought chaotic in the rooms upstairs of the barber, I now missed. In the long corridor footsteps arose and then died away. The lamp was too dark to read by. Before I realized it, I fell asleep."

Takuboku was first examined on February 1, 1911. The doctor said his case was serious, but when Takuboku went home, he did not believe what the doctor had told him, namely, that he would have to be hospitalized for three months. On February 3, Masao Ōta, a famous poet and doctor (1885-1945), examined Takuboku and informed him that even though his chest was all right, he should be hospitalized. It was then that Takuboku decided to enter the Tokyo University Medical School Hospital. Takuboku did not know at that time if his "tuberculosis" was contagious or not. Such a word as tuberculosis was dreaded in the old days, and it was not usually used by doctors because of the universal fear among Japanese regarding this disease. If a person in one's family was said to have tuberculosis, the family would be regarded as having a bad strain. Leprosy and tuberculosis ranked together in this area. The doctors told Takuboku he had chronic peritonitis.

On February 6, Takuboku felt too much at ease in the hospital. He tired of reading and could not write any poems. On February 7, the fluid in his abdomen was drained by a minor operation. About three liters of fluid were removed by syringe. Takuboku felt as if he had the urge to eat, but joking about the situation, he suddenly fainted. The fluid was the color of whiskey. This tanka reveals a kind of bravado on Takuboku's part. He is trying to show he can take it, no matter what happens, but in his diary he does indicate his fear about his illness.

On another level of interpretation: when a person is hospitalized, he is excited, so he usually cannot sleep the first night, but in this instance the poet was able to; therefore, he felt somewhat cheated, somewhat disappointed. One reason Takuboku was this relaxed was due to his ignorance about the real nature of his illness. He had little knowledge of medicine.

All three lines are formal. In colloquial Japanese the formal forms *irite* and *yū ni* are *haitte* and *yū noni* respectively.

98. This tanka may be considered to have no direct connection to these hospital poems, but since it was published in the March 1911 issue of *Waseda Bungaku*, it was probably written during the period of hospitalization, February 4-March 15, or very soon after. Once hospitalized, a patient remembers his past life because he now has enormous blocks of time. Takuboku reflected on his past pride. What a change has taken place, for he is now helpless in this hospital room. He realizes the limits life imposes on all men. Still, a kind of maturing has occurred in a short period of time. Perhaps only illness or crisis can bring on this awareness of self.

We must also take into consideration the fact that Takuboku was received as a free patient, as a charity case. Until that day he had enjoyed a certain prestige as a poet in spite of his poverty, but now he found himself among the lowest in the social scale. In a hospital, patients are made class-conscious in a strange way. The size of the room, its furnishings, the quality of bedding, the numbers of visitors and their own personal appearance, all these indicate social class. Furthermore, subtle differences in the attitudes of doctors and nurses toward patients make the sick aware of differences in financial and social status. A free patient naturally feels inferior.

99. According to Takuboku's diary entry for February 7, 1911, about three liters of fluid were drained from his abdomen that day. The following day the pain in his swollen belly was "greatly eased." On February 12, the swelling began again. On February 15, he was moved from the tuberculosis ward to a general ward because he was "clearly free from complications." Apparently he thought he was safe from pulmonary tuberculosis. On February 22, he felt some pain in his chest, which was diagnosed as due to pleurisy. In those days people believed pleurisy and tuberculosis were different diseases.

Peritonitis patients have a swollen belly. If tuberculosis appears in the lungs, the germs circulate through the blood stream, and sometimes these germs enter the kidneys and intestines. In peritonitis the membrane enveloping the intestines has become infected with germs from the lungs. Lymph is produced from the irritation.

Takuboku thought that to be ill was to be in pain, but in this tanka the poet feels no discomfort. He cannot go out since complete rest has been prescribed, so he can only lie in bed. He is sad, yet he is wondering about the nature of his illness, wondering if he is really ill. The simplicity of this tanka saves it from sentimentality. The speaker is restrained as he talks about himself, but it is as if he has objectified one Takuboku, a man stroking his stomach and feeling sad as he lies on a hospital bed.

The entire poem is formal. In this tanka the punctuation has real meaning. Takuboku deliberately put commas around the word *hitori* (alone, by myself, by oneself). Thus *hitori* attracts attention. If there were no punctuation, the experience would become ordinary, but the commas intensify the self, intensify the loneliness, the sadness, the sorrow.

100. As usually happens in a patient, especially one unused to a Western-style bed, Takuboku had pains in his back on his third day of hospitalization, but he writes that the pain disappeared after he got up, washed, and ate breakfast. On the night of February 25, 1911, however, he was sleepless due to high fever. On the following day his temperature was above 100 degrees the entire day. The high fever continued for about ten days. Though, he writes, he was told it was a cold he had, it must have been pleurisy. On March 6, he had the fluid that had accumulated in the pleural cavity drained. During this period he felt quite unwell. According to his diary, he was prohibited from writing and was often sleepless and suffered from loss of appetite. He writes about his disgust with the illness (March 4), and he even thinks of escaping from the hospital by breaking a window (March 5). The following entry is found on March 12: "For the first time the doctor gave me permission to write a little. But sitting up and making a clean copy of poems for three installments in my tanka column completely exhausted me. The fever which has continued for two weeks seems to have burnt all the strength out of my body."

Tanka 100 must refer to these experiences from February 25 to March 10. Except for that short period, however, Takuboku does not seem to have experienced much physical discomfort.

This tanka recaptures the helplessness a patient feels about pain not directly related to illness. A complete rest having been prescribed, the patient cannot walk around and must remain in bed. A stiffness develops throughout the body, not from the illness but from the mere fact of lying in bed. The pain first appears in the back and then spreads. The discomfort increases at night because all is quiet and there is nothing to do except concentrate on the pain one feels.

The first line of the Japanese is colloquial, the final two lines formal.

101. The Japanese have an enormous number of onomatopoetic words *(giseion)*, such as *bisshori* in this tanka (drenched, dampened). A synonym for *bisshori* is *gusshori*. For rustling sounds there are such words as *kasa-kasa* or *goso-goso*. See Oreste Vaccari's *Brush Up Your Japanese* (Tokyo, 1940), pp. 233-256, for a list of *giseion*.

A sick person sweats while asleep. What the Japanese call "night sweat" *(ne'ase)* comes out around midnight or early morning. It is, of course, a symptom of disease or fatigue, and when one wakes in such a state, he has a tired feeling, a feeling of heaviness. Note that Takuboku does not say the heaviness was from fatigue (which one would expect) but from sorrow. Thus, while the poet does not necessarily know he has tuberculosis, he does realize something is wrong with his system, and that saddens him.

This tanka was published in the March 1911 issue of the *Sōsaku* magazine together with seventeen others under the title "On a Hospital Bed." So this tanka was probably written while Takuboku was in the hospital. The other tanka in this series "On a Hospital Bed" are 82, 96, 99, 100 and 102 through 114.

102. In the daytime the poet is not sad, but the moment night comes, his sorrow suddenly appears. The poet makes his sorrow concrete—it steals in and settles on his bed. To use the word *noru* (to ride) is unusual in Japanese (sorrow steals into his room and climbs on his bed), but Takuboku wanted to express the feeling that his sorrow was indistinct and irrational—he does not know the what or why of that sorrow, yet it is immediate and direct and there, confronting him in the darkness. He did not invite the sorrow—it crept in on its own feet.

The word *nedai* indicates the bed was Western, not the Japanese *futon* or *toko* flat on the straw mats. The *nedai* was quite rare in Japanese homes in those days, only a few rich or a few Europhiles having one. Thus the poet is definitely in a hospital where *nedai* were common.

This tanka is mostly colloquial. *Yo to nareba* is slightly formal—to make "when night comes" colloquial, the poet would have had to write *Yoru ni nareba*.

103. Diary entry for February 9, 1911: "Leaning against the window of the hospital ward, I watched various kinds of people walking vigorously with big strides." Certainly this tanka is diary-like! Those who have been hospitalized can share the poet's feeling. But being hospitalized was a new experience for Takuboku. He had thought he was strong, yet suddenly for the first time in his life he found himself hospitalized. The strange, quite different from the world he lived in at the hospital. There is a sadness in this tanka, the sadness that comes from contrasting the world of the healthy and the world of the sick. But within the dimension of the world of the ill, Takuboku was attracted to this hospital world, its pace so different from the hectic, striving, struggling world he had known.

To make the third line in the Japanese colloquial, the poet would have had to write *aruku no o nagameru*. *Yoritsutsu* is formal, its colloquial form *yorikakatte* or *motarete*.

Another instance of Takuboku's revision before inserting a tanka in his notebook: the poem when it first appeared in *Sōsaku* in March

1911 has the third line *Genki yoku*, but Takuboku eliminated this slightly awkward rhythm by revising it to *Genki ni*.

104. At the time of composing this tanka, Takuboku was living in Tokyo with his family, but the poet was in the hospital. Earlier Takuboku had hated to send for his wife, daughter, and mother, who were living in Hokkaido and waiting for travel funds from him. Takuboku had not been able to forward the money, partly because of economic distress, but he had also hesitated because he did not want to lose his freedom. Subconsciously, though, he had felt guilty about his actions, and that guilt must have persisted even after their reunion. Alone in the hospital and weakened by disease, Takuboku could not suppress the guilt he must have been able to suppress while living in his narrow house with his family. In the dream described in this tanka, a dream he had in the hospital, perhaps his mother had rebuked him by saying, "You're going to desert me! I know how you really feel!" and then the tears came from her eyes.

Another interpretation is possible. Takuboku must have supported his mother, filial son that he was, in her discord with his wife. But subconsciously he may have felt anger toward his mother by believing she was the main cause of his estrangement from his wife. It may not be unreasonable to suppose this subconscious guilt produced the dream.

Some of Takuboku's poems on his parents are quite famous, especially the following two in *A Handful of Sand*:

> Out of the wall in this dark room/ My father and mother/ Leaning on sticks [Perhaps at this time Takuboku, poverty-stricken, was living alone. Sitting in the dark, he thinks of his parents, and once more a feeling of guilt takes hold of him. He has been unable to do anything for his old, worn parents.]

> ------

> Carrying my mother playfully on my back,/ I take one step, two, no more—/ How her lightness dims these eyes . . . [The poet could not carry his extremely light mother even three steps because of the weight of his sadness over her frail and emaciated condition.]

105. Takuboku was not afraid of his illness. Ordinarily one is, but he was optimistic about his chances for recovery, so this tanka is not concerned with the fear of the doctor's discovering something fatal about the poet's illness. No, the tone here is more playful. Takuboku wanted to hide something from the doctor, but when the man used his stethoscope, Takuboku felt as if his secrets were being pried loose. Perhaps Takuboku had some unkind thoughts about the doctor, or perhaps Takuboku was afraid the doctor would rebuke him for violating a hospital rule or for neglecting the doctor's advice.

Many doctors wrote poems in those days, so we cannot say this is the first time "stethoscope" appears in a tanka. But the word was fresh and new for Takuboku. Certainly he was not used to being examined in this way.

The word *chōshinki* is a prosaic scientific word, but its five syllables fit the tanka rhythm (Western readers may wonder why the word has five syllables and not three: *cho-o-shi-n-ki;* this is the way the syllables are counted in the *kana* syllabary).

Those parts of the stethoscope that enter the doctor's ears and that touch the patient's body were made of animal bone or ivory, the latter quite expensive. Since it is February or March, perhaps the poet anticipated the cold sensation of contact.

106. This tanka, like others, can be variously interpreted. The question is why the poet wanted his illness to worsen. We feel he was lonely—it was not that he was receiving no attention or was being completely ignored at the hospital. Even though there were two other patients in room 18, Takuboku felt isolated, removed from real human contact, especially during the long hospital night. If a nurse stays with him through the night, there will be greater attention given to him, more kindness. As Takuboku was at first thought to have a contagious disease, he was in a smaller room. A brief glance at his diaries shows his wife visited him almost every day (for example, February 5, 6, 7, 8, 9, 12, and 14); his daughter also visited him but less frequently. Obviously Takuboku did have visitors, but he wanted more contact, especially with some of the pretty nurses perhaps. Actually Takuboku does not really want to be ill but to be better cared for as a human being. A patient of his type who is not very ill and who can manage by himself is mostly left alone. Takuboku must have seen nurses diligently attending patients in serious condition.

107. From the moment Takuboku came up to Tokyo in 1908, he underwent a series of hardships: poverty, frustration, dissatisfaction. After the family was reunited in June 1909, he had to endure the discord between his mother and wife, which led to the latter's running away from home. Towards the end of 1910, the premature death of Takuboku's son occurred. In spite of these troubles his literary activities in 1909 and 1910 were remarkable. He published many tanka, short stories, articles, and reviews, the culmination of his effort the appearance of his tanka collection *A Handful of Sand.*

On the other hand, this period saw a sharp turn in his thought. After the so-called high treason trial of Shūsui Kōtoku and others was reported in the newspapers, his interest in socialism suddenly flared up. From the beginning of 1911 until he was hospitalized in February, he was very much engaged in investigating the Kōtoku case.

Under these difficult circumstances it seems natural to imagine he was indifferent to his family. Temporarily cut off from troubles when he entered the hospital, he must have felt as if he were in a kind of suspension. This transient release from stress must have restored him to his former feelings toward his wife. This tanka, then, is a simple, honest confession. Outwardly Takuboku had a number of unpleasant characteristics—he was bellicose, stubborn, proud. But inwardly he was straightforward, honest. The irritability he felt toward his illness declined while he was in the hospital. There he became more resigned and had more time to reflect on his life. Zen Buddhism uses the words "the true self," but *Makoto no ware* is Takuboku's coinage.

The first two lines are colloquial, the last line decidedly formal Japanese. *Itsukushimu* is an elegant (classical) word but can also be used in colloquial sentences.

108. "To lie" is a human trait, but in Takuboku's make-up this trait was marked. He thought it a real failing. Often in his *Romaji Diary*, which was written only for himself, we see the vacillating quality of the poet. Should he or should he not drink, buy, borrow, spend money, and, as in this tanka, lie? Takuboku was to himself an imp of perverseness.

109. Why did Takuboku shut his eyes? Because he was very much ashamed at that moment. When we feel ashamed, the cheeks are flushed. Takuboku could not bear the image of himself at that instant, an image of himself as a man who lied perpetually, so he shut his eyes. In his past he had told lies to get money, told lies to postpone payment of his debts, told lies to please others, told lies to ridicule others without their knowledge. A tanka of reflection and self-hatred.

110. In a moment of extreme distress the poet tried to escape through make-believe, but it did not work. The bright mood promised by pretense failed to materialize. To the Japanese, such an attempt sounds feminine, and there was something of the Japanese female in Takuboku's personality. Yet one feels moved by the intensity of the pain the poet must have felt in reviewing his past life.

Uso usually means "a lie," but in this instance it connotes "unreal" or "fabrication" or "invention."

111. An element of sadness in Takuboku's remembering his childhood days. His father and mother had wanted him to become a priest and to inherit his father's incumbency. But now Takuboku's strength and vigor have declined, so there is an added element of regret in the remembrance. All boys in those days wanted to be one of two things: a general or a prime minister. The Sino-Japanese War of 1894 occurred when Takuboku was eight or nine. The school textbooks contained anecdotes on courage, and sometimes teachers talked about their own experiences in war. Takuboku no doubt shared the same aspirations of many of the boys of his generation, and he probably did not know, at the time, that this childhood romanticism was against his father's cherished desire. Having abandoned that boyish dream, Takuboku, poor in health, remembers the old days and sympathizes with his parents.

112. Once more, as in tanka 111, we see Takuboku's nostalgia for his childhood years. That the man is riding a horse means he is an officer—being an officer, especially a general, was one of two ambitions schoolboys had when Takuboku attended school. It is doubtful if Takuboku feels any real regret in not choosing a heroic life, but the nostalgia is intense, real.

A well-known child's song in Taishō:

I like soldiers very much—
When I grow up
Decorations will hang from my chest
And I'll wear a sword and ride a horse
And cry "Giddyap!"

113. Diary entry for February 17, 1911: "After reading the newspaper, I suddenly felt unwell. A Diet member by the name of Motozō Fujisawa, who was scheduled to address an interpellation concerning the question of the southern and northern dynasties, suddenly tendered his resignation and after giving an ambiguous farewell speech went into hiding. The news made me feel that the extent to which this damnable oppression by the government might go is almost beyond imagination.

"The excitement I experienced was not pleasant, and I developed a slight fever."

In the fourteenth century the Japanese imperial house was divided into two factions—the southern dynasty and the northern, and the civil war that followed lasted about half a century. Actually the struggle was between the southern dynasty and the newly risen military class. The military ultimately prevailed and assumed the reins of power, and the two dynasties were then united. This historical situation gave rise to the controversy Takuboku refers to in his tanka, a controversy over an event that had occurred five centuries earlier.

In 1911, a dispute arose concerning the description of the two dynasties in the authorized history textbooks in the school system. Texts treated the northern dynasty as the legitimate line, but some scholars had asserted the southern line was the lawful one. The Katsura administration had decided the question, proclaiming the southern dynasty the rightful one. Diet member Fujisawa wanted to discuss this decision, but obviously pressure was asserted on him to prevent his speaking up on questions involving the imperial household. In those days such discussions were taboo. Though the question was purely academic, the authorities used their power for even that kind of triviality, so Takuboku, who had perpetually felt the restraining forces of society, family, friends, was outraged and looked upon Fujisawa as a fellow-sufferer.

For Diet membership, a man had to be at least thirty, though most members were certainly older. That Takuboku refers to Fujisawa as his younger brother is a characteristic touch. *Naite yarishi* (*Naite yatta* for the colloquial form) means to have cried for someone who is of lower status than the person crying, so Takuboku deliberately uses this verb after noting the member of parliament was like a younger brother (younger brothers being of lower status than elder brothers).

114. Takuboku was trained in the traditional ways of tanka. He tried to break away from the tradition through his choice of colloquial expressions and other techniques (for example punctuation and line division), but he could not do so completely. We believe Takuboku felt the necessity of retaining some of the formal elements of tanka, or tanka itself would disappear. Some poets after him (Aika Toki and Yōkichi Nishimura) tried to create perfectly colloquial tanka, but they did not succeed as real poets. One of the techniques Takuboku consciously retained was the very formal ending of the tanka—in this poem that formality occurs in the words *shite itaki kimochi kana.*

Colloquial Japanese easily falls into the 5-7-5-7-7 rhythm of tanka, but the effect of totally colloquial language is slightly different from tanka; still, that slightness makes all the difference. Perhaps the effect of totally colloquial language might be that of using no rhyme in the Shakespearean sonnet couplet "This thou perceiv'st, which makes thy love more strong,/ To love that well which thou must leave ere long," by substituting "shortly" for "ere long." Tanka is associated in the reader's mind with a long history of traditional models. Takuboku's attempt at transforming tanka was the limit he could go in breaking with tradition.

This tanka reveals Takuboku in one of his diabolic moods. The man who feels trapped often wants to destroy, to break, or to smash things. Takuboku, however, did not succeed in the wish he expressed in this tanka, for ultimately he could not look on with nonchalance toward crime, pain, death, destruction.

115. This kind of tanka, perhaps commonplace today, was new for Meiji and Taishō. The tone as a whole is quite colloquial, and like most of Takuboku's tanka in *Sad Toys*, the poet has decreased the formal element to its limit: *yū ga gotoku ni* is formal as is the final *kana.* The first line is what Japanese doctors actually do say to children or perhaps to all patients, who are as helpless as children when hospitalized.

One reason we think this tanka is a hospital poem is that the cost would have been too much for Takuboku if a general practitioner were to visit him at home. If he had been better off financially, a doctor's house call would have been easily within his means. Of course when Takuboku was quite ill at home, doctors were summoned.

In his notebook Takuboku begins the use of indentation from tanka 115. Tanka 1 and 2, though indented, were not in his notebook, for Toki had found them after Takuboku's death. They had been written on a slip of paper.

116. The formal ending of the second half of the last line, *hito o nikumeru,* is bold and forceful.

When a patient cannot sleep, he is often quite irritable. This tanka is typical of Takuboku's frustrated rebelliousness, a rebelliousness that must endure, that cannot lash out.

In those days an animal bladder or rubber bag was used to hold ice. Even today the icebag is held in place by a gadget behind and above the patient's head.

The fever may have been from a cold or perhaps from pleurisy. The diaries often note Takuboku had a high fever: February 25, 1911, he developed a high fever; February 26—104 degrees all day; February 27—from 100 to 101 degrees; March 1 until March 3—high fever.

Hito in Japanese usually refers to some particular man; *ningen* is often used for "mankind in general." In our translation of tanka 116, we have preferred the more forceful word "man," but we should regard the moment in this tanka as only temporary, for Takuboku had too warm a heart for such a theoretical wholesale hatred of mankind.

117. This tanka, a contrast with 116, which was strong and forceful, is conventional and sentimental. *Haru no yuki* (spring snow) means the end of winter and the coming of spring. During the spring the snow is wet and falls in large flakes. In midwinter the snow is fine, the flakes smaller. Falling spring snow is quite pleasant to behold. The flakes do not fall straight but flutter, dance, twist. It is not too cold at such moments.

Spring is near, and that means the coming of the festive cherry blossom season, but the poet is confined to his bed because of a fever. Outer and inner, hot and cold, movement and confinement—all are working in this tanka.

The tone of the tanka is formal. The first line in the Japanese is a traditional cliché; the last line, quite formal; and the middle line, colloquial.

118. What the greatest sorrow represents is not clear. It may be death or the hopeless wait of lying on a hospital bed. The poet's illness must have been extremely bad at this moment. He may have felt he was going to die, waiting in bed only for that. To block out the pain of the thought or the vision, he closes his eyes. The eyes are not closed to hold back tears, for the poet is lying in darkness where no one can see him. The ambiguity of "greatest sorrow" effectively intensifies what it must be. The indentation of *Kore ka to* equally intensifies the line and the ambiguity of the pain.

119. Perhaps this tanka was written at the same time as tanka 118. A pain in the chest is not from the lungs—but from pleurisy. And pleurisy is often attended by a high fever. At such moments the doctor is a patient's chief support. Seeing the doctor reassures one, even though little can be done. When we bear up under severe pain, the eyes are shut tight.

An indented line attracts the reader's attention and thus intensifies the line. But when two lines are indented, either the first and last lines or the first two or last two, the remaining unindented line is emphasized. This is the general rule in *Sad Toys*, though in some cases the impact of indentation is not so clear.

120. The poet's entire focus is on his doctor's face, trying to read it for signs. Is my condition serious or not? the poet wonders. He has doubts about the real nature of his illness. The poet feels doctors comfort and lie—mostly they console. Therefore, he is skeptical of words and looks for some hint on the doctor's face. Even in this very formal tanka, we feel the desperation of the speaker at this time as he hunts for some sign of truth on his doctor's face.

121. Several of these later hospital poems reveal Takuboku's weakness as a man. When one is seriously ill, a spiritual weakness evolves as well, and the emotions work overtime. Even this proud man cannot escape the sentimental, but to an outsider the situation is also moving.

Indentation of the first line intensifies it. The next two lines, except for the final *ki* in *nakitaki*, are rather colloquial.

122. That the book one reads in bed becomes too heavy to hold is a common experience for the weak and ill. Takuboku often refers in his diaries to reading in bed. But ill in the hospital now, his body weak, he easily tires. Reading, in one sense, stops us from thinking; but when the patient stops reading, there is time for reflection—and reflection about the unpleasant. The formal tone of this tanka suggests exhaustion and illness and weight of thought.

We must remember that Japanese books were often quite light in weight, especially when we contrast them with Western books. In the Meiji period, there were many books made of thin Japanese paper and bound in Japanese style, but those in use were mostly Chinese classics or books published during the Tokugawa period. Almost all books printed in Takuboku's day had a heavier Western look, but generally speaking, Japanese books, especially novels, weigh less than those published in the West. The fact that even this kind of Oriental book feels heavy underscores the poet's weakness. His strength has been sapped by disease in these later hospital poems, and there is no perverseness. The earlier hospital poems were more optimistic, but these poems during an attack of pleurisy show the poet's sadness. They are eloquent reflections on the nature of illness.

123. Gold watches were not common in Japan in those days. An imported gold watch was, of course, a status symbol. Was it mere whim that made the hospitalized Takuboku desire one? At this moment his fever must have gone down. He probably felt much better. But there were many occasions in the hospital during which he was keenly conscious of his poverty, so this poem may be a reaction to that kind of mentality. The rich also entered the hospital, and they probably had better rooms. The complicated hospital world must have provided Takuboku with painful moments of social awareness.

The tone of this tanka is colloquial, the last line containing only the formal *hoshi to omoeri*. Generally, when Takuboku wants to express some deep emotion, as in tanka 119 through 122, his poems are formal. While this moment in tanka 123 is almost prosaic, that prosaic experience is made into a poem that carries with it the texture of a life of poverty and pain. That Takuboku speculates on such a prosaic desire provides the poetic element.

124. This tanka was probably written while Takuboku was in the hospital or not long after he had left on March 15, 1911. Judging from his diary, we might conjecture he was comparatively well until the middle of April. He often went out for walks, visited friends, and once even viewed the cherry blossoms. The results of periodic examinations seem to have been fairly positive, and he was told the ointment for his abdomen was no longer necessary (April 10).

This tanka represents one of those rare, precious moments in Takuboku's life. Thinking he is better, he can dream of the future, make plans, prepare for the publication of his book. The binding of literary books was of serious concern to Japanese authors. Even today in Japan, the author has some say about the design of his book, though covers are simpler. Sōseki's *Kokoro* (1914) was green and vermilion in its binding, its design copied from the cover of a book of sutras. Sōseki had a favorite painter do the design.

Ordinarily there would be no comma between *Itsu ka* and *zehi*, but the fact that Takuboku put this rather awkward comma here shows he wanted to emphasize the words.

125. The medicine would be in powdered form, and Takuboku, not used to taking medication, did not have the knack of swallowing the powder directly from its paper wrapper (it is best to put some water into the mouth first). Medicine in those days was also available in liquid form; tablets were quite rare. The poet's illness is not disappearing. He had thought he was cured, yet fresh pains occurred in his chest and made him feel a kind of desperation. His eyes closed from the pain, but he also shut them to keep out thoughts about his illness. The choking comes from the powdered medicine, but the poet's condition is more serious than that. Takuboku packs into the limited thirty-one syllables of this tanka a whole world of complexity.

Sleet comes in comparatively warm weather. Pleurisy patients are apt to have chest pains during a sudden change in weather. Perhaps the poet's fear caused by pains in his chest made him choke on the medicine.

Diary entry March 17, 1911: "Sleet. Fever in the afternoon. Unwell."

126. *Sarado* in those days was potato salad with carrots, green peas, and mayonnaise. It was a new and somewhat exotic dish, and it was found at restaurants and some hospitals. Today *sarada* (not *sarado* as in this tanka) is sold at butcher shops in two varieties—potato and macaroni. In Takuboku's day, the Shirakaba School of poets (White Birch School) had great enthusiasm for the exotic and new and liked to use foreign words in its poems. Many Japanese at that time would not have known what *sarado* was.

Anyone who has been confined in a hospital recognizes the truth of this tanka moment. The eyes see and the nose smells, but the appetite cannot rise to the occasion. The dash lets the reader fill in the rest of the poem.

This tanka has a peculiar effect brought about by the combination of a very new and exotic subject *(sarado)* and the formal traditional diction in the last line. *Mi wa mitsuredomo* (though I did so and so) is a hackneyed phrase used in tanka. The *mi* in the expression, even though written in the Chinese character for "to see" does not mean "to see." It is the same *mi* (to try) commented on in note 87.

127. The language in this tanka is formal, as is that in tanka 128 through 134.

Aware, which may mean "pity" or "sorrow" or "compassion," is used here as a literary expression equivalent to "Ah!"

The poet has scolded his child, and his wife, true to her subordinate role in the Japanese family system, remains silent, but her gaze reveals her annoyance. In his mind the poet offers his own justification as he maintains his role of ruler of the family without the necessity of explaining his conduct. Of course, illness makes one irritable, but that is not the real reason behind the poet's rebuke to his child. He has transferred to the innocent child his anger against the world, his immediate surroundings, and his physical condition. Yet he feels guilty about his injustice to a child when he is basically raging against the injustice of the world.

The poet is not in the hospital but at home. With other patients around, no father would have reprimanded his own child.

128. *Unmei* (fate) was a word new to tanka. The poet here personifies fate, a Western conception, the Japanese thinking of fate not as a god or as a person but merely as "luck" or "chance." It was the vogue of the Myōjō School of poets to use this kind of personification, as Akiko Yosano did at times. Tanka 118 of her *Tangled Hair* personifies death: "My friend found poetry/ At the end of her ordeal,/ But for me/ Only black death/ Ahead." The Japanese do have names for the personification of poverty and death, for example, Binbōgami (god of poverty), pictured as shabby looking and rather comical, and Shinigami (god of death), a slightly comical figure.

The key point of this tanka is in the word *futon*, which means the entire Japanese-style bed on the mats including the quilts. In this tanka only the quilt is referred to. A Japanese *futon* in Takuboku's time was very heavy (some still are today, though there are much lighter ones). The *futon* is padded with cotton and covered with cotton cloth or silk. Takuboku's *futon* would have been made of coarse cotton. The older the *futon* is, the heavier it gets, for the cotton becomes compressed and contains less air. To a weakened invalid, the *futon* seems especially heavy. Japanese hospitals have a special device for easing the heaviness of the *futon*, especially for those patients who have undergone surgery. The device looks like an iron hoop cut in two; when it is placed on the bed, the patient is relieved of the pain which comes from the weight of the quilt. In this tanka we find the weight of the *futon*, the weight of the poet's illness, and the weight of his unknown destiny.

129. Thirsty people want water, but perhaps Takuboku felt that to reach for a cup or for a drink was too prosaic or flat for tanka. True, Takuboku did like fruit—tanka 4 notes his night walk to find a fruit store. We must remember that the thirst of a sick person is a different kind of thirst. The poet feels dull, languid, weary. The fresh taste of an apple might alleviate that languor. By some means or other he wants to get rid of this condition, but he cannot.

130. The cold icebag soothes one's fever, but once the poet drops off to sleep, he cannot help but wake suddenly after the ice melts and no relief is forthcoming. The high fever melts the ice, the fever causing pain throughout the body.

The poet was either at the hospital or at home. Ice was purchased in blocks for home use and was kept in a wooden tub. The ice was chipped with an auger or nail. Ice was not cheap, ten to fifteen sen per *kan* (four kilograms).

Me ga same kitari is slightly colloquial. To be perfectly formal, it would have to be written *me same kitari*, but then there would be only six syllables instead of the required seven. It can also be written formally as *me no same kitari*, seven syllables exactly.

131. The lack of indentation in the first line stresses it against the other two lines of the Japanese. In the Tōhoku district, the song of the cuckoo begins in mid-May and lasts through July. Perhaps the poet's fever made him feel summer was about to begin.

Generally the cuckoo would not be heard in Tokyo, so Takuboku dreamed of the beloved village of his youth. Beloved yes, for its quiet and for the beauty of its surroundings. Yet Takuboku disliked the people of Shibutami village, especially for their treatment of his father. Living in Tokyo and having become more cosmopolitan, Takuboku thought he had outgrown that earlier sentimentality related to home ties. But he has not been able to, and he feels sad that he cannot forget his early native place. Thus the *kanashiku* of the poet is complicated. He cannot break away, rebel, cast off the past, however much he desires to. That is sad, and so is his nostalgia for the old places.

The cuckoo here is a synecdoche for "home." Takuboku uses the indirect method rather than coming out so sentimentally with the word *home*. Akiko Yosano illustrates this kind of Japanese psychology in a tanka in which her heroine realizes she cannot directly ask about her "lover" but only about the "white wisteria" next door: "To the man come from my village/ I could only ask/ About white wisteria/ On the estate/ Next to my house" (see tanka 28, *Tangled Hair*).

132. Takuboku left Shibutami village in 1901, but he returned because of illness in 1903. The following year he again went to Tokyo; however, after his father's loss of his temple job, the poet went back home to get married in 1905. For a while he was a substitute teacher there as he was trying to help his father regain the position. Takuboku left Shibutami for Hokkaido in 1907.

In tanka 131 through 134, Takuboku reveals his nostalgia for Shibutami. This tanka is more simple and direct than 131, for Takuboku mentions *furusato* (native town). When the poet was strong and healthy, he did not think of his home, but now that he is ill, he does. This kind of nostalgia is a commonplace occurrence to those who are ill.

Takuboku often spoke as if he were an old man. He probably thought five years a vast time, but he is only twenty-five at the present moment. People in the Meiji period seem to have matured at a rapid rate.

133. *Sansō* is an elegant mountain villa. Takuboku's home, located at the foot of a hill, was about two hundred meters from the village highway, but he poeticizes his residence into *sansō*. The Japanese tend to beautify the plebian. *Sansō* also has the four syllables necessary for the five-syllable division of *sansō o*. The temple Takuboku's family lived in was surrounded by mountains and would thus have some of the characteristics of a *sansō*!

The cuckoo sings during the day. In these four tanka on the cuckoo (131 through 134), Takuboku is trying a variety of ways to make the same point about his nostalgia for Shibutami. But each poem in a tanka sequence, while connected to other poems, is to be considered an independent, autonomous poem.

134. The *hiba* is a strong tree, but it is not as elegant as the *hinoki* (Japanese cypress). Unfortunately *hiba* (the *hiba arborvitae*) does not translate as poetically as *hinoki*. The latter, which has the best and costliest timber, is produced mostly in the middle part of Japan; the *hiba*, which is as strong but less elegant, is produced in the Tōhoku district.

This kind of tanka is rare. The noun *cuckoo* is preceded by an adjective clause. The number of syllables makes this effort a tanka, but it is very close to being a haiku, which often uses this grammatical structure of noun preceded by its modifying clause.

A rare quiet mood of nostalgia for the usually troubled Takuboku. The reference to temple adds to the quiet of the cuckoo's song in the early summer morning.

135. Takuboku does not have many poems of this kind in *Sad Toys*. That is, in this instance he is gentle and sympathetic, whereas he often focuses on stronger feelings tinged with irony or cynicism. He had in him feelings of great tenderness, but his struggle with the world and art and illness hardened him.

In the Taishō period, the position of a nurse, like that of women in general, was quite subordinate to the male's. A nurse was a nurse, not a servant. But in those days, some nurses, especially those employed by general practitioners, were expected when not busy to do chores usually done by servants. She was trained at the hospital, for nursing schools as we know them today were nonexistent. Perhaps this nurse is sixteen or seventeen or slightly older.

136. The first line in the Japanese is formal, the second and third lines colloquial.

The Japanese say a cold hand signifies a warm heart, but that is not Takuboku's meaning in this tanka. A patient identifies the various nurses by their hands as the pulse is taken. The "cold hand" may be typical of the distance between nurse and patient, of the impersonality and indifference. Since Takuboku was hospitalized a month, he must have seen many nurses and thought about their attitudes toward the patients. That Takuboku gives the initial F means he definitely remembers the nurse's name but suppresses it. It is of course possible that she may have been anemic—there must have been in her something which attracted his attention.

137. A typical moment in the hospital world. Japanese hospitals have enormously long corridors. When a man has been in bed keeping absolutely quiet for three days, he is unsteady in walking; if he spends a week without moving, walking is almost impossible. At home Takuboku remembered that long corridor. It was an impressive challenge for a patient determined to get well, but Takuboku had been too weak then to walk it. Now that he is at home, he probably feels he could have made the walk to the very end of the corridor.

138. In those days the tulip was not as common in Japan as it is today. It was imported into Japan during the Tokugawa period.

Once more Takuboku uses a noun (tulip) preceded by its adjective clause.

To touch and smell the tulip would have been pleasant for the poet, but he was too weak, so he could only admire the flower from a distance. Takuboku tried to walk about to hasten his recovery, but he soon tired; probably even the short distance to the tulip was too much for him at this particular moment. Out of the hospital now, the poet remembers that terrible moment of weakness made vivid by the color of the flower.

139. Once more we find Takuboku in a moment of weakness, yet it is the self-pity of the ill, a common experience. Takuboku uses synecdoche, the hands representing the total decline of the power of his body.

140. This poem was published in the July 1911 issue of the *Shin-Nippon* magazine as one of a series of twenty-six poems entitled "After Illness."

What Takuboku was thinking as the cause of his disease is a matter of conjecture. Of course, he did not know the nature of his mother's illness at the time of writing this tanka, but the following entry in his diary for January 23, 1912, may not be irrelevant. For several days his mother had hemorrhaged:

> A polite "locum tenens" [the doctor's deputy, in this instance, may have been a person studying medicine but without a medical license] about thirty years old came to see her. After examining my mother, he made the following diagnosis: She had had chronic tuberculosis for many years. As she was old, its progress was very slow, but her left lung had almost lost its ability to function.
>
> I suspected the nature of my mother's illness as she had hemorrhaged, but the doctor's words gave me a shock. Unfortunately I knew many facts which corroborated his statement. I had heard from my mother herself that she had had "emaciation," i.e. consumption, when she was fifteen or sixteen. Moreover, she had been saying for some years that she couldn't sleep on her left side because of coughing. And I was told she had coughed up a small amount of blood while I was in the hospital last year. I also had to consider the cause of my eldest sister's death.
>
> ... The fact that the nature of my mother's illness has been found means that the cause of the misfortune enveloping my home has become clear. Today I had to admit I was in a desperate situation. Coexisting in my mind with the desire that she live as long as possible is the fear that if she does, I will be in real difficulties.

When Takuboku wrote this poem, he did not know that his mother had tuberculosis, but he must have suspected the nature of his own disease. On April 25, 1911, he writes: "Why is it that I have not yet been cured forty days after being released from the hospital? And the fear of hunger is drawing near." On May 10, he writes: "In the afternoon I summoned up the courage to go to the hospital. The doctor said the aftereffects of pleurisy still persist, but my lungs are intact . . . ." The fact that Takuboku had to summon up his courage to undergo a medical checkup reveals he had guessed how serious his illness was. It would be natural if he thought about his sister's death in 1906 and his mother's evident weakening since 1910. This kind of speculation is part of the background of tanka 140.

The critic Katsuichiro Kamei (see Introduction) makes the assertion that Takuboku was not referring to physical ailment when he said the cause of his sickness was deeply complicated but was probably deploring his fate since his birth in having an overabundance of aspirations, which Kamei considers a manifestation of what he calls Takuboku's "general aggressiveness." At the same time, Kamei believes Takuboku was perhaps referring to a loneliness which nothing could alleviate and to a despair which stemmed from that loneliness. On the other hand, Kamei wonders if Takuboku did not have a presentiment of the shortness of his life, a corollary to which might be that extraordinary outburst of creativity which enabled the poet to write more than 240 tanka in three days (see Introduction, footnote 7).

We might say that the cause of Takuboku's "sickness unto death" is too tangled, too complicated, to unravel.

Probably "sickness" in this tanka includes the physical as well as this added suggestion by Kamei. Zen Buddhism often notes the impossibility of the rational method in getting back to the source, to the cause, of anything. Analysis and dissection of this kind may well lead to an intense closing of the eyes.

Takuboku's division of his tanka into three lines is his own invention—probably a division into two lines or even five will give the same effect. But in this tanka the threefold division works quite well. A different arrangement in only a few places provides this poem with the usual tanka characteristics of rhythm and emphasis. But the second line has almost the rhythm of prose. The line is in the *kanbunchō* style—that is, in the Chinese style with its forceful and manly and cryptic emphasis. Japanese prose is softer, perhaps even feminine, when it is compared with *kanbunchō*. The latter is the style in which classical Chinese writings were "read" in a special way in Japanese. As the Japanese borrowed Chinese characters, each character had its Japanese way of pronouncing it. So a technique of reading Chinese sentences in Japanese was developed with minimum changes in word order, and these changes were indicated by several signs. This Japanized Chinese style is forceful and manly in its cryptic emphasis. An educated Japanese in the Meiji period or even today would instantly recognize the style in the second line.

141. *Nan no kokoro zo* is an exclamatory sentence meaning "What a mind I have!" In colloquial Japanese, the line would be *Nan to yu kokoro darō!*

The poet is rebuking himself for his weakness. Sadly aware that the situation surrounding him would be the same even if he were cured and forseeing the continuation of a life of pain and fatigue, the poet, in this weak moment, desires to die as he is. Of course, he knows that he ought not to be this weak and irresponsible, so he rebukes himself. But the rebuke is a weak one; the general tone of the poem is the poet's despondency over his sad condition.

The second and third lines in the Japanese are in the weighty, masculine, and cryptic style, the *kanbunchō* (see note 140).

142. On February 7, 1911, Takuboku underwent minor surgery for peritonitis. He writes in his diary on that day: "The operation was performed to make a small hole in the lower abdomen in order to drain the fluid accumulated in the belly. When about three liters of that whiskey-colored fluid had come out that rubber tube, I felt as if I had suddenly become hungry, and I fainted while joking about that hungry feeling. The operation was suspended. I was made to lie on my back. Still cracking forced jokes, I sipped the wine I was ordered to drink. After that I felt good, but all my strength was gone."

Certainly the scar must have been very small. Probably it was not only that Takuboku minded the scar—he wanted a stronger body. In Meiji Japan, the word *chūkō* (loyalty to the emperor and filial piety) was uppermost in the mind of every schoolboy, each student knowing the Chinese classical statement, "Our body, our hair, our skin, we have been given by our parents. The first of the filial duties is to keep these intact." When Takuboku's body was unharmed, he might not have remembered these words, but as he pats his operation scar at this moment in this tanka, he may have been thinking about them.

143. The slight humor of this tanka reveals another of the many facets of illness. Those who have been ill a long time recognize the poet's psychology. At the beginning stages of illness, a patient is quite regular in taking his medicine. At this point Takuboku was perhaps still cavalier about his illness.

144. Tanka 144, 146, and 147 reveal Takuboku's interest in things Russian. He often read Turgenev and other Russian writers. Many Russian novels were translated during the Meiji period by the famous writer Futabatei Shimei (1864-1909).

Immediately before Takuboku entered the hospital, he read with deep interest Kropotkin's *An Appeal to Youth*, the first of a series of revolutionary books secretly published in the United States. Sakae Ōsugi (1885-1923) translated this book in 1907. In the hospital Takuboku copied into his notebook Kropotkin's *Terror in Russia*, which had been published in 1909. Takuboku also copied Tolstoi's essay on the Russo-Japanese War. One of Takuboku's poems in *Yobuko to Kuchibue (The Whistle and Whistling)* has the refrain *V Narod!* (see Introduction).

Kropotkin used the assumed name Borodin while he engaged in underground activities. From Takuboku's interest in Kropotkin, the name Borodin must have held a kind of fascination for the poet. Takuboku's dissatisfaction with society must have led him to think of this alias on the day he wrote tanka 144.

145. It seems Takuboku had admirers and friends wherever he lived, but he had few lifelong friends. Towards the end of his life he was estranged even from his closest companions.

146. *Kakumei* (revolution) was a powerful and dangerous word during the Meiji period.

Apart from the question of whether Takuboku should be called a socialist poet, it is clear that in his last years he was an enthusiastic socialist and revolutionary, at least in theory. But bound by the bonds of family and poor health, he had to remain a bystander's bystander. To him tanka was a "sad toy," a toy with which he consoled his frustration and despair. Still, Takuboku's spirit of rebelliousness seemed to be innate. He was dissatisfied with the order of Japanese society at the time and intuitively felt it had to be changed before anything else. His reading in socialism was haphazard, as was inevitably the case in those days, so his socialist ideas were not consistent. It is perhaps as inadequate to put too much stress on his socialism as it is to utterly disregard it. The fact remains that his ideas definitely turned socialistic in his last years and that he wrote some good poems decidedly socialist in sentiment. But if he is remembered, and that seems quite likely, it will be for his tanka. His socialist poems are incomparably smaller in number than his tanka, and even if these socialist poems can be regarded as creations of the highest quality—and on this point opinion is sharply divided—he did not create enough of them for these to guarantee him lasting fame. These poems, however, are quite significant from the viewpoint of literary history.

147. In his memorandum of important events during the previous year, which he inserted at the end of his diary for 1911, Takuboku has the following entries:

> June: The conspiracy case involving Shūsui Kōtoku came to light causing a significant change in my thought. From that time on I began to sporadically collect books and magazines related to socialism . . . .

> This year was very important as far as my thought was concerned. I found a key with which to unify my character, tastes, inclinations: socialism. Very often I thought, read, and talked about it. But the repression of the government was unreasonable in the extreme, making it impossible for me to publish my views.

In Takuboku's famous poem "A Spoonful of Cocoa" (June 15, 1911) in his series of socialist poems entitled *Yobuko to Kuchibue*, we find the lines "I know/ The sad heart of the terrorist."

148. Takuboku does not explicitly explain this moment of plight. Perhaps it was some humiliating experience, perhaps something financial, perhaps some lack of creative energy.

Do what you like with me, Fate, the poet says. Yes, there is despair here, but is there not as well something powerful in its resignation?

149. The "comfort" in this tanka is purely economic. Takuboku's *Asahi* salary at this time must have been twenty-eight yen a month, a raise of three yen a month from his starting salary. Takuboku had no genius for guarding his funds. At the end of 1910, he had received a fifty-four-yen bonus and other income so that he had actually earned 165 yen 65 sen for that month, but at the end of this period he had only 1 yen 21 sen left, his diary entry for December 1910 continuing: "I spent the rest on payment for debts incurred because of unexpected happenings, long-standing debts to the boardinghouse, and medication....By the way, I have to pay back 40 yen to the Kyōshinkai [a mutual financing association formed by *Asahi* employees] and 100 yen or so to the Gaiheikan [a boardinghouse] next year." For only a moment the poet dreams in this tanka of the ease with which he could live in the countryside on thirty yen a month, but he knows, equally well, that he would have difficulty finding a job which would pay that much. Seeing his salary of nearly thirty yen gone, he imagines he can live very comfortably on that figure in the country. He is concentrating on the additional expenses city life involves, but he is blind to the fact that with his debts and loose spending, he will be in difficulties even in rural Japan.

150. Nostalgia for home is an important motif in Takuboku's poetry. Though his family was obliged to leave Shibutami village "as if pelted with stones," Takuboku could never forget that region during his wandering life. In his heart it was a haven of rest, a sanctuary, its symbols the Kitakami River and Mount Iwate:

> Like tears/ The banks of Kitakami with willows softly green/ Before my eyes

---

> Face to face with the mountain of my home,/ I am wordless—/ How kind this mountain of my home!

In his poems, Shibutami is always his old dear home, but note the contrast in the *Romaji Diary* entry for April 18 (p. 93).

151. The date of this poem is not clear, but it must have been written after Takuboku left the hospital in March 1911.

Nareri (literally "became" or "has become") has the same meaning as *narerikeri*, but *keri* serves as an intensifier. It intensifies the fact that summer has come. The day before, the speaker did not realize summer was so near. What brought the awareness to him was the rain. The fact that it is light outside even during the rain indicates the season. The spring rainy season is almost at an end. In Tokyo, the rainy season varies with the year (the calendar marks the beginning of each rainy season but not its end); normally the rainy season in Tokyo is from early June to the end of June or the beginning of July. Usually when it rains, the day grows darker; especially during the rainy season are the days dark and gloomy. But the added element in this tanka is the convalescent's vision. To a convalescent the sunshine of summer is too strong, so the rain that falls on a day which retains its light is pleasant to Takuboku's weakened vision.

152. Usually painful experiences become sweeter with time's passage. The poet is obviously recuperating, for if he were still ill, the taste of medicine would remain vile. Thus the poet is happier; he feels safer, better. Part of the time of his illness was spent in the hospital, part at home. Was it the same medicine, though, that altered its flavor from the first stages of illness through the passage of time? Most likely new medicine was prescribed according to the state of the patient's illness, so the taste changed accordingly. A moment of reminiscence.

153. The poet's sorrow is perhaps caused by lost time and by the fact that he could not help his daughter, Kyōko, during that period. In the previous poem the poet was happy about his recovery, but one's life is a series of shifting, contradictory moments. Here the sadness intensifies the period of incapacitation of four long months. A child at certain ages may grow an inch or so in a short period, but in the everyday life of the healthy, such changes are not perceptible. Kyōko's increase in height thus intensifies the enormous length of those four months. Perhaps while the poet was in bed, the time seemed shorter, but the shock of recognition from Kyōko's growth makes a psychological extension of that time.

154. Like tanka 151, 152, and 153, this poem is also formal.

The question is why the poet feels sad to see his child growing taller and becoming quite healthy. The sadness is complex due to several levels of interpretation. The poet may feel the contradiction between his child's healthy state and his own unhealthy one. He probably feels his inability to help her grow in other ways, for the poet is weak from his own failing health. And if the poet is aware of the seriousness of his own illness, he may see the shadow of that illness falling hereditarily on his offspring's now-healthy body. Or perhaps the intense healthiness of the child emphasizes the decline of the poet's body and his own approaching death. Whatever the sadness is, it is complex.

155. *Makurabe* (by one's bed) indicates the poet is ill. A young child would not necessarily be frightened by a parent's illness, but the staring would cause the fright. Kyōko was not accustomed to her father's intense gaze. The reasons for the staring may be the same as those in note 154.

156. A chance moment when the poet is struck by the passage of time. Like our indifference to a plant until we find a bud on it, parents too can be indifferent to their children until some special moment. The change was in the child—perhaps Kyōko did something or said something that brought the poet to this realization of some transformation in his daughter. But he could also indulge in such reflections because, ill in bed, he was temporarily released from the hectic life of his healthy days. A sick person is apt to find his children noisy and bothersome, especially if the illness is bad, but this moment goes beyond that kind of annoyance.

157. No Japanese father would say such words to a child. The child, who would normally respect her father and grandfather, would not understand these words; and the father would be ashamed to say these things about himself and about his own father. Thus the poet is probably watching his child busily at play, and these words form an internal stream in his mind.

The first line finds the poet looking at the child objectively, for *Sono oya* means "its parent" or "her parent." In the last line the poet moves closer to his own child by using the word *ko*, which means in this instance "my child." The repetition of *oya* and the use of the word *chichi* are interesting. *Oya* is equivalent to "parent," *chichi* to "father." The difference is not in intimacy but in the situation in which one refers to the father. A son uses the word *chichi* in referring to his own father while speaking to a third party. When a third party refers to the father of another man, the speaker will use the word *oya* or *chichi-oya* with the proper honorific attached. A father during the Meiji period called himself *chichi* when he wrote to his children. In the moment of this tanka, the poet is speaking to himself as if speaking to the child in a formal way.

This tanka is in the weighty "kanbunchō" style, which, we believe, saves it from sentimentality.

158. That his child is as stubborn as he himself was makes the poet sad. His child is lacking in what the Japanese call *sunaosa* (its adjective form *sunao* meaning yielding, obedient, docile, compliant, mild). Ordinary children will of course cry if scolded, and even more tears will come from a spanking. The poet laments the lack of that childlike quality in his daughter. The criticism by the poet of his own child is equally a criticism of himself. Kyōko at this time was probably four or five (see note 159). She was born December 29, 1906.

159. The Kōtoku Incident of 1910 (see Introduction) began Takuboku's pursuit of socialist learning. But certainly Takuboku's interest was basically theoretical. A real revolutionary would have kept such a word as "revolution" secret, especially before his family, for it was a dangerous term in those days. Takuboku may have been enthusiastic about slogans, but he was more romantic and idealistic in their usage than in being deeply committed to them. The light tone of this tanka belies any profound commitment.

Kyōko was probably four at this time. This puzzling situation comes from the difference in the way the Japanese count a man's age. Before World War II, the Japanese used to count a fraction of a year as one year; therefore, a child born in February was two years old on January 1 the next year. A man's age had nothing to do with his birthday. He became one year older every January 1. Hence the special importance attached to the New Year by children. Some critics refer to Takuboku as twenty-seven, but he was a little less than two months past his twenty-sixth birthday when he died.

160. Takuboku is often at his most natural in his poems about his child Kyōko. Kyōko is singing a Western song with Japanese lyrics, for the *shōka* is a song taught at school as distinguished from traditional songs called *uta*. Most *shōka* were songs using Occidental music. Many Irish and Scottish folk songs, for example, came into Japan during the Meiji period, and to their melodies the Japanese added lyrics in Japanese. Sometimes a folk song about love for a sweetheart was changed into love for one's native town, as in "Comin' thro' the Rye," its Japanese title "The clear evening sky." To "Annie Laurie" was added a lyric about three famous court ladies of the Heian period, and "Killarney" was turned into a song about mountain life. When the Meiji government decided to incorporate music into the primary school curriculum, the schools were obliged to adopt Western music, for Japanese music hardly had any musical scores. Furthermore, the samurai, still influential in the new government, had disdained Japanese music as vulgar and effeminate, the only exception being *yōkyoku*, the music of the Nōh play. Of course, some *shōgaku shōka* (songs for primary schools) were by Japanese composers trained in the Western way, "Kōjō no Tsuki" ("The Moon on the Ruined Castle") and "Sumidagawa" ("The Sumida River") still sung with great affection. "Sakura-sakura" ("Cherry Blossoms") was composed from ancient Japanese music.

161. Though objective and seemingly prosaic, this tanka has an undercurrent of keen pathos. The moment we know the situation in which Takuboku had been placed because of illness and other factors, the joyful surprise felt by the poet can be appreciated.

Contrasted to Japanese fathers today, fathers in Meiji and Taishō were much more aloof and rarely revealed their affection for their young children. Thus the tenderness on the part of Kyōko is a rare moment for Takuboku. The father was lord in his family. His position varied somewhat with social class—the higher his status in the outer world, the more elevated his position in the family. Among the working classes and small shopkeepers, positions of father and mother were almost equal, and children were intimate with both. But in the upper classes and in rich families, fathers were given special homage and kept their distance from offspring. Still, like the king or queen in modern Britain, the father reigned but did not rule. He left everything concerning the children's education to his wife. Though the highest policies were decided by the father, it was only the mother who trained and scolded children. The father's role was to praise on special occasions or to chastise when the children were exceptionally unruly.

At meals silence was encouraged. It was unmannerly to talk while eating. In many families the father had a special dish or two for himself. The mother deferred to him, and she personally served him in many cases, even if the family had maids to wait on everyone. No one began eating until the father did. He rarely played with his children, though he sometimes took them on outings. The New Year was an exception in terms of games, but even then he was often busy entertaining visitors. To the children his was an august existence, but their love for him was instinctive, mixed with respect and fear. Outwardly the father's position was similar to that of his counterpart in Victorian England, but generally speaking, the atmosphere in Japanese homes was not as dismal as we find it in some Victorian novels.

162. Children usually remember snack time. Like most events in Japan, it is regulated—ten in the morning, three in the afternoon.

Kyōko was so fascinated in looking out the window that she forgot it was time for her *oyatsu*. *Yatsu* means eight. In the Tokugawa period, noon and midnight were called *kokonotsu* (nine); 2 a.m. or p.m. was called *yatsu*; 4 a.m. or p.m. was referred to as *nanatsu* (seven) and 6 a.m. or p.m. *mutsu* (six). As *yatsu* covered the period two to four, 3 p.m. was called *yatsu* and hence the name with honorific *oyatsu*.

This tanka is like a *shaseibun* (a sketched nature scene). Though the picture is domestic, it is accurate and concise. We see the eyes of the child looking from the second-story window down at the by-street pedestrians. The poet, however, gives this moment dramatic impact, for the child is not conscious she is being watched by her father, who is himself all too aware of the time. What he felt would be merely momentary has suddenly turned into a period of intense concentration.

163. Normally a smell would irritate the nose, but the fresh ink is so strong it penetrates to the very eyes of the poet. Was Takuboku reading a new book or fresh newspaper, and did he suddenly notice the irritation and turn to look out the window for some fresh air only to find the garden had turned green without his having been aware of the seasonal change? Or, more likely, did he sit down at his desk to write some tanka, not with brush and inkstone and Chinese ink but with his pen and a bottle of ink beside him? If the latter, then he was jarred from the tanka he had in mind, and his eyes went toward the window where the contrast of the green garden and the black ink immediately formed this spontaneous rendering of a moment.

If the poet had been in good health, he might not have noticed the smell or been irritated by it. This is probably the focus of the poem—the fact that the poet is so susceptible to the slightest stimulus, that he is so weakened, gives him sorrow. He had been unable to go out because of his illness. At this moment he is made aware of his weakened state by the way his eyes smarted, and looking outside, he realizes sadly that the spring passed while he was in bed and that now it is early summer.

Akira Kawano in "Amy Lowell and Haiku" (Bulletin of Fukuoka University of Education, vol. 22, part I, February 1973) notes the use of the *kireji* (cutting word) in haiku—that is, the division of the haiku into two contrasting parts. Kawano cites Ezra Pound's famous "In a Station of the Metro" ("The apparition of these faces in a crowd;/Petals on a wet, black bough"). The cutting word in this instance, says Kawano, is the semicolon, but obviously, as the critic points out, there is a contrast between the two lines, really a gap between them which (quoting Earl Miner) "must be imaginatively leaped between the statement and the vivid metaphor." In Takuboku's tanka 163, there is a transitional jerk between the eyes smarting and the ink and the fresh garden. This is part of the *kireji* of tanka.

164. In this formal tanka the impossibility of communication is stressed. The intense concentration on the poet's face as he focused his gaze on a particular area of the *tatami* straw mats in his room made the wife ask her question, but the answer cannot be as easily expressed as the question. Such a serious or gloomy thought might have been about his failures, his hopeless future, his nearness to death. He is slightly irritated by the ease with which his wife asks the question—the formality of language suggesting that annoyance; for to his wife his action seemed mere absentmindedness or daydreaming.

165. *Yuku haru* is a cliché in Japanese literature (the passing of spring or the end of spring). *Yuku aki* is also used (the passing of fall), but *yuku fuyu* (the passing of winter) is never said, nor is summer included in this idiomatic expression.

The question in this tanka involves the mislaid shaded or smoked glasses a patient wears for conjunctivitis. This irritation of the eyes is common in the spring, probably because of dust or sand particles. The illness is also referred to as "spring catarrh." Since the eyes are sensitive to light, dark glasses are used. Today such patients usually wear an eye patch.

The poet is thinking about a former time when he was in much better health. He could then walk around outdoors, for conjunctivitis is not serious. In that earlier period only the poet's eyes were weak. How much better he was that year compared to his serious illness now! He remembers nostalgically that earlier time. Spring itself is a nostalgic season for the Japanese. There are many spring flowers then, but with the passing of spring the rainy season comes and then the long hot summer. In this tanka it is summer now, and the poet in his weakened condition finds his eyes too sensitive to the glare of summer. These special glasses had metal frames, so they were not too fragile. Unless they were broken, he would not have thrown them away. There is obviously a very practical need for the glasses at this moment, but there is nostalgia too, and mixed into that nostalgia is an annoyance over not being able to find what he is looking for.

166. *Omoeru* (I felt) is formal literary Japanese; normally one would say *to omotta*.

An earlier event of a boyhood scolding is momentarily relived when the poet, seriously ill now, is scolded by his elderly mother for failing to take his medicine. A joy lingers in that moment of nostalgia as the poet recalls his early days when he was young, not so ill, and not so frustrated and disillusioned about his health and his family and the world. His joy also comes partly from his discovery that his elderly mother is still spirited enough to scold him.

167. *Akesasete* means the speaker had someone open the paper sliding doors for him; thus the word emphasizes the poet's illness.

The Japanese home consists of numerous partitions for dividing rooms, separating rooms from corridors, keeping out the cold, offering protection from the glare of sunlight, and maintaining privacy within rooms. The *fusuma* or *karakami* partitions divide a guest room into two halves, the major half containing the alcove. These partitions are opaque, the sliding doors on both sides covered with heavy decorated paper. Some rooms are separated from the corridor by a wall and are therefore entered by way of the *fusuma* or *karakami*, some rooms by the *shōji*, the papered sliding doors with latticed wooden frames. Only one side of the *shōji* is covered with a thin, white rice paper. Light can filter through this paper, but not through the *fusuma* or *karakami*. At the same time, the light filtering through can either keep out the strong glare of the sun or can aid the dark Japanese room in becoming much lighter. Another kind of *shōji* covers a window or the *amado*, glass sliding partitions to keep out cold, rain, and snow. The Japanese can also use a two-fold opaque screen *(byōbu)* for maintaining privacy in a room. The *makura-byōbu*, a smaller, opaque two-fold screen, maintains privacy and shuts out draughts around beds. A single-leaf screen *(tsuitate)* is used either for privacy in a room or for decoration in the hall at the entrance; this screen is either blank or ornamented with calligraphy in Chinese ink or with some beautiful scene from nature.

In this tanka the *shōji* referred to can be either sliding doors opening off a corridor of windows or *shōji* covering the sliding glass partition of the *amado*. Whatever the type, the fact remains that the poet had someone open the *shōji* so that the sky could be observed. During Takuboku's long illness, that was all he could do while lying quietly in bed. This viewing of the sky is not analyzed in terms of the Western idea of searching for God or an image of eternity but represents merely the longing to go outdoors, to move in the world of nature, to feel free by confronting the living, pulsing, organic world.

Usually Takuboku indents a line to emphasize it. In this tanka his long illness is emphasized. The season is not indicated in this poem because even if it were winter, the sliding shutters in front of the *amado* could be opened, the sky visible. Whatever the season, seeing the sky became a real necessity for the poet.

168. Takuboku was not the typically obedient patient, so it must have been extremely difficult for him to remain quietly in bed. Even those patients who ignore their high fever may be putting on a kind of bravado, for it is human nature to worry about a fever. In consumptive patients the temperature fluctuates. The doctors themselves do not worry about these variations, but patients do. Consumptive patients are nervous and irritable during such moments, as is Takuboku in this instance. All they can do is rely on the doctor by waiting submissively for his visit and for the fever to go down. Takuboku catches the essence of just this kind of moment.

169. The flowers in this poem must be *nageire*, that is, giving the appearance of having been casually thrown into a vase though in reality the flowers have been deliberately arranged. Probably the poet's wife had bought the flowers even though she could not afford them. The poet on waking was surprised to find them, and they inspired him to write something. The suggestion in desiring to write "something" is that he wanted to create something immediate, spontaneous. An essay or short story would have required too much thought, so we feel that "something" must have been a tanka, something that could be handled and perhaps finished without too much labor. This poem was probably written when Takuboku felt comparatively well. Takuboku spent many drab days in bed, but from his diary we learn he sometimes took walks, went flower-viewing, and frequently talked for long hours with friends.

Buying flowers is a kind of extravagant waste if the family is poor.

But some Japanese women, and perhaps women not unlike Takuboku's wife, Setsuko, will buy them simply because they are fond of flowers. Setsuko did like the beautiful—she played the violin, wrote tanka herself, and found enjoyment in literature and singing. A diary entry for April 27, 1911: "In the evening Setsuko bought some tulips and freesia."

From *A Handful of Sand*: "Feeling close to my wife/ On this day in which all my friends seemed superior to me/ I bought her some flowers"

170. Women's liberation was very much in vogue in the late Meiji and early Taishō periods. Such women as Noe Ito (1895-1923), Raichō Hiratsuka (1886-1971), Akiko Yosano, and Ichiko Kamichika (b. 1881) may be considered part of the women's liberation movement in the early years of this century.

It is difficult to imagine the gentle, obedient, and loving Setsuko as such a woman, but there must have been moments when she wanted to rebel. Once she actually ran away from Takuboku (October 2, 1909). She left with their daughter, but she returned on October 26 at the urging of Kindaichi and Takuboku's teacher. In June 1911, she wanted to return to Morioka to help her family move to Hakodate, but Takuboku refused to let her go. Setsuko borrowed five yen from a friend; then she lied to her husband that her parents had sent the money in a letter, a letter she claimed she had lost. Takuboku discovered the real situation and in a rage told her to leave and not return, having forfeited by her act the right to be a mother and wife. See note 178 on this situation.

In this tanka she does rebel on one such day. Takuboku, bed-ridden, is helpless to control her. He gazes at the dahlias in order to remain calm in much the same way Raskolnikov in *Crime and Punishment* traces the scalloped edges of the wallpaper flowers to keep his mind steady after the murder of the pawnbrokeress.

Biographer Iwaki offers another interpretation of this tanka. The main argument lies in the meaning of the word *hanatareshi*. Most critics have interpreted the word to mean "liberated," but Iwaki believes Takuboku used it in the original sense of "banished," namely "divorced." The sixth poem in the series entitled "Death" (see note 5) uses *hanatareshi* in this obsolete sense: *Hanatareshi onna no gotoki kanashimi o yowaki otoko mo kono hi ima shiru.* Takuboku included this tanka in *A Handful of Sand*, but in a slightly different version: *Hanatareshi onna no gotoki kanashimi o/ Yowaki otoko no/ Kanzuru hi nari.* The poem may be translated as follows: "I, a weak man, today feel the same sorrows as does a woman cast away," (i.e. a divorced woman). If the word *hanatareshi* is given this meaning, tanka 170 must be interpreted in the following way: "Today my wife behaves as if she has been divorced [i.e. forlornly and abjectly], and I gaze at these dahlias." This interpretation seems to correlate well with Setsuko's character. Tanka often have more than one possible interpretation, so we offer both possibilities, though we favor the earlier version.

Like tanka 163, this too has its *kireji* organization, the first two lines violent in movement, the last line quiet, steady, focused. The indented line draws the reader's attention to the dahlias, a new flower—Western and exotic. The new woman and the new flower seem a conscious arrangement on the part of the poet.

171. Takuboku often found the money he needed—and from an unexpected source. At this moment the poet is actually waiting for some money to come, though he has no reasonable grounds for expecting it. *Kane nado* means money or something equivalent to money. *Netsu, okitsu shite,* suggests the speaker is ill, but he may not be very ill. He is hard-pressed for money, but because he is in poor health, he cannot bustle about trying to raise funds. Restlessly he is waiting for a windfall.

Without the comma after *Netsu* in the second line, the rhythm flows smoothly; with the comma the rhythm becomes heavier, harmonizing with the tone of the entire poem.

172. It is perhaps dangerous to make generalizations about a people as complicated as the Japanese, yet it may be characteristic of the Japanese to be weak-willed, to lack tenacity, to despair. Suicide exists for them as a real way out of a dilemma, and perhaps there is in the Japanese a lack of attachment to life. The violent impact of natural disasters have added to Japanese resignation and/or acceptance of the world as it is. Certain aspects of Buddhism also stress the ephemerality, the transitory element, and the nothingness of man's life. "To strive, to seek, to find, and not to yield," Tennyson's line in "Ulysses," seems to be the antithesis of the Oriental frame of mind. The Japanese do not even like the strong primary colors—they seem to prefer the delicate shades. Japanese food is bland. Resignation is a Japanese virtue. On the other side of the coin, the stress on the transitory and ephemeral may intensify the Japanese immersion into the moment of now, into seizing the moment and enjoying it to the full.

In this tanka the poet smokes a cigarette to calm himself. He is in some crucial moment of desperation in which no matter how he analyzes his problem, he cannot grasp it. As he smokes, he becomes more and more disgusted, so disgusted that he even forgets to light up again. The poet is headed toward a failure of will, the shock of recognition of the limitation of everything in his bleak life.

173. The first line in the Japanese sounds awkward with its expression *ishi koro* (about the time when he was). Colloquially *ishi koro* is *ita koro*.

A number of situations can be imagined in this dramatically ambiguous tanka. Did the friend actually have an affair in "some town," or did it actually take place in Tokyo? Did the event happen, or was the friend merely bragging? If the love affair was so painful to the friend, he might not have revealed it, so perhaps the lie was in the speaker's feigned intensity of affection. Whatever the situation or whatever the lie, it is the poet's sadness that moves the reader. The cause of that sadness is somewhat ambiguous. Was it because the poet saw the weakness of a friend who brags or misrepresents his feelings? Perhaps the poet's sadness arose in seeing the man's need to tell lies about an event of this sort.

174. Humorous on the surface, this poem reveals the poet's sadness, the darkness of his actual life. Ill, he found his home miserable due to the tension between his wife and mother, and he could only give himself over to this image of a fly cleaning its legs—a kind of temporary relief for the poet, a looking-the-other-way at the trivial, the insignificant. On another level of interpretation, all Takuboku could do was wring his own hands much like the fly, for it was impossible for Takuboku to change his life style.

Waraite minu has a special connotation. "I laughed" in formal Japanese is *warainu* or *waraitari*, but *waraite minu* (I tried laughter) connotes that the poet *dared* to laugh. With his home in the condition it was in, he probably had few occasions to laugh, but even when he laughed, he must have restrained himself, his laughter not too loud. Tuberculosis patients fear to laugh aloud lest the effort induce coughing.

175. The word play in *sutegataki* and *tabako* appeals in this tanka. *Sutegatai* is a common expression meaning "having a charm of its own" or "charming in its own way." The word is composed of *suteru* (throw away) and *katai* (difficult). In saying that the sadness of the day in which he has chest pains is not altogether bad because the sorrow has a charm of its own, Takuboku introduces a simile. That sorrow is as charming as a cigarette which has a good taste. Here the word play enters. A cigarette is thrown away after a few puffs, but if it is of especially good flavor, the smoker will be reluctant to dispose of it. The *sutegataki* applies literally to cigarettes; when we say "sorrow" is *sutegataki*, the expression is used figuratively. Thus the word play is in the literal and figurative use of the same word. Takuboku's pleurisy gave him chest pains, but he has lived with them a long while, and at some psychological moment those pains are an extension of himself, his sensitivity, his poetic insight.

176. A desperate moment for the poet. He wanted to do something violent—quarrel, break something, strike a girl, anything to rid himself of the irritation, the discontent, he feels. The mood of violence took place a moment ago, but now the poet is quiet. Usually after such thoughts of violence, one will say how foolish he has been, but the poet reverses this stereotyped reaction. He understands quite well why he was so desperate. He knows the condition could not be helped, could not be avoided. And that is cause enough for the pity he feels for himself.

177. *Soniya* is the Japanese Romaji spelling of Sonia. The first two lines in the Japanese are colloquial.

It is mere whim for the poet to call his daughter Sonia, but we know Takuboku loved Turgenev and Tolstoi, especially the former. Sonia is of course a common Russian name. Perhaps he was thinking of the Sonia in *Crime and Punishment*.

A blank space was left on a page in the notebook between tanka 177 and 178.

178. To the artists of the period the conflict between loyalty to one's family and loyalty to oneself was a real problem. Writers very often wanted to be liberated from the bonds of the family, and many naturalistic novels were written on the theme of this bitter struggle, the hero under the insidious influence of the system. Takuboku was one of those who suffered from the struggle most heavily, though he never more than hinted at it in his writing. He never made it a theme of his stories. On the contrary, he avoided facing this problem in his writing. His *Romaji Diary*, however, is a frank confession of his attempt to liberate himself from his family, but he did not have the strength to cut the bonds completely. He retained the traditional Japanese attitude toward parents—he loved his family too much. Accordingly, the contradiction left him in misery.

The "discord" in this tanka is not simple. There was discord between Takuboku's wife and mother, between his parents, and between his wife and himself.

The rift between his wife and mother intensified during the period of hardship when Takuboku had travelled alone to Kushiro, his family left at Hakodate. In the Japan of those days, the conflict between a bride and her mother-in-law did not flare out into the open. The bride had to unconditionally obey the wishes of the parents of her husband, so under the surface grudges were formed and rankled the parties concerned. When Setsuko ran away from home in October 1909, she was probably prompted by the pain of poverty and ill health, but clearly her relationship with her mother-in-law was partly responsible.

As for the discord between Takuboku's parents, his father could no longer support the family after he was deprived of his incumbency, the burden falling on Takuboku. Because of the father's desertion in 1907 to live with his former teacher (his wife's brother), we can easily imagine the parent's ambiguous position in his family. He did rejoin the family in 1909, and when Takuboku wrote tanka 178, his father was living with him. But the poet wrote in his diary for May 3, 1911, that in a fit of anger his father had struck his own wife. In September of the same year, Takuboku's father again ran away from home and returned only when he heard his son was dying.

At the end of the *Romaji Diary*, Takuboku comments on the arrival of his family in Tokyo on June 16, 1909. Reading his wife's letter reporting their arrival at Morioka on their way to Tokyo, Takuboku writes in his diary on June 10: "I thought: 'And so at last!'" The expression, however, is by no means one of relief and happiness but of resigned despair.

Within less than four months after the family had arrived in Tokyo, Setsuko ran away from home. It is true that the conflict with her mother-in-law was one of the causes for this action, but Takuboku's attitude was also responsible. Perplexed by the arrival of his family and actually reluctant to find himself once more in charge of its well-being, he had, nevertheless, rented rooms above a barbershop. His entire family had to live in a small area; the women had to go downstairs to cook meals. Setsuko's ill health was looked on with indifference by her mother-in-law. Takuboku himself was aloof—rather he ignored the family. Not that he had ceased to love his wife. He was confident of her unchanged love for him. Perhaps he could not for a moment imagine she would desert him. Setsuko returned to him, thanks to the efforts of Kindaichi and Takuboku's former teacher, but the poet had been shocked by the action he took. In a letter dated March 8, 1910, addressed to his friend and brother-in-law Miyazaki, Takuboku wrote: "Since I received the blow at the end of last autumn, my thought underwent a sudden change. I felt every single part of my mind had been transformed."

In June 1911, Setsuko wanted to visit her parents' home as the Horiai family had decided to leave Morioka to move to Hakodate. In order to acquire the necessary funds for the journey, she borrowed five yen, lying to her husband that her sister Takako had sent the money. Takuboku had his doubts, and finally Setsuko had to tell him the truth. Her sister wired her then, requesting her to come and sending a telegraphic money order. Takuboku sent back the sum.

The following entries in Takuboku's diary are relevant:

June 4, 1911: I could not forgive Setsuko for trying to deceive me with her chicanery. I declared I divorced her, but she would not go. [Westerners may find these words strange; in those days, however, Japanese husbands used such words in the same way a judge does. The wives usually acquiesced, so there was no need to go to court.] Thus our relationship has become nothing but a means of life for each of us.

June 6, 1911: I ordered her to give me the purse. She said she couldn't find it, though she was sure she had put it somewhere temporarily .... I ordered her to absolutely find the purse because, I said, she might be concealing something else. She sobbed out that she felt she was going mad. I wrote a letter to Takako enclosing in it a money order for five yen. In the letter I censured her for sending the telegram, and I added that if they wanted to exercise parental power, it was entirely inconsistent with my ideas of the family system, and so I would divorce her.

Behind Takuboku's tyrannical attitude, we can sense the irritation of an invalid and his fear of again being deserted by his wife. After this event the entries in Takuboku's diary are short and rather sporadic. He developed a high fever in July, and Setsuko too was unwell. In spite of her condition she continued to keep house with her mother-in-law and often went to the *Asahi* to borrow money on her husband's salary. On July 27, Setsuko went to the Miura section of Internal Medicine of Tokyo Imperial University and was told that her left lung was slightly affected. The following day she went to the Aoyama division of Internal Medicine (see note 97). Her reason for doing so is not clear, but she may have hoped the other department would negate the previous day's diagnosis. Dr. Arima, who saw her, diagnosed her as having "catarrh of the pulmonary apex," and he told her the disease was contagious. In his diagnosis Dr. Arima used a euphemistic expression which was usual in those days to lessen the shock.

What the actual relationship was between Setsuko and Takuboku at this time is not clear, but the following entry written on August 2, 1911, several days after Setsuko's diagnosis, is suggestive: "Of late Setsuko frequently keeps to her bed. And so the burden of cooking and other chores falls on my aging mother. Going up and down stairs must be trying to an old woman."

In September 1911, Takuboku broke off his relationship with Miyazaki, Setsuko's sister's husband and his own friend and patron of many years. A letter from Miyazaki had infuriated the poet. According to the husband of Takuboku's sister Mitsuko in the April 19, 1947 issue of the *Mainichi* newspaper, the cause of the split was due to Takuboku's belief that illicit relations had gone on between Setsuko and Miyazaki. It is now impossible to verify this assertion, but Yukinori Iwaki, Takuboku's biographer, believes Mitsuko was misinformed about the nature of the dispute between the two friends. Even though Miyazaki liked Setsuko very much and sympathized with her, it is utterly groundless, Iwaki says, to infer there were clandestine relations between them. Some very warm and rather careless expressions of sympathy toward Setsuko in Miyazaki's letter to Takuboku's wife hurt the poet very much. Miyazaki had written the letter to Setsuko on behalf of her parents for, because Takuboku had severed relations with her family (probably in June), there was no other channel through which they could inquire after Setsuko. Miyazaki, as Setsuko's brother-in-law, tried to know the state of her health and to persuade her, if possible, to come to see her parents. His solicitude and his affection for her seem to have led him to use some expressions which might incur misunderstanding. The supposition that he had a liaison with Setsuko originates from what Seiichi Miura (Mitsuko's husband) said after World War II and from a book written by Mitsuko. But biographer Iwaki convincingly denies this theory, saying it resulted only because of Mitsuko's misunderstanding. At any rate, this incident seems to have dealt Takuboku a crushing blow, for from that time on he did not publish anything.

In his diary entry for January 7, 1912, he writes:

I cannot help lamenting the misfortune of having to spend yesterday and today in unutterable unpleasantness. Recently my wife is rather unwell. Going around with her hair uncombed and wearing some shapeless nightgown over her old clothes, she looks quite dispirited and listless. And she often keeps coughing incessantly. Every time I see her god-awful appearance, I cannot help being seized by some indescribable brooding anger and desperation.

Today when I was lying by the brazier and warming myself, she seemed to be out on the verandah in the cold wind. Twice I asked her, "Aren't you cold out there?" The first time I heard only her answer, "No." When I repeated the same question about half an hour later, I was greeted by the brusque retort, "Why should I be on the verandah?" She seemed to be lying in the next room, warming herself by using the *kotatsu* [in Takuboku's day, a device for warming oneself economically by covering an earthenware case containing a few pieces of live charcoal with a quilt under which one sat]. I felt I had to make some sort of angry reply, but lying on my back at the time, I utterly lacked the strength to get angry.

At night when Kyōko went to bed, my wife had another violent fit of coughing. "You go to bed too," I ordered. She lay down in bed. Then I asked her, "I'm going out to buy something for a cough. Will you take it or not?" "I'll buy something tomorrow," she replied. With the words, "No. My kindness seems to be annoying to you, but your coughing is maddening," I went out into the cold wind to buy some medicine and some cough drops. I was overpowered by self-pity.

Setsuko was a dutiful wife to the end. Her death, reported by Miyazaki in a letter to Kindaichi, is pathetic:

On May 5, 1913, she died in the hospital. When she was dying, she wrote in pencil that she hoped we would take care of Kyōko.... Then she wrote down the names of Mr. Yosano, Mr. Kindaichi, Mr. Toki, Mr. Mori, and Mr. Natsume, asking me to tell them about her death and to beg them to be kind to Kyōko. Next she stared at me and asked me to love her sister (my wife). Then closing her eyes, she said, "I'm dying. Good-by, all of you." But a few moments later she opened her eyes again and said, "It takes a long time to die." By that time we were already crying. Then once more she said, "Good-by, all of you," and closed her eyes. A small amount of yellow foam came out of her mouth. And that was the end. [Quoted from Koyō Yoshida, *People Around Takuboku* (Kaizōsha, 1929).]

The weighty *kanbunchō* style adds gravity to this tanka and saves it from sentimentality.

179. The reading for home as *ie* instead of the other possible reading *ya* gives this line one syllable too many, but the heaviness caused by the extra syllable makes the impact stronger.

Even something as trivial as a household pet will bring on the usual conflict between mother and daughter-in-law. Had Takuboku's home been a little larger, the tension would have been eased, but his poverty made a large home with many rooms an impossibility.

180. This tanka once more emphasizes the bitterness of the discord between Setsuko and Takuboku's mother. It was unendurable to Takuboku, but he had to hold back his feelings, for he loved his mother and his wife, and he was too ill, too powerless, to remedy the situation.

A boardinghouse may be one of two kinds, either a *shirōto-geshuku* or (as in tanka 180) a *geshukuya*. The former is run by some widow or elderly couple needing money and having a spare room in their home. A more personal relationship is possible in such a home. In the *geshukuya* the boardinghouse is run as a business by professionals —there are many rooms, food is served, maids wait on the boarders, and a large bath is provided. Takuboku stayed at the Gaiheikan when he came up to Tokyo in 1908. The rude, business-like treatment he received is recorded in his *Romaji Diary*.

The comma after *mo* in the second line adds to the staccato rhythm intentionally wanted by Takuboku.

181. This tanka is similar to tanka 174 in which Takuboku amused himself by watching a fly, and while tanka 181 is as humorous on its surface, it too has a deeper level. Takuboku imitates the cow to forget his illness, but it is not the illness alone that oppresses him. As usual, he could not support the heavy burden of his family. No relief was in sight for him, so he had to create his own whims, his own antics. On the surface the tanka suggests that the poet is feeling better, that he can forget his illness, that he can create his own diversions, but that he had to employ such devices implies the weight of the oppression he was perpetually under. Of course, he is quite aware that he cannot imitate a cow in the presence of his wife and child—the indented line reveals how difficult the constant presence of his family was. When Setsuko and Kyōko went out, he could breathe easier, could find release, could whip out a good moo—there was no longer the possible intrusion of the tension between his mother and wife.

182. A poem of real pathos. Takuboku's father had no real place in Takuboku's Tokyo home. The aging Zen priest who had lost his incumbency and had later deserted his family can now only idle away his hours, playing in this instance with ants in the garden. The poem shows Takuboku's filial piety. There is no harsh criticism of his father, but an image of love is generated in the selection of the detail. The poet is watching a broken old man.

This poem must have been written after Takuboku moved from the two rooms over a barbershop, for no garden would have been available there for the family. Thus this moment must have occurred after Takuboku rented a small independent house on August 7, 1911. On September 3, however, Takuboku's father again ran away because of his son's poverty and because of the emotional strain in the household.

183. The formal *kanashikaruran* is in colloquial usage *kanashii darō* (must be sad).

Another tanka of Takuboku's self-scorn, but one in which he once more reveals his sympathy and compassion for his aging parents.

As the only male child Takuboku was doted upon by his parents, so much so that his sisters were jealous of him. Tora, the second eldest sister, said, "After my brother was born, my mother loved him alone, forgetting our existence. Though only a small child, I remember I was dissatisfied" (see Yoshida, note 178).

Mitsuko, Takuboku's younger sister, said: "My brother was such a spoiled child that on those nights he wanted to eat *yuzu-manjū* [a kind of steamed bun flavored with the grated rind of Japanese lemons], he did not stop insisting on having one until he woke up everyone. My mother was obliged to get up and make him some. He did not mind how cold it was or how late. I hear that she denied herself tea when she was near her death, praying to God to alleviate his disease in exchange for her abstention [see tanka 184]. I don't know if this was true or not as I was not with her at the time. But I remember that she never ate chicken or eggs when I was a child. I was told that she forswore them so that my brother, who was very delicate, might grow healthy" [see Mitsuko Miura, *My Sad Brother Takuboku* (Tokyo, 1948)].

Such blind love for Takuboku was shared by his father. Thus in Takuboku's childhood the child lacked nothing to make his life comfortable. His parents' infatuation with him, together with his precocity, contributed a great deal toward making the poet an arrogant young man proud of his talent.

184. In Japan, people often abnegated what they liked best when they prayed to the gods for something, such as recovery of their dear ones from illness. *Sake o tatsu* (to give up sake) or *otoko o tatsu* (to abstain from sexual relations) were common expressions. Some Japanese even vowed to give up salt.

Takuboku's mother is so self-sacrificing for her son that she is willing to give up tea, a real necessity for the Japanese. But in spite of the mother's kind intentions toward Takuboku, she is also human and cannot help becoming angry. In this household the main problem concerns her daughter-in-law. When the mother is angry with Setsuko, the former cannot help being stiff toward her son. She cannot help sulking, and that in turn must affect her attitude toward her son moment by moment. Perhaps this tanka is not this complicated, but it may suggest the irony that in spite of praying for her son's recovery, she does not realize how much pain she has been causing him through the discord with her daughter-in-law.

185. Usually the children in the neighborhood responded when the poet called them, but at this moment no one came up to him. The poet, who has been troubled by the psychology of both his wife and mother, recognizes that even the simple mind of a child cannot be guessed, cannot be calculated. Yes, the child is father of the man!

The first two lines in the Japanese without a comma between them contain two actions by the poet and a reaction on the part of the children, and these lines have an effect very similar to that of prose. That is to say, the poetry of this tanka is concentrated in the last indented line. What seems like awkward prose suddenly changes into a poem as the reader reaches the last line.

186. The division of the lines in this tanka is unusual, for even while there is only one extra syllable in the Japanese, the first two lines contain only nine syllables, the last line twenty-three. The length of this last line suggests the building up of extreme tension in the poet's mind over this long period of illness in which he can neither recover nor die. The second line, composed as it is of only one word of strong impact, is also effective. There is in this moving tanka the bitterness of a mind deteriorating.

187. That Takuboku's friend sent him a money order just as the poet's medicine ran out saddens the speaker. Most people would be happy because of the coincidence, but Takuboku says the money order (*kawase* may be a money order sent either by mail or wire) made him sad. He is sad to be reduced to such helplessness by illness. At this period in his life Takuboku was undergoing a severe financial crisis. He had been taking Pyramidon, a medicine tuberculosis patients use to reduce fever. Made in Germany, Pyramidon must have been very expensive, but though it was very efficacious in bringing down the fever of tuberculosis patients, the drug did have some bad side effects. Most doctors did not worry about fever in tuberculosis patients, for the fever usually fluctuates. But the patient himself worried about his Pyramidon, so the money Takuboku received at this time was quite fortuitous.

Takuboku's diary entry for January 23, 1912, notes he had Setsuko buy five packs of Pyramidon. On January 28, 1912, Takuboku wrote: "I took Pyramidon pills three times yesterday and the day before for fever, but as my fever rose to over 100 degrees at bedtime, I didn't take the medicine this morning or afternoon. I finally took one dose at 3 p.m. when my fever rose to over 100 degrees. It seems my condition is very bad."

In September 1911, Takuboku's father again deserted his home, taking with him two lined and two unlined kimonos, a tobacco pouch, a hat, one yen fifty sen from Mitsuko plus fifty sen of household money. On July 17, 1911 (the year Takuboku was hospitalized), an old friend had wired Takuboku money. On August 2, 1911, Miyazaki had wired Takuboku forty yen. At this time Takuboku's wife was ill, her sickness having been diagnosed as tuberculosis. Takuboku himself was ill in bed. August 1, 1911, Setsuko had gone to Takuboku's office to get an advance on her husband's salary—even though she herself was ill. Takuboku's mother had to do the cooking during this period. On August 6, Takuboku borrowed twenty yen from a usurer. On August 7, he moved from the upstairs rooms over a barbershop to an independent house with three rooms (three, six, and eight mats respectively) plus a kitchen and garden. This period was one of intense financial struggle. Certainly we can understand Takuboku's sadness on receiving a money order from a friend.

Kawase no kanashisa is a kind of shorthand to reduce the complexity of the emotions involved in receiving the money order. If this tanka were translated into prose, it might read: "I was very reassured on receiving a money order, but at the same time I was very sad because I was reduced to being dependent on the sympathy of my friend."

188. The psychology of this tanka is common to *nagabyōnin* (persons with a long illness). The ill are apt to be irritable and to scold in spite of knowing they ought not to. After the poet's child, exhausted from the torment of her tears, fell asleep, the poet could then touch her—a kind of caress gentle enough not to wake her. If the child were awake, Takuboku could not have performed this gesture of sympathy. The restraint of Japanese fathers in showing affection toward their children is stressed in this tanka.

189. Logically, breathing will be harder with the lungs contracted, but this tanka clearly describes the freshness of a late summer morning when the weather suggests the coming of autumn. To a patient stricken with tuberculosis, summer is a bad season, for when the weather is hot, he feels as if his lungs are edematic, as if he cannot take in enough air. Of course this reaction is more psychological than physiological. When the weather turns cooler, the patient feels as if his lungs have been restored to their full activity. The poet, having suffered from the heat, was joyous in perceiving a sign of autumn in the cool morning breeze. The following entry appears in Takuboku's diary for August 21, 1911: "I created 17 poems, sending them to Yūgure Maeda of *Shiika* magazine. This morning it was cool like autumn." Tanka 189 then follows.

190. The last poems of *Sad Toys* (tanka 190 through 194) are quiet, pure. They contain an afterglow, a twilight glimmer. In tanka 190, we feel something of the expectation of a patient waiting for the passing of summer. Usually the warmth of an electric lamp is unpleasant in summer, but when the temperature is falling, we get a pleasant sensation from the warmth of a bulb. Of course, today's bulbs cannot be touched, but in those early Takubokian days, the candle power of an electric bulb was only five to ten.

Bulbs in those days had carbon filaments, not those of tungsten. The bulbs were dark, five to sixteen candlepower at most, though the size of the bulb was rather large. The bulbs were shaped like eggplants with a protuberance at the top which was formed when the small hole from which the air had been sucked was fused after producing a vacuum. The bulbs were of transparent glass, and the carbon filaments forming a double loop could easily be seen.

191. The poet wanted to surprise his daughter with the doll he bought for her, but he found her taking a nap. There is a calm here, a resignation, as the poet quietly amuses himself with the toy doll. The mood of this tanka contrasts with that of tanka 186.

192. Once more in these last poems of *Sad Toys*, we feel the change in Takuboku's mood. If he had been stronger and his health had not declined, he would have been sarcastic or angry over the look his sister gave. In this instance he felt sad because she seemed bigoted to him, the two lines in the Japanese interpreted as "She gave me a pitying look, making me sad." A materialist, Takuboku could not regard Christ as divine, but only as a human being. Even though Takuboku is near death, he cannot believe in Christ, though the poet was interested in the Bible during his younger days. Buddha was a man, so it is easy for a Japanese to regard Christ in the same way. If Mitsuko had not been his beloved sister and if his health had been better, Takuboku might have ridiculed her. At this stage in his life, however, Takuboku has lost his former acerbity, and his mind is quieter, the way the evening sky is after a storm.

In order to become a missionary, Takuboku's sister Mitsuko entered Seishi Jogakuin, a mission school for women in Nagoya. When she was staying with a Miss Evans living in Asahikawa in Hokkaido, she was sent for by her brother to help keep his house, for both his mother and wife were ill. Mitsuko arrived on August 10, 1911, and returned to Nagoya in October. During her stay at her brother's, her father ran away from home taking some of her money. Miyazaki, Takuboku's friend who later married Setsuko's sister, first fell in love with Mitsuko, but she seems to have been indifferent, and Takuboku did not approve of the marriage; instead the poet recommended Miyazaki marry Setsuko's sister. Later Mitsuko married a Mr. Miura.

Kurisuto is a new pronunciation in Japanese. Earlier, uneducated Japanese had said *Kirisuto* on hearing the word Christ or Christus, but from the end of the Meiji period to Taishō, intellectuals changed the pronunciation to *Kurisuto*. Japanese has no such combination as *kri*—the sound has to be *kuri* or *kiri*, the latter nearer to the combination *kri* than the former when pronounced by a Japanese. Meiji intellectuals found that the sound of *ch* is *k* and not *ki*, but they equated the European *k* sound to the Japanese *ku*. The result was that the pronunciation of Christ by Japanese became more removed from the original sound than it had been earlier.

193. The poet was ill in bed, perhaps with a fever, but he asked his wife or mother to bring his pillow out to the verandah (the *engawa*), usually a corridor inside the house downstairs facing the garden. The poet could not look up at the strong sun during the day, but the evening sky provided the exact light and calm for a weak man. In his stronger days Takuboku would have explicitly stated his sorrow over the fact that he could not enjoy the sky, but here there is no anger or sorrow that he must ask others to put out his pillow and perhaps even his bedding. He simply describes the fact amid a deepening quiet of resignation, of acceptance.

During this season the glass doors of the *engawa* remain open.

194. Compare this tanka with tanka 179.

In this poem, as in these last several poems, there is a natural formality, an effortless ease. The poet knows he cannot afford the luxury of a dog, but he consults his wife, who is inside the house watching him—consults her immediately after he sees the dog pass along the outside of the bamboo fence of the garden. In the natural ease of this consultation with his wife, the poet forgets his poverty, illness, and frustration. There is no flippancy in the question; rather there is a calm acceptance of things as they are, perhaps the calm acceptance of things as they are before one dies.

The fact that *Sad Toys* closes with these serene poems seems significant. Did Takuboku intentionally arrange these poems to be the final ones in his gray notebook, or did the poet undergo a radical change of mood at the end of his life?